I0047617

Introduction to C++ Programming

CADCIM Technologies

525 St. Andrews Drive
Schererville, IN 46375
USA
(www.cadcim.com)

Contributing Author
Sham Tickoo
Professor
Purdue University Calumet
Hammond, Indiana
USA

CADCIM Technologies

Introduction to C++ Programming
CADCIM/TICKOO Publication

ISBN 978-1-942689-28-7

www.cadcim.com

DEDICATION

*To teachers, who make it possible to disseminate knowledge
to enlighten the young and curious minds
of our future generations*

*To students, who are dedicated to learning new technologies
and making the world a better place to live*

THANKS

To staff of CADCIM Technologies for their valuable help

Online Training Program Offered by CADCIM Technologies

CADCIM Technologies provides effective and affordable virtual online training on various software packages including Computer Aided Design and Manufacturing (CAD/CAM), computer programming languages, animation, architecture, and GIS. The training is delivered 'live' via Internet at any time, any place, and at any pace to individuals as well as the students of colleges, universities, and CAD/CAM training centers. The main features of this program are:

Training for Students and Companies in a Classroom Setting

Highly experienced instructors and qualified engineers at CADCIM Technologies conduct the classes under the guidance of Prof. Sham Tickoo of Purdue University Calumet, USA. This team has authored several textbooks that are rated "one of the best" in their categories and are used in various colleges, universities, and training centers in North America, Europe, and in other parts of the world.

Training for Individuals

CADCIM Technologies with its cost effective and time saving initiative strives to deliver the training in the comfort of your home or work place, thereby relieving you from the hassles of traveling to training centers.

Training Offered on Software Packages

CADCIM provides basic and advanced training on the following software packages:

CAD/CAM/CAE*: CATIA, Pro/ENGINEER Wildfire, PTC Creo Parametric, Creo Direct, SOLIDWORKS, Autodesk Inventor, Solid Edge, NX, AutoCAD, AutoCAD LT, AutoCAD Plant 3D, Customizing AutoCAD, EdgeCAM, and ANSYS*

Architecture and GIS*: Autodesk Revit Architecture, AutoCAD Civil 3D, Autodesk Revit Structure, AutoCAD Map 3D, Revit MEP, Navisworks, Primavera, and Bentley STAAD Pro*

Animation and Styling*: Autodesk 3ds Max, Autodesk Maya, Autodesk Alias, The Foundry NukeX, MAXON CINEMA 4D, Adobe Flash, and Adobe Premiere*

Computer Programming*: C++, VB.NET, Oracle, AJAX, and Java*

*For more information, please visit the following link: **http://www.cadcim.com***

Note

If you are a faculty member, you can register by clicking on the following link to access the teaching resources: ***www.cadcim.com/Registration.aspx***. The student resources are available at ***www.cadcim.com***. We also provide **Live Virtual Online Training** on various software packages. For more information, write us at ***sales@cadcim.com***.

Table of Contents

Chapter 3: Control Statements

Chapter 4: Functions and Arrays

Chapter 5: Strings, Pointers, and Structures

Chapter 6: Union, Enumeration, and Preprocessor

Chapter 7: Data Structures

Chapter 8: Classes and Objects

Chapter 9: Constructors, Destructors, and Operator Overloading

Chapter 10: Inheritance

Chapter 11: Virtual Functions and Polymorphism

Chapter 12: The C++ Console I/O Operations

Chapter 13: Exception Handling

Chapter 14: The File I/O System

Preface

C++

Welcome to **Learning C++ Programming Concepts**, an example based textbook, written to cater to the needs of beginners and programmers. C++ is an object-oriented programming language, which is a preferred programming approach followed by the software industry. C++ enjoys the distinction of being the most popular and widely used OOP language in the world. The syntax, style, features and philosophy of the language form the basis of many other programming languages such as Java and C#.

Created by Bjarne Stroustrup in the early 1980s, C++, over the period, has undergone many changes and improvements. In 1998, the language was standardized by the American National Standards Institute (ANSI) and the International Standards Organization (ISO). The textbook confirms to these standards and explains various features of the language in a simple and easy style.

The highlight of the textbook is that each concept introduced in it has been exemplified by a program to clarify and facilitate better understanding. Also, the line-by-line explanation of each program ensures that the users with no previous programming experience are able to master the programming techniques and concepts and use them with flexibility while designing other programs.

The main features of the book are as follows:

Programming Approach: This textbook introduces the key ideas of object-oriented programming in an intuitive way. The concepts are illustrated through best programming examples, covering all aspects of OOP and C++.

Notes: Additional information is provided to the users in the form of notes.

Illustrations: There is an extensive use of examples, schematic representation, flow-charts, tables, screen capture images, and programming exercises.

Learning Objectives: The first page of every chapter summarizes the topics that are covered in it.

Self-Evaluation Test, Review Questions, and Exercises: Each chapter ends with a Self-Evaluation test so that the users can assess their knowledge. The answers of the Self-Evaluation test are given at the end of the chapter. Also, the Review Questions and Exercises are given at the end of each chapter that can be used by the Instructors as test questions and exercises.

Chapter 1

Introduction to C++

INTRODUCTION

In the early 1980's, a new programming language was developed by Bjarne Stroustrup at Bell Laboratories, USA. This language, an extended version of C language, is known as C++. This object-oriented programming language is also known as the superset of the C language. Apart from the features of the C language, C++ also has some additional features such as classes, objects, and so on. When C++ language was developed, it was known as 'C with classes'. In 1983, the name was changed to C++. The **++** sign specifies that it is an incremented version of the C language. This means that the code written in C can also be executed in the C++ environment. Basically, C++ was developed to eliminate some of the limitations of the C language and also to provide some new features to the user.

In this chapter, you will learn about procedure-oriented programming, key concepts of object-oriented programming, and also some C++ fundamentals.

PROCEDURE-ORIENTED PROGRAMMING

Procedure-oriented programming (POP) is a programming technique in which a problem is divided into subparts. These subparts are solved by using different functions or procedures. In this type of programming technique, all the programs are developed around functions or procedures. These functions or procedures work on the global data (data that can be accessed by all the members of a program) and can also manipulate it. In this type of programming technique, the primary focus is on the functions. For example, you may want to solve a problem that performs three different operations such as reading data from the user, processing the data, and printing the output. Three different functions are created to handle these operations, see Figure 1-1.

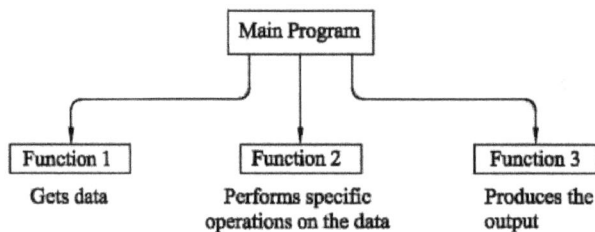

Figure 1-1 *Representation of an example*

The above figure illustrates that all the three operations are performed by three different functions.

In procedure-oriented programming, the data that can be accessed by all the functions is declared as global. Each function can also have its own local data.

A major drawback of procedure-oriented programming is that the data is not treated as a critical element and can be manipulated by any of the functions. Another drawback is that you cannot solve the real world problems by using the procedure-oriented technique. As the size of the program increases, it becomes more complex and difficult to understand.

OBJECT-ORIENTED PROGRAMMING

Object-oriented programming (OOP), developed to overcome the limitations of the procedure-oriented programming, is an improved technique for developing the programs. In case of OOP, the data is treated as the most critical element and the primary focus is on data and not on procedures. In this technique, the data is grouped together with the functions that operate on it. A problem is divided into entities known as objects. Each object maintains its own copy of data and functions. The data cannot be accessed directly by the other objects of the program. It can only be accessed through a proper interface such as functions, as shown in Figure 1-2.

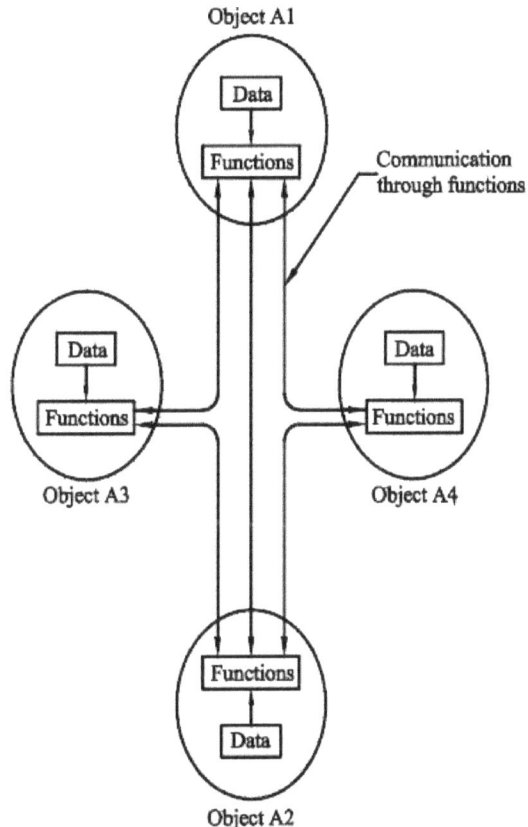

Figure 1-2 *Representation of OOP*

Features of Object-Oriented Programming

There are certain features that have made object-oriented programming very popular. These features are as follows:

1.   Objects
2.   Classes
3.   Encapsulation

4. Inheritance
5. Polymorphism

Objects

In object-oriented programming, a problem is divided into certain basic entities called objects. The objects can be used to represent real life objects such as people, bank account, and so on. In this type of programming, all communication is carried out between the objects. When a program is executed, the objects interact with each other by sending messages. The objects contain the data and the functions that can be used to manipulate the data. Each object maintains its own copy of the data and methods, which can communicate with each other through a proper channel or interface.

Classes

A class is a user-defined data type, which is used to group the data and the functions together. These objects are the instances of a class. A class can also contain important members such as a constructor, which is used to create objects. The objects that belong to the same class must have certain properties in common. For example, a table and a chair are the objects of the class furniture. Both the objects have certain properties in common. For example, both are made of wood and so on.

Encapsulation

Encapsulation is the mechanism used for wrapping up the data along with the functions that can operate on the data directly. This mechanism is used to keep the data safe from the outside interferences. The encapsulation hides the internal data and only provides the external interface (functions) through which it can be accessed. Encapsulation also provides the concept of data hiding or information hiding so that it cannot be accessed directly.

Inheritance

Different kinds of objects often have certain amount of properties in common with each other. Inheritance is the process by which one object can acquire the properties of another object. This is called the reusability of code. In inheritance, whenever a new object is created, it can only define those properties that make it unique from the other objects. Inheritance supports the concept of the hierarchical classifications. For example, the fruit 'Apple' is a part of the class 'Fruits', which is again a part of the class 'Food', as shown in Figure 1-3.

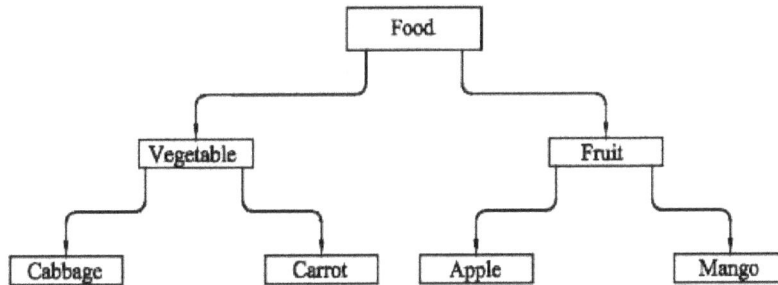

Figure 1-3 *Hierarchical classification*

In the above figure, the two classes Fruits and Vegetables, apart from inheriting certain properties from the class Food, also add some properties of their own. The classes Apple and Mango inherit the properties of the Fruits class while the classes Cabbage and Carrot inherit the properties of the Vegetables class.

Polymorphism

Polymorphism is another feature of object-oriented programming. Polymorphism is a Greek term that consists of two words, poly and morph. Poly means many and morph means forms. So, polymorphism means 'one name many forms'. In polymorphism, an operation shows different behaviors depending on the type of data used in it. In polymorphism, the internal structure (functioning) of the operation is different but the external interface (name) is the same. When an operator shows different behaviors in different contexts, it is known as operator overloading. When a single function name is used to perform different operations, it is known as function overloading, see Figure 1-4.

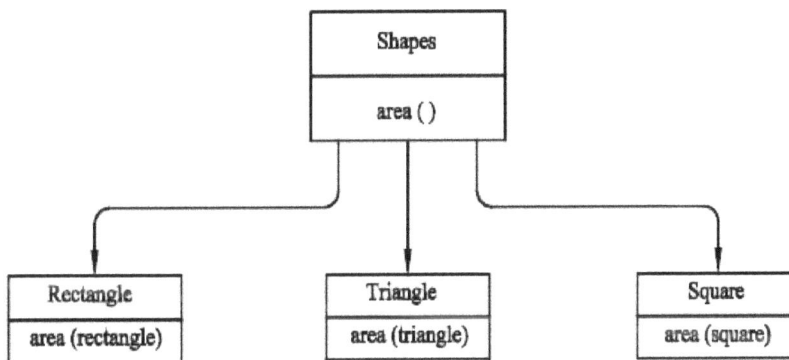

Figure 1-4 *Polymorphism*

FUNDAMENTALS OF C++

In this section, you will learn about some basic fundamentals of C++ and also the process of writing a program in C++.

First C++ Example

The following example illustrates a simple C++ program through a line-by-line explanation.

Example 1

Write a program to perform the addition of two numbers.

The following program will prompt the user to enter two numbers, add them, and then display the output on the screen. The line numbers on the right are not a part of the program and are for reference only.

```
//Write a program to add two numbers                              1
#include<iostream>                                                2
using namespace std;                                              3
int main( )                                                       4
{                                                                 5
     int  i, j, k;                                                6
     cout<<"Enter two numbers: "<<endl;                           7
     cin>>i;                                                      8
     cin>>j;                                                      9
     k=i+j;                                                       10
     cout<<"The result of the addition is: "<<k<<endl;           11
     return 0;                                                    12
}                                                                 13
```

Explanation

Line 1

//Write a program to perform the addition of two numbers

This line starts with two forward slash (//) lines, which represent a single-line comment. This comment is ignored by the compiler (a software program that translates the high-level language into a machine-level language) until the end of the line is encountered. The basic purpose of the comments is to provide short remarks during programming, wherever needed. You can also use multiline comments by using the symbols **/*** and ***/,** as follows:

```
/*   This line
     represents multiline
     comments.
*/
```

Line 2

#include<iostream>

In this line, the contents of the header file **iostream** are included in the program. This header file contains functions that support the C++ Input/Output (I/O) operations. This header file should be included in a program that contains the I/O statements.

Line 3
using namespace std;
This line directs the compiler to use the **std** namespace. A **namespace** provides a region in which all the program elements can be placed. The mechanism of namespaces is used to organize large programs. The keyword **using** specifies to the compiler that you want to use the **std** namespace. The standard library of C++ is declared in the **std** namespace, so it must be included in all the C++ programs.

Line 4
int main( )
In this line, the **main( )** is a function and the keyword **int** specify that an integer value must be returned by the **main( )** function to the operating system. In each program, the execution begins from the **main( )** function. Here, the argument list of the **main** function does not contain the arguments as represented by the empty parenthesis ( ).

Line 5
{}
These are the curly braces, which indicate the start ({) and the end (}) of the **main( )** function. The statements, which are written in between these two ({}) braces, are associated with the **main( )** function and must be executed whenever a call is made to it.

Line 6
int i, j, k;
In this line, the keyword **int** represents the integer data type that can only take numeric values. The variables **i**, **j**, and **k** are the names given to the memory locations that are used to store the integer values assigned to them.

Line 7
cout<<"Enter two numbers: "<<endl;
This is an output statement that causes the string Enter two numbers: to be displayed on the screen. The identifier **cout** is a predefined object of an output stream. It is attached to an output device, which is usually a screen. The **<<** operator is known as the insertion operator or an output operator, which is used to send the string Enter two numbers: to the object **cout**. The keyword **endl**, also known as **endline**, directs the compiler to end the current line and transfer the control to the next line.

Line 8
cin>>i;
This is an input statement that is used to read a number from the user. In this line, the identifier **cin** is a predefined object of an input stream that is connected to an input device, usually a keyboard. The **>>** operator is known as the extraction or an input operator that is used to extract the value from an input device. The value, which is entered by the user from an input device (keyboard) is stored in the variable **i**.

Line 9
cin>>j;
The working of line 9 is the same as line 8.

Line 10
k=i+j;
In this line, the value stored in the variable **i** is added to the value in the variable **j** with the help of the addition operator (**+**). After the addition, the resultant value is assigned to the variable **k** with the help of the assignment operator (**=**). You will learn more about operators in the next chapter.

Line 11
cout<<"The result of the addition is: "<<k<<endl;
This line is used to display the string The result of the addition is:, and also the value of the variable **k** on the screen.

Line 12
return 0;
In this line, the **return** statement is used to return a value (0) to the operating system. This statement is treated as a termination statement, which indicates that the program is terminated normally.

The output of the program is as follows:
Enter two numbers:
10
20
The result of the addition is: 30

The output will be displayed on the screen as follows:

More About I/O Operators

In the previous program, you have already learned about two I/O operators: **<<** (insertion) and **>>** (extraction). These operators can handle any type of data such as **float**, **int**, **char**, and so on. In this section, you will learn more about the working of the I/O operators.

The >> (extraction) Operator

The **>>** (extraction) operator is used with the **cin** statement. The purpose of this operator is to get data as input from the user. The **>>** operator is used to extract the data from an input device through the **cin** object and assign it to the variable on its right.

For example:

        int i;
        cin>>i;

In this example, the **>>** (extraction) operator extracts a value such as 20 from the keyboard and assigns it to the variable **i**, as shown in Figure 1-5.

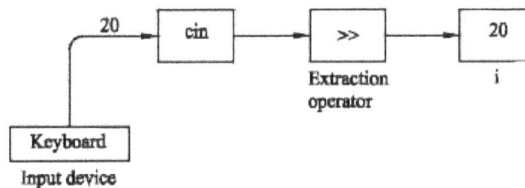

Figure 1-5 *Working of an extraction operator*

The << (insertion) Operator

The **<<** (insertion) operator is used with the **cout** statement, which is used to send the result to an output device. The **<<** (insertion) operator is used to insert the contents of a variable on its right to the object on its left.

For example:

        int avg=10;
        cout<<"Average is: "<<avg<<endl;

In the above example, the **<<** operator first sends the string Average is: to **cout**. Next, the content of the variable **avg** is sent to **cout** and finally the keyword **endl** is sent, which transfers the control to the end of the line, as shown in Figure 1-6.

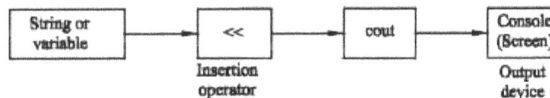

Figure 1-6 *Working of an insertion operator*

The following example illustrates the use of the **>>** (extraction) and **<<** (insertion) operators. Write a program to calculate the average of three numbers.

Example 2

The following program will prompt the user to enter three numbers, calculate their average, and display the resultant value on the screen.

```
//Write a program to find the average of three numbers        1
#include<iostream>                                            2
using namespace std;                                          3
int main( )                                                   4
{                                                             5
        int sub1, sub2, sub3;                                 6
        float avg;                                            7
        cout<<"Enter the points scored in Physics: "<<endl;   8
        cin>>sub1;                                            9
        cout<<"Enter the points scored in Biology: "<<endl;  10
        cin>>sub2;                                            11
        cout<<"Enter the points scored in Chemistry: "<<endl; 12
        cin>>sub3;                                            13
        avg = (sub1+sub2+sub3)/3;                             14
        cout<<"The average is: "<<avg<<endl;                  15
        return 0;                                             16
}                                                             17
```

Explanation

Line 6
int sub1, sub2, sub3;
In this line, **sub1**, **sub2**, and **sub3** are declared as integer type variables.

Line 7
float avg;
In this line, **avg** is declared as a **float** type variable (You will learn about the C++ data types in the next chapter).

Line 8
cout<<"Enter the points scored in Physics: "<<endl;
This line is an output statement, which will display Enter the points scored in Physics: on the screen.

Line 9
cin>>sub1;
In this line, the **cin** statement is used to read an integer value from the user. Next, the resultant value is assigned to the variable **sub1**.

The working of the lines from 10 to 13 is the same as the lines 8 and 9.

Line 14

avg = (sub1+sub2+sub3)/3;

In this line, first the addition operation is performed on the values of the variables **sub1, sub2**, and **sub3**. Next, the resultant value of the addition operation is divided by 3 and is assigned to the variable **avg**.

Line 16

return 0;

In this line, the **return** statement is used to return a value (0) to the operating system. This statement is treated as a termination statement, which indicates that the program is terminated normally.

The output of the program is as follows:

Enter the points scored in Physics:

68

Enter the points scored in Biology:

72

Enter the points scored in Chemistry:

70

The average is: 70

The output will be displayed on the screen as follows:

Self-Evaluation Test

Answer the following questions and then compare them to the answers given at the end of this chapter:

1. In the _____ programming technique, all the programs are developed around the _____ or _____.

2. In object-oriented programming, the _____ is treated as the most critical element.

3. In object-oriented programming, all communication is carried out between the _____.

4. _____ is the process by which one object can acquire the properties of the other objects.

5. The program execution begins from the _____ function.

Answer the following questions:

Review Questions

1. Differentiate between procedure-oriented and object-oriented programming.

2. Explain polymorphism.

3. Explain inheritance.

4. Explain encapsulation.

5. Explain the working of the **<<** (insertion) and **>>** (extraction) operators.

Exercises

Exercise 1

Write a program that prompts the user to enter a number and checks whether it is even or odd. The program should display the result on the screen.

Exercise 2

Write a program that prompts the user to enter two numbers, multiplies them, and then displays the result on the screen.

Answers to Self-Evaluation Test
1. procedure-oriented, functions, procedures, **2.** data, **3.** objects, **4.** Inheritance, **5. main( )**

Chapter 2

Getting Started with C++

After completing this chapter, you will be able to:
- *Understand various data types.*
- *Understand the concept of variables.*
- *Learn about the concept of identifiers and keywords.*
- *Understand various types of constants or literals.*
- *Understand various types of operators.*
- *Understand the concept of expressions.*
- *Understanding type conversions.*

INTRODUCTION

In this chapter, you will learn about the fundamentals of C++ such as variables, data types, identifiers, keywords, constants, operators, and expressions.

VARIABLES

A variable is a named location where data is stored. It is a location in the computer's memory with a specific address, where a value can be stored and retrieved, when required. The value of a variable can vary while the program is being executed.

Variable Name

While naming a variable, you must follow certain rules. The rules are as follows:

a.   Only alphabetic characters, both uppercase and lowercase, digits from 0 to 9, and the underscore (_) can be used.
b.   The name can start with an alphabet or an underscore but not with a digit.
c.   Uppercase and lowercase characters are considered separately by the compiler.
d.   Keywords cannot be used as identifiers.

The following variable names are invalid in C++:
9_count
count#

The following variable names are valid in C++:
count_9
my_account

DATA TYPES

While programming, you need to store variables in the computer's memory. The memory of a computer is organized in bytes. Before storing the variable, the compiler should know the type of value to be stored in the variable and the amount of memory to be allocated to it. For this purpose, C++ provides the concept of data types whose representation depends on the machine architecture.

Table 2-1 lists the fundamental data types, their sizes, and ranges.

Integer Type (int)

The integer data type can store only numeric data and that too, in the form of whole numbers. The data, which is of integer type can be signed or unsigned.

The syntax is as follows:

```
signed int a;
unsigned int b;
int c;
```

In this syntax, **a**, **b**, and **c** are the variables and **signed int**, **unsigned int**, and **int** specify the data type.

A **signed** integer, written as **signed int** in the program, can hold a positive or a negative value, whereas an **unsigned** integer, written as **unsigned int** in the program, can only hold a positive value. By default, an integer is always signed. Depending on the size of the value, the integer type can be **int**, **short int**, and **long int**, see Table 2-1. The range of the values depends on the machine architecture. For example, the range of the values that an integer can store is greater than a short integer but less than the long integer.

Signed and **unsigned** integers can be long or short. For example:

    signed long a;
    unsigned short b;

Data Type	Bytes	Value Range
char	1	-128 to 127
unsigned char	1	0 to 255
signed char	1	-128 to 127
int	2	-32768 to 32767
unsigned int	2	0 to 65535
signed int	2	-32768 to 32767
short int	2	-32768 to 32767
unsigned short int	2	0 to 65535
signed short int	2	-32768 to 32767
long int	4	-2147483648 to 2147483647
unsigned long int	4	0 to 4294967295
signed long int	4	-2147483648 to 2147483647
float	4	3.4e-38 to 3.4e+38
double	8	1.7e-308 to 1.7e+308
long double	10	3.4e-4932 to 1.1e+4932
bool	1	True or False

Table 2-1 *Fundamental data types, values, and their ranges*

Character Type (char)
The character data type can store only a single character, mostly ASCII (American Standard Code for Information Interchange) values. The syntax is as follows:

    char a;
    char b;

In the above syntax, **a** and **b** are the variable names and **char** specifies the character data type.

The value, which is assigned to a character variable, should be enclosed in single quotes. For example:

    char a= 'c';

In the above example, the character value **c** is assigned to the character variable **a** with the help of the assignment operator (**=**). The assignment operator will be discussed later in this chapter.

Table 2-2 lists the ASCII characters and their corresponding values.

Value	Char	Value	Char	Value	Char	Value	Char
33	!	54	6	75	K	96	`
34	"	55	7	76	L	97	a
35	#	56	8	77	M	98	b
36	$	57	9	78	N	99	c
37	%	58	:	79	O	100	d
38	&	59	;	80	P	101	e
39	'	60	<	81	Q	102	f
40	(	61	=	82	R	103	g
41	)	62	>	83	S	104	h
42	*	63	?	84	T	105	i
43	+	64	@	85	U	106	j
44	,	65	A	86	V	107	k
45	-	66	B	87	W	108	l
46	.	67	C	88	X	109	m
47	/	68	D	89	Y	110	n
48	0	69	E	90	Z	111	o
49	1	70	F	91	[	112	p
50	2	71	G	92	\	113	q
51	3	72	H	93	]	114	r
52	4	73	I	94	^	115	s
53	5	74	J	95	_	116	t

Table 2-2 *ASCII characters and their corresponding values*

Floating-point Type (float)

The floating-point data type is used to store decimal point numbers such as 10.23, -0.676, and so on. Depending on the size of the value, there are three sizes for floating-point variables: **float**, **double**, and **long double**. The syntax is as follows:

    float a;
    double a;
    long double a;

The range of **double** is greater than **float** but less than a **long double**.

Boolean Type (bool)

The **bool** data type can hold a **Boolean** value, true or false.

For example:

    bool a=true;
    bool b=false;

The numeric value corresponding to true is 1 and to false is 0.

Declaring a Variable

A variable must be declared before it can be used in the program. The syntax for declaring a variable is as follows:

    data_type var_name;

Each declaration has two parts. The first part is the data type, which specifies the type of value to be stored in the variable and the amount of memory to be allocated. The second part of the declaration is the variable name. While naming a variable, you must follow certain rules. These rules have been described earlier in this chapter.

You can also declare multiple variables of the same type in a single statement. These variables are separated by commas. The syntax is as follows:

    data_type var1, var2, var3;

In the above syntax, the variables **var1**, **var2**, and **var3** are of the same type.

Initializing a Variable

Initialization means to assign an initial value to a variable. You can assign a value to a variable by using the assignment operator (**=**). The assignment operator will be discussed later in this chapter.

The syntax for initializing a variable is as follows:

    data_type var_name = value;

In the above syntax, the **data_type** specifies the type of data, **var_name** specifies the name of the variable, and **value** specifies the initial value that is assigned to the variable. The value on the right side of the operator is assigned to the variable that is on the left side.

Note

If you cannot assign an initial value to a variable, by default, it is initialized to zero.

Scope of a Variable

The scope of a variable refers to that part of the program within which it can be accessed and manipulated. The scope also specifies when to allocate or deallocate memory to the variable. The scope is of the following two types:

a. Global scope
b. Local scope

Global Scope

The variable that is declared outside the **main** function is referred to as a global variable. A global variable can be used anywhere in the program. The memory is allocated to this variable when the program execution begins and deallocated after the program terminates normally.

The following example illustrates the use of the global variable.
Write a program to add two numbers.

Example 1

The following program will prompt the user to enter a number, add it with a global value, and display the output on the screen. The line numbers on the right are not a part of the program and are for reference only.

```
//Write a program that shows the use of the global variable        1
#include<iostream>                                                 2
using namespace std;                                               3
int x=10;//Global variable                                         4
int main()                                                         5
{                                                                  6
        int y,z;                                                   7
        cout<<"Enter a value "<<endl;                              8
        cin>>y;                                                    9
        z=x+y;                                                     10
        cout<<"The total is: "<<z<<endl;                           11
        return 0;                                                  12
}                                                                  13
```

Explanation

Line 4
int x=10;
The variable **x** is defined as a global variable because it is outside the main( ) function of the program. The initial value assigned to this variable is 10.

Line 7
int y,z;
In this line, **y** and **z** are declared as integer type variables.

Line 8

cout<<"Enter a value "<<endl;
This line will display the following on the screen:
Enter a value

Line 9
cin>>y;
This line is used to accept the value of variable **y** from the user.

Line 10
z=x+y;
In this line, the value of the variable **x** is added to the value of the variable **y** by using the addition operator (**+**). The resultant value will be assigned to the variable **z** by using the assignment operator (**=**). These operators will be discussed later in this chapter.

Line 11
cout<<"The total is: "<<z<<endl;
This line will display the following on the screen:
The total is: value of the variable **z**

Line 12
return 0;
In this line, the value 0 is returned to the **main( )** function and the program is terminated.

The output of the program is as follows:
Enter a value
10   (This value is entered by the user)
The total is: 20

Local Scope
The local scope variable can be used in a particular block of a program within which it is defined. The lifetime of a local scope variable is as long as the block that is being executed.

The following example illustrates the use of the local variables.
Write a program to add two numbers.

Example 2

The following program will prompt the user to enter two numbers, add them, and display the output on the screen.

```
//Write a program to illustrate the use of local variables        1
#include<iostream>                                                 2
using namespace std;                                              3
int main()                                                        4
{                                                                 5
```

```
        int x,y,z;//Local to the main function                        6
        cout<<"Enter the value of x"<<endl;                           7
        cin>>x;                                                       8
        cout<<"Enter the value of y"<<endl;                           9
        cin>>y;                                                      10
        z=x+y;                                                       11
        cout<<"The total is: "<<z;                                   12
        return 0;                                                    13
}                                                                    14
```

Explanation

Line 6
int x,y,z;
In this line, **x**, **y**, and **z** are declared as integer type variables. These variables are local to the **main( )** function. They cannot be used outside the **main( )** function.

Line 7
cout<<"Enter the value of x"<<endl;
The line will display the following on the screen:
Enter the value of x

Line 8
cin>>x;
This line is used to accept the value of the variable **x** from the user.

Line 9
cout<<"Enter the value of y"<<endl;
The line will display the following on the screen:
Enter the value of y

Line 10
cin>>y;
This line is used to accept the value of variable **x** from the user.

Line 11
int z=x+y;
In this line, the value of variable **x** is added to the value of the variable **y** by using the addition operator (**+**). The resultant value will be assigned to the variable **z** by using the assignment operator (**=**).

Line 12
cout<<" The total is: "<<z;
The above line will display the following on the screen:
The total is: value of the variable **z**

Line 13
return 0;
In this line, the value 0 is returned to the **main( )** function and the program is terminated.

The output of the program is:
Enter the value of x
10
Enter the value of y
20
The total is: 30

IDENTIFIERS AND CONSTANTS

Identifiers are the names that the programmer uses to represent variables, functions, and labels in a program. While naming an identifier, you need to follow certain rules. The rules are the same as that for naming a variable and these have been described earlier in this chapter.

The following are the examples of identifiers:

    int acc_num
    int roll_num

In the above example, **int** specifies the data type, while **acc_num** and **roll_num** are the identifiers.

The following are some examples of invalid identifiers:

9var_name	Should not start with a number
var#name	Only letters, numbers, and the underscore character (_) can be used
int	Keywords cannot be used as identifiers

Constants are the program elements whose values remain fixed throughout the program. Constants, also called literals, can be of basic data types such as integer, character, and so on. The representation of a constant depends on the type of data. For example, 'v' is a character constant, 10.23 is a floating-point constant, and so on.

KEYWORDS

Keywords are the words that are predefined in any programming language. These words are used for a specific purpose and cannot be used as names for defining variables. For example, **int** refers to an integer data type. The list of the C++ keywords is as follows:

asm	do	if	return	typeid
auto	double	inline	short	typename
bool	dynamic cast	int	signed	union
break	else	long	sizeof	unsigned
case	enum	mutablestatic	using	
catch	explicit	namespace	static_cast	virtual

char	export	new	struct	void
class	extern	operator	switch	volatile
const	false	private	template	wchar_t
const_cast	float	protected	this	while
continue	for	public	throw	
default	friend	register	try	
delete	goto	reinterpret_cast	typedef	

ESCAPE SEQUENCE

Escape sequence is a sequence of characters that are used to send a command to a device or a program. These characters are preceded by a backslash (\ ), which is called an escape character. These characters are not only used for text formatting but they also serve a special purpose. For example, **\n** is used for switching the control to the next line. The list of escape sequence characters is as follows:

\n   newline
\r   carriage return
\t   tab
\v   vertical tab
\b   backspace
\f   form feed
\a   alert(beep)
\'   single quote
\"   double quote
\?   question mark
\\   backslash

Example 3

The following example illustrates the use of the escape sequence characters.
Write a program to illustrate the working of the escape sequence characters.

The following program will display the string (specified in the program) in the next line by using the escape sequence characters.

```
//Write a program that shows the working of the escape sequence characters    1
#include<iostream>                                                            2
using namespace std;                                                          3
int main( )                                                                   4
{                                                                             5
        cout<<" \t This is used for tabular space"<<endl;                     6
        cout<<" \n This shifts the control to the next line"<<endl;           7
        return 0;                                                             8
}                                                                             9
```

Explanation
Line 6

cout<<" \t This is used for tabular space"<<endl;
This line will display the following on the screen:
> This is used for tabular space

> **Note**
> *In the above output, the space before the output statement is because of the \t (tabular space)*
> *character.*

Line 7
cout<<" \n This shifts the control to the next line"<<endl;
This line will display the following on the screen:
This shifts the control to the next line

The output of the program is:
> This is used for tabular space

This shifts the control to the next line

In the above output, the output statement will be printed in the next line because of the **\n** (new line) character, which shifts the control to the next line.

The output will be displayed on the screen as follows:

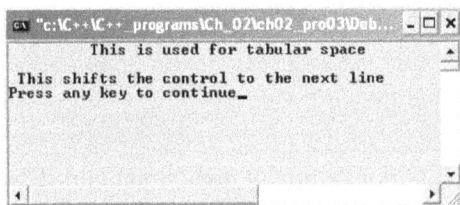

OPERATORS

Operators are defined as the symbols that are used when an operation is performed on the variables or constants. C++ provides a variety of operators, which are as follows:

a. Assignment operator
b. Arithmetic operators
c. Increment or decrement operators
d. Relational and equality operators
e. Logical operators
f. Conditional operators
g. Compound assignment operators
h. sizeof () operator
i. Scope resolution operator

Assignment Operator

The assignment operator is used to assign a value to a variable. The equal (=) symbol is used as the assignment operator. The syntax for using the assignment operator is as follows:

    variable_name = value;

In the above syntax, the **value** on the right of the assignment operator (=) is assigned to the variable **variable_name** that is on the left. The left value should always be a variable. The right value can be a variable, a constant, or the result of an operation.

You can also use the assignment operator (=) for multiple assignments. The syntax is as follows:

    var1 = var2 = var3 = value;

In the above syntax, the same value is assigned to all the three variables.

Arithmetic Operators

There are five arithmetic operators in C++. These are as follows:

Operators	Operation
+	Addition
-	Subtraction
*	Multiplication
/	Division
%	Modulus

A modulus operator returns the remainder after the division of two numbers. The percentage symbol (%) is used as the operator.

The syntax for using the modulus operator is as follows:

    var1 = var2 % var3;

In the above syntax, after the division of the **var2** and **var3**, the remainder is assigned to **var1**.

The following example illustrates the use of the modulus operator (%).

Example 4

Write a program to divide two integers and store the remainder into the third integer.

The following program will prompt the user to enter two numbers, divide them, store the remainder, and display the output on the screen.

//Write a program that divides two integers and stores the remainder
//into the third integer by using the modulus operator

```
                                                                           1
#include<iostream>                                                         2
using namespace std;                                                       3
int main()                                                                 4
{                                                                          5
        int a, b, c;                                                       6
        cout<<"Enter two numbers "<<endl;                                  7
        cin>>a>>b;                                                         8
        c=a%b;                                                             9
        cout<<"The remainder is: "<<c<<endl;                              10
        return 0;                                                         11
}                                                                         12
```

Explanation

Line 6
int a, b, c;
In this line, **a**, **b**, and **c** are declared as integer type variables.

Line 7
cout<<"Enter two numbers "<<endl;
The line will display the following on the screen:
Enter two numbers

Line 8
cin>>a>>b;
This line is used to accept the value of variables **a** and **b** from the user.

Line 9
c=a%b;
In this line, the value of variable **a** is divided by the value of variable **b** and the remainder is assigned to the variable c.

Line 10
cout<<"The remainder is: "<<c<<endl;
This line displays the following on the screen:
The remainder is: the value of variable **c**

Line 11
return 0;
In this line, the value 0 is returned to the **main( )** function and the program is terminated.

The output of the program is as follows:
Enter two numbers
12
3
The remainder is: 0

The output will be displayed on the screen as follows:

```
"c:\C++\C++_programs\Ch_02\ch02_pr...
Enter two numbers
12
3
The remainder is: 0
Press any key to continue_
```

Increment and Decrement Operators

In C++, there are two operators: increment (++) and decrement (--). The increment operator (++) increases the value by one and the decrement operator (--) decreases the value by one. You can use these operators in two notations, which are as follows:

a. Prefix increment and decrement operators
b. Postfix increment and decrement operators

Prefix Increment and Decrement Operators

The prefix increment operator (++) increases the value of its operand by one. So, in prefix notations, the value of the operand is increased by one and then it is assigned to the variable on the left side. In these notations, the operator is used before the operand (++a). The syntax for using the prefix increment operator is as follows:

    var1 = ++var2

In the above syntax, the value of the **var2** is increased by one and then it is assigned to **var1**.

The prefix decrement operator (--) is the same as prefix increment operator, except that in the former the value of the operand is decremented by one.

Postfix Increment and Decrement Operators

The postfix increment operator (++) also increases the value of its operand by one. In the postfix notations, the increment is done after the value of the operand is assigned to the variable on the left side of the assignment operator. In these notations, the operator is used after the operand (a++).

The syntax for using the postfix increment operator is as follows:

    var1 = var2++

In the above syntax, the value of the variable **var2** is assigned to the variable **var1**. Next, the value of the variable **var2** is incremented by one.

The following example illustrates the use of the increment operators.

Example 5

Write a program to illustrate the working of the prefix and postfix increment operators.

The following program will increment the value of a variable, assign the resultant value to another variable, and display the output on the screen.

```
//Write a program that illustrates the use of the prefix and postfix    
//increment operators                                                    1
#include<iostream>                                                       2
using namespace std                                                      3
int main()                                                              4
{                                                                       5
        int a=5,b,c;                                                    6
        b=a++;                                                          7
        c=++a;                                                          8
        cout<<"Value of b is: "<< b <<endl;                             9
        cout<<"Value of a is: "<< a <<endl;                            10
        cout<<"Value of c is: "<< c <<endl;                            11
        return 0;                                                      12
}                                                                      13
```

Explanation
Line 6
int a=5,b,c;
In this line, **a**, **b**, and **c** are declared as integer type variables and the value 5 is assigned to the variable **a**.

Line 7
b=a++;
In this line, the value of variable **a** (5) is assigned to variable **b.** Next, the value of variable **a** is incremented by one and it becomes 6.

Line 8
c=++a
In this line, the value of variable **a** (6) is incremented by one and it becomes 7. Next, it is assigned to variable **c** and it becomes 7.

Line 9
cout<<"Value of b is: "<< b <<endl;
This line will display the following on the screen:
Value of b is: 5

Line 10

cout<<"Value of a is: "<< a <<endl;
This line will display the following on the screen:
Value of a is: 7

Line 11
cout<<"Value of c is: "<< c <<endl;
This line will display the following on the screen:
Value of c is: 7

Line 12
return 0;
In this line, the value 0 is returned to the **main( )** function and the program is terminated.

The output of the program is as follows:
Value of b is: 5
Value of a is: 7
Value of c is: 7

Relational Operators

The relational operators are used to evaluate the relationship between two expressions or variables such that they are equal or one of them is greater or less than the other. The value returned by these operators is true or false.

The list of the relational operators is as follows:

Operators	Description
==	Equal
!=	Not equal
>	Greater than
>=	Greater than or equal to
<	Less than
<=	Less than or equal to

Note
The equality operator (==) is not the same as the assignment operator (=). The equality operator (==) is used to check the equality between two expressions or variables.

Logical Operators

C++ provides the following three logical operators:

a. AND (&&)
b. OR (||)
c. NOT (!)

These operators are used to join two relational expressions. The operators AND (**&&**) and

OR (||) are used when a single relational result is obtained from two expressions. The value returned by these operators is either true or false. The NOT (!) operator reverses the resultant value such that true is converted into false and false into true.

The relational and logical operators are explained with programming examples in Chapter 3.

Conditional Operator (? :)

The conditional operator (? :) is also known as the ternary operator. The syntax for using the conditional operator is as follows:

conditional expression ? statement 1 : statement 2

In the above syntax, if the conditional expression is true, **statement 1** will be executed. Otherwise, **statement 2** will be executed.

The following example illustrates the use of the conditional operator.

Example 6

Write a program to find the greater of the two numbers.

The following program will prompt the user to enter two numbers, compare them, and display the greater of the two on the screen.

```
//Write a program that finds the greater of the two numbers        1
#include<iostream>                                                  2
using namespace std;                                               3
int main()                                                         4
{                                                                  5
        cout<<"Enter two numbers"<<endl;                           6
        cin>>a>>b;                                                 7
        (a>b) ? cout<<"a is greater" : cout<<"b is greater"<<endl; 8
        return 0;                                                  9
}                                                                  10
```

Explanation
Line 6
cout<<"Enter two numbers"<<endl;
This line will display the following on the screen:
Enter two numbers

Line 7
cin>>a>>b;
This line is used to accept the value of variables **a** and **b** from the user.

Line 8
(a>b) ? cout<<"a is greater" : cout<<"b is greater"<<endl;

This line shows the working of the conditional operator. In this line, the condition (a is greater than b) is checked. If the condition is true, a is greater will be displayed. Otherwise, b is greater will be displayed.

Line 9
return 0;
In this line, the value 0 is returned to the **main( )** function and the program is terminated.

The output of the program is as follows:
Enter two numbers
56
65
b is greater

The output will be displayed on the screen as follows:

Compound Assignment Operators

The compound assignment operators are used when an operation is performed on the value currently stored in a variable and the modified value is again stored in the same variable. The list of these operators is as follows:

    Operators

    +=
    -=
    *=
    /=
    %=
    >>=
    <<=
    &=
    |=
    ^=

The syntax of these operators is as follows:

    var1 += value or expression

In this syntax, the value or the result of the expression is added to the current value of the variable **var1**. After that, it is assigned back to the same variable **var1**.

The following example illustrates the use of compound assignment operators.

Example 7

Write a program that will add two numbers by using the compound assignment operators. The following program will perform the addition operation on two numbers, assign the resultant value to the first variable, and display the result on the screen.

```
//Write a program to illustrate the working of the
//compound assignment operators                          1
#include<iostream>                                        2
using namespace std;                                      3
int main( )                                               4
{                                                         5
        int a=4,b=5;                                      6
        a+=b;                  //same as a=a+b            7
        cout<<"The value of a is: "<<a<<endl;             8
        return 0;                                         9
}                                                        10
```

Explanation
Line 6
int a=4,b=5;
In this line, **a** and **b** are declared as integer type variables. Value 4 is assigned to the variable **a** and value 5 is assigned to the variable **b**.

Line 7
a+=b;
In this line, the value of the variable **b** (5) is added to the current value of the variable **a** (4) and the resultant value 9 is assigned back to the variable **a**.

Line 8
cout<<"The value of a is: "<<a<<endl;
This line will display the following on the screen:
The value of a is: 9

The output of the program is as follows:
The value of a is: 9

sizeof() Operator
In C++, the amount of memory used by a variable or a data type depends on the machine architecture and on the compiler. To know the amount of memory used by a variable or a data type, you can use the **sizeof()** operator. The **sizeof()** operator returns the amount of memory used by a variable or a data type in terms of bytes.

The syntax for using the **sizeof( )** operator is as follows:
    sizeof(variable or datatype)

The following program illustrates the use of the **sizeof( )** operator.

Example 8

Write a program to illustrate the working of the **sizeof( )** operator.

The following program will display the memory space (in terms of bytes) used by an integer type variable.

```
//Write a program to display the number of bytes                1
//used by an integer type variable                              2
#include<iostream>                                              3
using namespace std;                                           4
int main( )                                                     5
{                                                               6
        int a;                                                  7
        a=sizeof(int);                                          8
        cout<<"Value of a is: "<<a;                            9
        return 0;                                              10
}
```

Explanation
Line 6
int a;
In this line, **a** is declared as an integer type variable.

Line 7
a=sizeof(int);
In this line, value 2 is returned by the operator. This is because two bytes of memory is used by an integer. Next, the value 2 is assigned to variable **a**.

Line 8
cout<<"Value of a is: "<<a;
This line will display the following on the screen:
Value of a is: 2

The output of the program is as follows:
Value of a is: 2

Note
The memory space (in bytes) used by a datatype varies from compiler to compiler.

Scope Resolution Operator (::)

The scope resolution operator (**::**) directs the compiler to use the global variable rather than the local variable. By default, the local variable is used by the compiler.

The syntax for using the scope resolution operator is as follows:

:: var1;

In the above syntax, **var1** refers to the global variable. In the case of a local variable, you do not have to use the scope resolution operator.

The following program illustrates the use of the scope resolution operator.

Example 9

Write a program to illustrate the working of the scope resolution operator.

The following program will display the values of the global and local variables on the screen.

```
//Write a program to illustrate the use of the scope resolution operator      1
#include<iostream>                                                            2
using namespace std;                                                          3
int x=234;       //Global variable                                           4
        int main()                                                           5
{                                                                            6
        int x=10;        //Local variable                                   7
        cout<<"The value of the global variable is: "<<::x<<endl;           8
        cout<<"The value of the local variable is: "<<x<<endl;             9
        return 0;                                                           10
}                                                                           11
```

Explanation

Line 4
int x=234;
In this line, **x** is defined as a global variable and the initial value assigned to it is 234.

Line 7
int x=10;
In this line, **x** is declared as a local variable and the initial value assigned to it is 10.

Line 8
cout<<"The value of the global variable is: "<< ::x <<endl;
In this line, the scope resolution operator is used with variable **x**. So, the value of the global variable **x** will be accessed from the particular memory location. This line will display the following on the screen:
The value of the global variable is: 234

Line 9
cout<<"The value of the local variable is: "<< x <<endl;
This line will display the following on the screen:
The value of the local variable is: 10

The output of the program is as follows:
The value of the global variable is: 234
The value of the local variable is: 10

Operator Precedence

The operator precedence determines the order of execution of operators by the compiler. An operator with a high precedence is used before an operator with a low precedence.

For example:

x=a+b*c

In the above example, the multiplication operator (*****) has a higher precedence than the addition (**+**) and the assignment operators (**=**). So, the value of the variable **b** is multiplied by the value of variable **c** and then the resultant value is added to the variable **a** (because the addition operator has a higher precedence than the assignment operator). Next, the resultant value of the expression (a+b*c) is assigned to the variable **x**.

Operator Associativity

When two or more operators have the same precedence in an expression, the order in which the operation is performed is defined as the associativity of an operator. The following are the two types of associativity:

a.   Left to Right
b.   Right to Left

Left to Right Associativity
In the left to right associativity, all the operations are performed from the left to the right. For example:

x=a+b+c

In the above example, the addition operator has the left to the right associativity. So, the value of variable **a** is added to the value of variable **b.** Next, the resultant value is added to the value of the variable **c**.

Right to Left Associativity
In the right to left associativity, all the operations are performed from the right to the left.

For example:

x+=y

In the above example, the compound assignment operator has the left to the right associativity. So, the value of variable **x** is added to the value of variable **y**. Next, the resultant value is assigned back to variable **x**.

Table 2-3 shows all the operators, their precedence, and their associativity. In this table, **R to L** is used for Right to Left and **L to R** is used for Left to Right.

Precedence	Operator	Associativity
1	:: ( ) [] . -> dynamic_cast type_id	**L to R**
2	++ -- + - ! ~ & * (type) sizeof( ) new delete	**R to L**
3	.* ->*	**L to R**
4	* / %	**L to R**
5	+ -	**L to R**
6	<< >>	**L to R**
7	< > <= >=	**L to R**
8	== !=	**L to R**
9	&	**L to R**
10	^	**L to R**
11	|	**L to R**
12	&&	**L to R**
13	||	**L to R**
14	? :	**R to L**
15	= += -= *= /= <<= >>= %= &= ^= |=	**R to L**
16	,	**L to R**

Table 2-3 *Operators, their precedence, and associativity*

EXPRESSIONS

An expression is a combination of variables and operators. These elements are combined according to the specified rules of the language.

For example:

    a=b+c   //Expression

In the above example, the expression contains three variables, **a**, **b**, and **c** and two operators, addition (**+**) and assignment (**=**). The operators specify the type of operation that is to be performed on the values of the variables.

In an expression, there can be one or more variables and one or more operators to perform an operation on the variables.

TYPE CASTING OR CONVERSION

Type casting means the conversion of one data type to another data type. For example, a float value can be converted into an integer value. There are two types of type casting that are discussed next.

a.   Implicit type casting
b.   Explicit type casting

Implicit Type Casting

In implicit type casting, the conversion is done automatically by the compiler. In this type of conversion, a smaller data type is converted into a larger data type. For example, a float value can be converted into a double value because the size of the float value is 4 bytes and the size of the double value is 8 bytes. So, it is possible for a double variable to take a float value. No operator is required in an implicit conversion. This is done without any intervention of the programmer.

Explicit Type Casting

In explicit type casting, the conversion is carried out between two incompatible types. For example, a float value can be converted into an integer value. This is done with the help of the **(type)** operator. The syntax is as follows:

    data_type var1 = (type) var2

For example:

    int i = (int) 10.23

In the above example, the value (10.23) is converted into an integer value (10) and after that the resultant value (10) is assigned to the variable **i**. Here **int** is used as a **(type)** operator to convert the float value into an integer value.

The following example illustrates the implicit and explicit conversions.

Example 10

Write a program to illustrate the conversion from one data type to another.
The following program will convert a **float** type value into **double** and then the same value into an **int** data type. It will also display the resultant values on the screen.

```
//Write a program to convert a float value to a double value
//and also a float value to an integer type          1
#include<iostream>                                    2
using namespace std;                                  3
int main()                                            4
{                                                     5
        int i;                                        6
        float a= 10.23;                               7
        double b;                                     8
        b=a;    //Implicit conversion                 9
        cout<<"Value of b is: "<<b<<endl;            10
        i=(int) a;          //Explicit conversion    11
        cout<<"Value of i is: "<<i<<endl;            12
        return 0;                                    13
}                                                    14
```

Explanation
Line 6
int i;
In this line, **i** is declared as an integer type variable.

Line 7
float a= 10.23;
In this line, **a** is declared as a **float** type variable and the value 10.23 is assigned to it.

Line 8
double b;
In this line, **b** is declared as a **double** type variable.

Line 9
b=a;
This line shows implicit type casting. In this line, the value of the float variable **a** is assigned to the double type variable **b.** This is done automatically by the compiler because the size of the float data type is smaller than the double data type.

Line 10
cout<<"Value of b is: "<<b<<endl;
This line will display the following on the screen:
Value of b is: 10.23
Line 11

i=(int) a;
This line shows the explicit type casting. In this line, a **float** value (10.23) is converted into an integer value (10). The conversion is done with the help of the **(type)** operator. Here **(int)** is used as the **(type)** operator.

Line 12
cout<<"Value of i is: "<<i<<endl;
This line will display the following on the screen:
Value of i is: 10

The output of the program is as follows:
Value of b is: 10.23
Value of i is: 10

Self-Evaluation Test

Answer the following questions and then compare them to the answers given at the end of this chapter:

1. A variable is a _____ storage location.

2. The _____ cannot be used as identifiers.

3. The _____ are the program elements whose values remain fixed throughout the program.

4. The _____ operator is used to assign a value to a variable.

5. The _____ operator returns the amount of memory used by a variable or a data type.

Review Questions

Answer the following questions:

1. The modulus operator (%) returns the remainder after the division of two numbers. (T/F)

2. The equality operator (==) is the same as the assignment operator (=). (T/F)

3. The logical operators are used to join two relational expressions. (T/F)

4. The scope resolution operator is used to access the global variable. (T/F)

5. The implicit conversion is done automatically by the compiler. (T/F)

Exercises

Exercise 1

Write a program to find whether the number entered by the user is even or odd.

Exercise 2

Write a program to divide two numbers entered by the user and also display the quotient.

Answers to Self-Evaluation Test

1. named, 2. keywords, 3. constants, 4. assignment, 5. **sizeof( )**

Chapter 3

Control Statements

In this chapter, you will learn about the flowcharts and the control structures.

FLOWCHART

A flowchart is a graphical representation of the steps that constitute a program. It shows how the control moves in a program. A flowchart is drawn using some special symbols, which are as follows:

Oval

The oval symbol represents the start and the end of the program. The symbol is as follows:

Figure 3-1 *An oval symbol*

Rectangle

The rectangle symbol represents the process box in which actions such as calculations are performed. The symbol is as follows:

Figure 3-2 *A rectangle symbol*

Diamond

The diamond symbol represents the decision box in which a condition is checked. The symbol is as follows:

Figure 3-3 *A diamond symbol*

Arrow

The arrow symbol represents the path through which the control passes from one symbol to another symbol. The symbol is as follows:

Figure 3-4 *An arrow symbol*

Parallelogram

The parallelogram symbol represents the input or the output box. The symbol is as follows:

Figure 3-5 *A parallelogram symbol*

CONTROL STRUCTURES

The programs, during execution, may need to take decisions and repeat a particular block of code a number of times. C++ provides **control structures** or **control statements** that specify the order of the execution of the statements. The control structures control the flow of the execution in a program. The control structures are of three types:

a. Sequential control structure
b. Selection or Decision control structure
c. Repetition, Iteration, or Loop control structure

Sequential Control Structure

In a sequential control structure, the program statements are executed one after the other in the same order as they appear in the program. In all programming languages, the sequential control is used as the default control. All the programs that have been described in the earlier chapters are sequential.

Selection or Decision Control Structure

The selection or decision control structure is used to alter the flow of control in a program. The flow of control depends on the result of a particular condition applied to it. C++ supports three different types of selection control structures:

a. if statement
b. if-else statement
c. switch statement

The if Statement

The **if** statement is a single path statement, which means it will execute a statement or a block of statements only if the condition is true. The syntax for the **if** statement is as follows:

    if(condition or expression)
        statement1;

In the above syntax, the condition or expression can be true or false. If the condition or expression is true, **statement1** will be executed. Otherwise, the control will be transferred to the next statement after the **if** block.

In case there is more than one statement that must be executed if the condition is true, then the statements should be grouped together in braces {}. The syntax for the **if** statement is as follows:

```
if(condition or expression)
{
        statement 1;
        statement 2;
        _____
        _____
        statement n;
}
```

In the above syntax, all the statements from 1 to n will be executed, if the condition or expression within the **if** statement is true. Otherwise, they will not be executed and the control will be transferred to the next statement after the **if** block.

The following example illustrates the use of the **if** statement.

Example 1

Write a program to find the greater of the two numbers.

The following program will prompt the user to enter two numbers, compare them, and display the greater of the two on the screen. The numbers on the right are not a part of the program and are for reference only.

```
//Write a program to find the greater of the two numbers
1
#include<iostream>                                              2
using namespace std;                                           3
int main()                                                     4
{                                                              5
        int a,b;                                               6
        cout<<"Enter two numbers"<<endl;                       7
        cin>>a>>b;                                             8
        if(a>b)                                                9
        cout<<"a is greater than b"<<endl;                     10
        cout<<"b is greater than a"<<endl;                     11
        return 0;                                              12
}                                                              13
```

Explanation
Line 6
int a,b;
In this line, **a** and **b** are declared as integer type variables.

Line 7
cout<<"Enter two numbers"<<endl;
This line will display the following on the screen:
Enter two numbers

Line 8
cin>>a>>b;
This line is used to accept the values of variables **a** and **b** from the user.

Line 9
if(a>b)
In this line, the **if** statement is used to check the
condition whether it is **true** or **false**. If the condition
a>b (a is greater than b) is true, the next line (line 10)
will be executed. Otherwise, line 10 will be skipped
by the compiler and the control will be transferred
to line 11.

Line 10
cout<<"a is greater than b"<<endl;
This line will display the following on the screen:
a is greater than b

Line 11
cout<<"b is greater than a"<<endl;
This line will display the following on the screen:
b is greater than a

The output of the program is:
Enter two numbers
3
2
a is greater than b

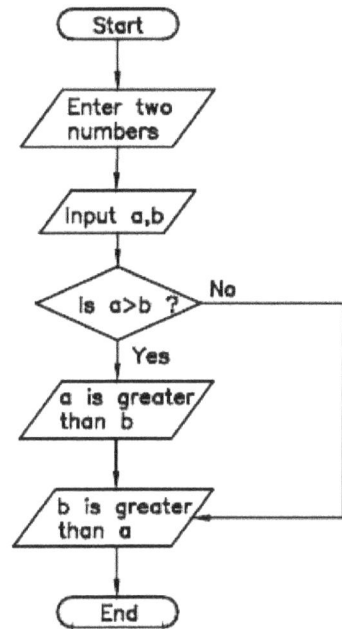

Figure 3-6 *Flowchart of Example 1*

The flowchart in Figure 3-6 gives a diagrammatic representation of the program described
in Example 1.

The if-else Statement
The **if-else** statement is a dual path statement, which means if the condition given within the
if statement is true, the statements associated with the **if** block will be executed. Otherwise,
the statements associated with the **else** block will be executed. The syntax for the **if-else**
statement is as follows:

```
if(condition or expression)
{
    statement 1;
```

```
        statement 2;
    }
    else
    {
        statement 3;
        statement 4;
    }
```

In the above syntax, if the given condition or expression is true, **statements 1** and **2** will be executed and the **else** block will be skipped. Otherwise, the **if** block will be skipped and the **statements 3** and **4**, which are associated with the **else** block, will be executed.

The following example illustrates the use of the **if-else** statement.

Example 2

Write a program to find the greater of the two numbers by using the **if-else** statement.

The following program will prompt the user to enter two numbers, compare them, and display the greater of the two on the screen.

```
//Write a program to find the greater of the two numbers        1
#include<iostream>                                              2
using namespace std;                                            3
int main()                                                      4
{                                                               5
        int a,b;                                                6
        cout<<"Enter two numbers"<<endl;                        7
        cin>>a>>b;                                              8
        if (a>b)                                                9
                cout<<"a is greater than b" <<endl;            10
        else                                                   11
                cout<<"b is greater than a" <<endl;            12
        return 0;                                              13
}                                                              14
```

Explanation
Line 6
int a,b;
In this line, **a** and **b** are declared as integer type variables.

Line 7
cout<<"Enter two numbers"<<endl;
This line will display the following on the screen:
Enter two numbers

Line 8
cin>>a>>b;
This line is used to accept the values of variables **a** and **b** from the user.

Line 9
if (a>b)
In this line, the **if** statement is used to verify whether the condition within the **if** statement is **true** or **false**. If the condition **a>b** (a is greater than b) is true, the next line (line 10) will be executed. Otherwise, line 10 will be skipped and the control will be transferred to line 11.

Line 10
cout<<"a is greater than b" <<endl;
This line will display the following on the screen:
a is greater than b

Line 11
else
This statement and the block of code associated with this will be executed only if the condition given in the **if** statement is false. Otherwise, the whole **else** block will be skipped.

Line 12
cout<<"b is greater than a" <<endl;
This line will display the following on the screen:
b is greater than a

The output of this program is as follows:
Enter two numbers
2
3
b is greater than a

The flowchart in Figure 3-7 gives a diagrammatic representation of the program described in Example 2.

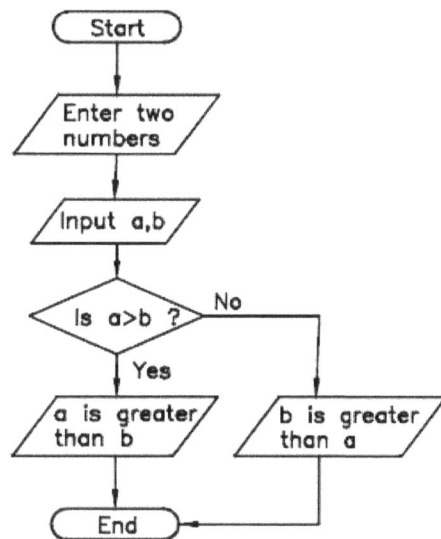

Figure 3-7 *Flowchart of Example 2*

Nested-if statement

When an **if** statement is used within another **if** statement, the resulting statement is known as a **nested-if** statement. In the **nested-if** structure, the last **else** statement is always associated with the **if** block that precedes it. The syntax for the **nested-if** statement is as follows:

```
if(condition)
{
        if(condition)
        {
```

```
                          statements;
                          if(condition)
                          else
                          {
                                  statements;
                          }
                }
        }
```

The following program illustrates the use of the **nested-if** statement.

Example 3

Write a program to find the greatest of the three numbers by using the **nested-if** statement.

The program given next will prompt the user to enter three numbers, compare them, and display the greatest of the three numbers on the screen.

```
//Write a program to find the greatest of the three numbers          1
#include<iostream>                                                   2
using namespace std;                                                 3
int main()                                                           4
{                                                                    5
        int a,b,c;                                                   6
        cout<<"Enter three numbers"<<endl;                           7
        cin>>a>>b>>c;                                                8
        if(a>b)                                                      9
        {                                                            10
                if(a>c)                                              11
                {                                                    12
                        cout<<"a is the greatest number"<<endl;      13
                }                                                    14
                else                                                 15
                {                                                    16
                        cout<<"c is the greatest number"<<endl;      17
                }                                                    18
        }                                                            19
        else                                                         20
        {                                                            21
                if(b>c)                                              22
                {                                                    23
                        cout<<"b is the greatest number"<<endl;      24
                }                                                    25
                else                                                 26
                {                                                    27
                        cout<<"c is the greatest number"<<endl;      28
                }                                                    29
```

```
        }                                                      30
}                                                              31
```

Explanation

Line 6
int a,b,c;
In this line, **a**, **b**, and **c** are declared as integer type variables.

Line 7
cout<<"Enter three numbers"<<endl;
This line will display the following on the screen:
Enter three numbers

Line 8
cin>>a>>b>>c;
This line is used to accept the values of variables **a, b,** and **c** from the user.

Line 9
if(a>b)
In this line, the **if** statement is used to check whether the value of variable **a** is greater than the value of variable **b**. If the condition is true, the control will be transferred to line 11. Otherwise, the control will be transferred to line 20**.**

Line 10
{
This line indicates the start of the **if** statement (line 9).

Line 11
if(a>c)
If the condition given in line 9 is true, the control will pass to line 11. Otherwise, this line will be skipped by the compiler. In this line, the **if** statement is used to check whether the value of variable **a** is greater than the value of variable **c**. If the condition is true, the control will be transferred to line 13. Otherwise, the control will be transferred to line 15.

Line 12
{
This line indicates the start of the **if** statement (line 11).

Line 13
cout<<"a is the greatest number"<<endl;
This line will display the following on the screen:
a is the greatest number

Line 14
}
This line indicates the end of the **if** statement (line 11).
Line 15
else

If the condition given in line 11 is true, the control will pass to line 15. Otherwise, the entire **else** block will be skipped by the compiler.

Line 16
{
This line indicates the start of the **else** statement (line 15).

Line 17
cout<<"c is the greatest number"<<endl;
This line will display the following on the screen:
c is the greatest number

Line 18
}
This line indicates the end of the **else** statement (line 15).

Line 19
}
This line indicates the end of the **if** statement (line 9).

Line 20
else
This **else** block is associated with the **if** statement given in line 9. If the condition given in line 9 is false, the control will pass to the **else** statement. Otherwise, the entire **else** block will be skipped by the compiler.

Line 22
if(b>c)
In this line, the **if** statement is used to check whether the value of variable **b** is greater than the value of variable **c**. If the condition is true, line 24 will be executed. Otherwise, it will be skipped and the control will be transferred to line 26.

Line 24
cout<<"b is the greatest number"<<endl;
This line will display the following on the screen:
b is the greatest number

Line 26
else
This **else** block is associated with the **if** statement given in line 22. If the condition given in line 22 is false, the control will pass to the **else** statement. Otherwise, the entire **else** block will be skipped by the compiler.

Line 28
cout<<"c is the greatest number"<<endl;

This line will display the following on the screen:
c is the greatest number

The output of the program is as follows:
Enter three numbers
12
23
34
c is the greatest number

The output will be displayed on the screen as follows:

```
c:\C++\C++_programs\Ch_03\ch03_pr...  _ □ ×
Enter three numbers
12
23
34
c is the greatest number
Press any key to continue
```

The flowchart in Figure 3-8 gives a diagrammatic representation of the program described in Example 3.

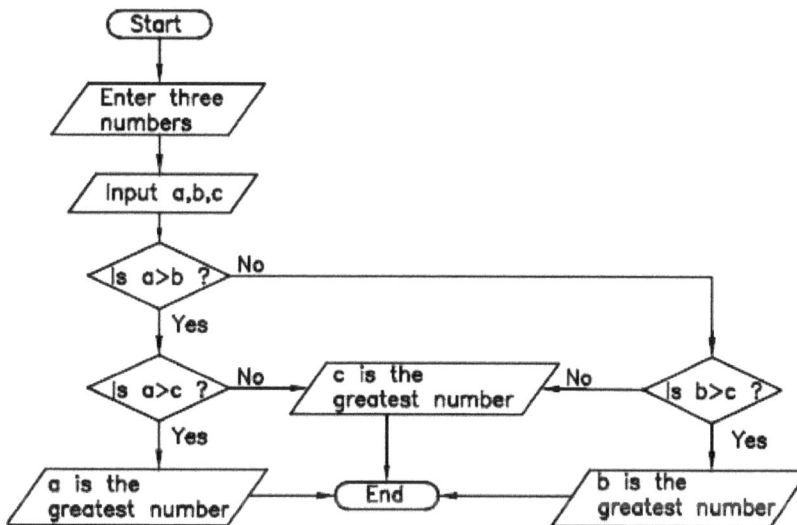

Figure 3-8 *Flowchart of Example 3*

The else if Statement

The **else if** statement is a conditional statement that is used when you want to verify more than one condition. The working of the **else if** statement is the same as that of the **if** statement, except that the **else if** statement must be preceded by an **if** statement. The syntax for the **else if** statement is as follows:

```
if(condition)
     statement1;
else if(condition)
     statement2;
else
     statement3;
```

In the above syntax, the condition given in the **if** statement is checked if it is true or false. If the condition is true, **statement1** will be executed. Otherwise, the condition given in the **else if** statement will be checked. If it is true, **statement2** will be executed. Otherwise, **statement3** will be executed.

The following program illustrates the use of the **else if** statement.

Example 4

Write a program to display the grades based on the points scored by the user.

The following program will prompt the user to enter the points scored, calculate the grades, and display the equivalent grade on the screen.

```
//Write a program that displays the grades according to the points scored    1
#include<iostream>                                                           2
using namespace std;                                                         3
int main()                                                                   4
{                                                                            5
     int points_scored;                                                      6
     cout<<"Enter the points scored"<<endl;                                  7
     cin>>points_scored;                                                     8
     if(points_scored>=90)                                                   9
          cout<<"Grade A"<<endl;                                             10
     else if(points_scored>=80)                                             11
          cout<<"Grade B"<<endl;                                             12
     else if(points_scored>=70)                                             13
          cout<<"Grade C"<<endl;                                             14
     else                                                                    15
     cout<<"FAIL"<<endl;
               16
     return  0;                                                              17
}                                                                            18
```

Explanation

Line 6

int points_scored;

In this line, **points_scored** is declared as an integer type variable.

Line 7

cout<<"Enter the points scored"<<endl;

This line will display the following on the screen:

Enter the points scored

Line 8

cin>>points_scored;

This line is used to accept the value of the variable **points_scored** from the user.

Line 9

if(points>=90)

In this line, the condition (the value of the variable **points_scored** is greater than or equal to 90) within the **if** statement is checked. If the condition is true, the next statement (line 10) will be executed. Otherwise, the next statement (line 10) will be skipped and the control will be transferred to the **else-if** statement (line 11).

Line 10

cout<<"Grade A"<<endl;

This line will display the following on the screen:

Grade A

Line 11

else if(points_scored>=80)

If the condition given in the **if** statement is false, the control will pass to line11. In this line, the condition (the value of the variable **points_scored** is greater than or equal to 80) within the **else-if** is checked. If the condition is true, **line 12** will be executed. Otherwise, the control will be transferred to **line 13**.

Line 12

cout<<"Grade B"<<endl;

This line will display the following on the screen:

Grade B

Line 13

else if(points_scored>=70)

If the condition given in **line 11** is false, the control will pass to this line (line 13). In this line, the condition (the value of the variable **points_scored** is greater than or equal to 70) within the **else if** is checked. If the condition is true, line 14 will be executed. Otherwise, the control will be transferred to line 15.

Line 14
cout<<"Grade C"<<endl;
This line will display the following on the screen:
Grade C

Line 15
else
If the compiler cannot find any conditional match in the program, the control will be transferred to line 15 and the statements associated with it will be executed.

Line 16
cout<<"FAIL"<<endl;
This line will display the following on the screen:
FAIL

The output of the program is as follows:
Enter the points scored
85
Grade B

The output will be displayed on the screen as follows:

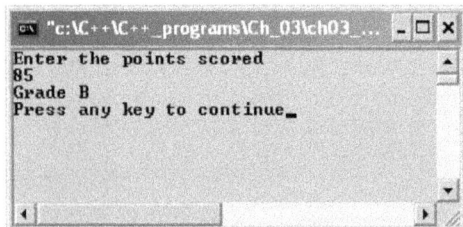

The switch Statement

The **switch** statement is a selection or a case control statement, which makes it possible for the compiler to transfer the control to different statements within the **switch** body depending on the value of a variable or expression. In a **switch** statement, the flow of execution is controlled by a value of the variable or expression. This variable or expression is known as the control variable. In the same **switch** body, two case constants cannot have identical values. Also, the upper and lowercase character constants are differentiated by the compiler.

The syntax for the **switch** statement is as follows:

```
switch(expression)
{
    case constant 1:
    statement;
    break;
    case constant 2:
```

```
        statement;
        break;
        case constant n:
        statement;
        break;
        default: //Optional
        statement;
    }
```

In the above syntax, the value of the **switch** expression is matched with the case constants one by one. If a match is found, the control will be transferred to the statement associated with that particular case label. If no match is found, the default case will be executed in case it exists. If, on the other hand, a match is not found and also there is no default case in the **switch** body, no case will be executed.

In the above code, the **break** statement is optional. The **break** statement is used to transfer the control to the end of the **switch** body. If the **break** statement is not used in the **switch** body, then all the cases from the one matched will be executed.

The following example illustrates the use of the **switch** statement without using the **break** statement.

Example 5

Write a program to display a message according to the value entered by the user.

The following program will prompt the user to enter a number, compare it with the given cases, and display the statement associated with the particular case.

```
//Write a program that illustrates the use of the switch statement     1
#include<iostream>                                                      2
using namespace std;                                                    3
int main()                                                             4
{                                                                       5
    int i;                                                              6
    cout<<"Enter a number"<<endl;                                       7
    cin>>i;                                                             8
    switch(i)                                                           9
    {                                                                  10
        case 1:                                                        11
        cout<<"GOOD MORNING"<<endl;                                    12
        case 2:                                                        13
        cout<<"GOOD AFTERNOON"<<endl;                                  14
        case 3:                                                        15
        cout<<"GOOD EVENING"<<endl;                                    16
        case 4:                                                        17
```

cout<<"GOOD NIGHT"<<endl;	18
default:	19
cout<<"HAVE A NICE DAY"<<endl;	20
}	21
return 0;	22
}	23

Explanation

Line 6
int i;
In this line, **i** is declared as an integer type variable.

Line 7
cout<<"Enter a number"<<endl;
This line will display the following on the screen:
Enter a number

Line 8
cin>>i;
This line is used to accept the value of the variable **i** from the user.

Line 9
switch(i)
In this line, the **switch** statement is used to match the value of the variable **i** with all the case constants one by one. If a match is found, the control will be transferred to the statement associated with that particular case.

Line 10
{
This line is used to indicate the start of the **switch** body.

Line 11
case 1:
This line begins with the **case** keyword, which is followed by an integer value **(1)**. This value is matched with the value of the control variable **(i)**. If a match is found, line 12 will be executed. Otherwise, the control will be transferred to **case 2.**

Line 12
cout<<"GOOD MORNING"<<endl;
This line will display the following on the screen:
GOOD MORNING

The functionality of lines 13 to 18 is the same as that of lines 11 and 12.

Line 19
default:
In this line, the **default** keyword is used. If no match is found, the code or statement associated with the **default** case will be executed. This statement is optional.

Line 20
cout<<"HAVE A NICE DAY"<<endl;
This line will display the following on the screen:
HAVE A NICE DAY

The output of the program is:
Enter a number
2
GOOD AFTERNOON
GOOD EVENING
GOOD NIGHT
HAVE A NICE DAY

Note

In this program, no break statement has been used. Therefore, all the cases from the one matched, including the default, are executed, as shown in the output of the program.

The following example illustrates the use of the **switch** statement with the **break** statement.

Example 6

Write a program to display a message according to the value entered by the user.

The following program will prompt the user to enter a number, compare it with the given cases, and display the statement associated with the particular case.

```
//Write a program that illustrates the use of the switch statement
//with a break statement                               1
#include<iostream>                                      2
using namespace std;                                    3
int main()                                              4
{                                                       5
        int i;                                          6
        cout<<"Enter a number"<<endl;                   7
        cin>>i;                                         8
        switch(i)                                       9
        {                                              10
                case 1:                                11
                cout<<"GOOD MORNING"<<endl;            12
                break;                                 13
                case 2:                                14
                cout<<"GOOD AFTERNOON"<<endl;          15
                break;                                 16
                case 3:                                17
                cout<<"GOOD EVENING"<<endl;            18
                break;                                 19
```

```
        case 4:                                                    20
        cout<<"GOOD NIGHT"<<endl;                                  21
        break;                                                     22
        default:                                                   23
        cout<<"HAVE A NICE DAY"<<endl;                             24
    }                                                              25
    return 0;                                                      26
}                                                                  27
```

The functioning of Example 6 is the same as Example 5. In Example 6, the **break** statement has been used. As a result, the program executes only the matched case and its associated statements. For example, if the user enters 3, only **case 3** will be executed and all the other cases will be skipped by the compiler.

The output of the program is as follows:
Enter a number
2
GOOD AFTERNOON

The output will be displayed on the screen as follows:

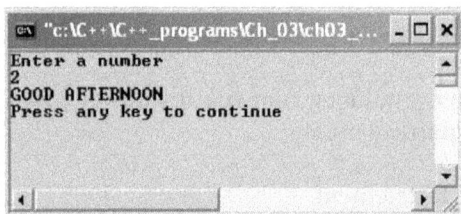

The flowchart in Figure 3-9 gives a diagrammatic representation of the program described in Example 6.

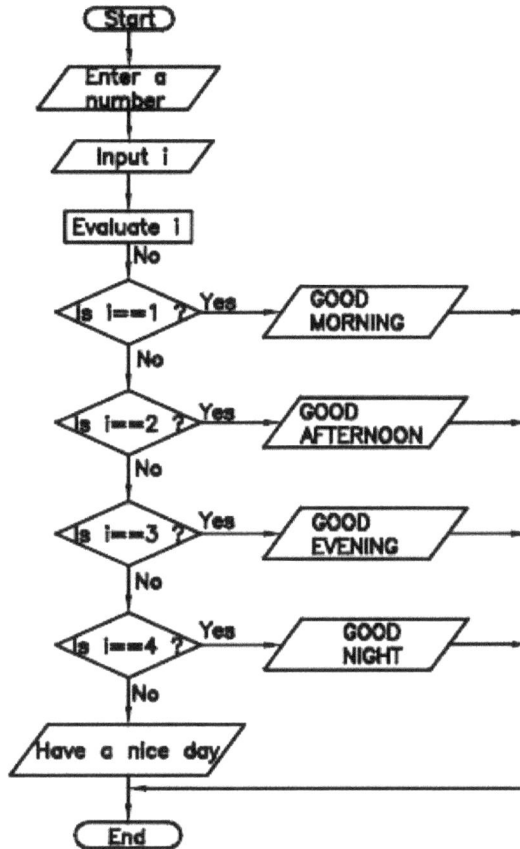

Figure 3-9 *Flowchart of Example 6*

Repetition, Iteration, or Loop Control Structure

Loops are used to repeat a particular block of code for a certain number of times. The block of code is repeated while the condition is true. If the condition is false, the loop ends and the control is transferred to the next statement immediately after the loop. In C++, there are the following three kinds of loops:

1. while loop
2. for loop
3. do-while loop

The while Loop

The **while** loop is a flow control statement that is used to execute a particular block of code as long as a certain condition is true. The **while** loop is mostly used in cases when you do not know how many times the loop will be repeated. The syntax for the **while** loop is given next.

```
while(condition)
{
    statement or block of code;
}
```

In the above syntax, the condition within the **while** statement is evaluated first. If the condition is true, the next statement or the block of code is executed. This code will be repeated until the condition evaluates to false.

The following example illustrates the use of the **while** loop.

Example 7

Write a program to illustrate the working of the **while** loop.

The following program will prompt the user to enter a number, compare it with a particular condition, and display the resultant value on the screen.

```
//Write a program that will prompt the user to enter a number          1
//and then repeat the block of code until it is not equal to zero.      2
#include<iostream>                                                      3
using namespace std;                                                    4
int main()                                                             5
{                                                                      6
    int n=1;                                                           7
    while(n!=0)                                                        8
    {                                                                  9
        cout<<"Enter a value"<<endl;                                   10
        cin>>n;                                                        11
        cout<<"The value entered by you is: "<<n<<endl;                12
    }                                                                  13
    cout<<"Exit from the while loop"<<endl;                            14
    return 0;                                                          15
}
```


Explanation
Line 7
int n=1;
In this line, **n** is declared as an integer type variable and the value one is assigned to it.

Line 8
while(n!=0)
From this line, the **while** loop begins. The code associated with the **while** statement will be executed as long as the condition **n!=0** (n is not equal to zero) is true. In this program, the variable **n** is initialized to one, as mentioned in line 7. So the code associated with the while statement must be executed at least once and then the control will be transferred to line 9.

Line 9
cout<<"Enter a value"<<endl;
This line will display the following on the screen:
Enter a value

Line 10
cin>>n;
This line is used to accept the value of variable **n** from the user.

Line 11
cout<<"The value entered by you is: "<<n<<endl;
This line will display the following on the screen:
The value entered by you is: value of the variable n

Line 13
cout<<"Exit from the while loop"<<endl;
When the **while** condition is false, the control is directly transferred to this line. This line will display the following on the screen:
Exit from the while loop

The output of the program is as follows:
Enter a value
4
The value entered by you is: 4
Enter a value
0
The value entered by you is: 0
Exit from the while loop

The flowchart in Figure 3-10 gives a diagrammatic representation of the program described in Example 7.

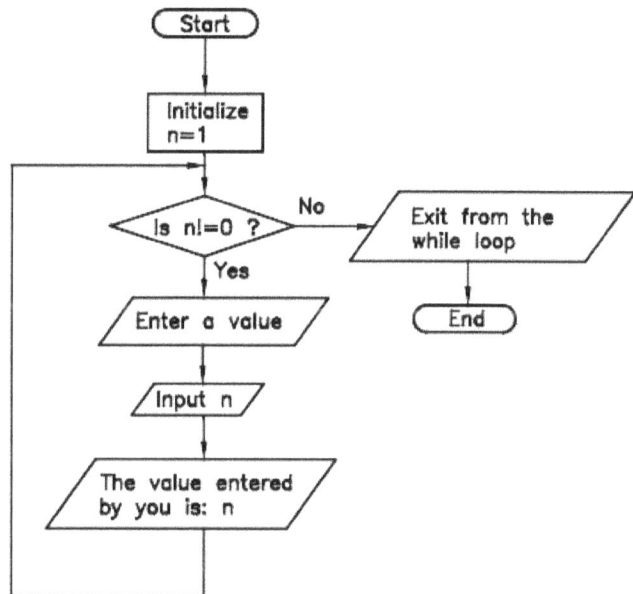

Figure 3-10 *Flowchart of Example 7*

The for Loop

The **for** loop is also a flow control statement that is used to execute a particular block of code for a specific number of times. The **for** loop is mostly used when you know the number of times the body of the loop will be executed. The **for** loop is easy to understand because all the control elements (initialization, condition, and increment or decrement) are placed together at one place. The syntax for the **for** loop is as follows:

for(initialization; condition; increment or decrement)

In the above syntax, the **for** loop consists of three expressions: initialization, condition, and increment or decrement. These three expressions must be separated by using a semicolon (;).

Initialization Expression
The initialization expression executes only once at the start of the loop. It is used to set the initial value of the loop control variable such as **int x=1**.

Condition Expression
The condition expression is evaluated each time before the execution of the body of the loop. The execution of the body of the loop depends on the condition whether it is true or false. If the condition is true, the body of the loop will be executed. Otherwise, it will be skipped and the control will be transferred to the next instruction after the **for** loop.

Increment or Decrement Expression
The increment or decrement expression is used to increase or decrease the value of the loop control variable by one or some other value, which is specified by the programmer. This expression is always executed after the body of the loop has been executed.

The following example illustrates the use of the **for** loop.

Example 8

Write a program to display the multiplication table of a number.

The following program will prompt the user to enter a number, calculate its multiples, and display the table on the screen.

```
//Write a program that displays the multiplication table of a number       1
#include<iostream>                                                          2
using namespace std;                                                        3
int main()                                                                  4
{                                                                           5
        int num,i,c;                                                        6
        cout<<"Enter a number"<<endl;                                       7
        cin>>num;                                                           8
        cout<<"The multiplication table is as follows: "<<endl;            9
        for(i=1;i<=10;i++)                                                 10
        {                                                                  11
```

c=num*i;	12
cout<<c<<endl;	13
}	14
return 0;	15
}	16

Explanation

Line 6
int num,i,c;
In this line, **num**, **i**, and **c** are declared as integer type variables.

Line 7
cout<<"Enter a number"<<endl;
This line will display the following on the screen:
Enter a number

Line 8
cin>>num;
This line is used to accept the value of variable **num** from the user.

Line 9
cout<<"The multiplication table is as follows: "<<endl;
This line will display the following on the screen:
The multiplication table is as follows:

Line 10
for(i=1;i<=10;i++)
This line shows the working of the **for** loop. The variable **i** (loop control variable) is initialized to one and the condition **i<=10** is checked. If the condition is true, the body of the loop will be executed and the control will be transferred to line 12. Otherwise, the body of the loop will be skipped and the control will be transferred to line 15.

Line 12
c=num*i;
In this line, the value of the variable **num** is multiplied by the value of variable **i** and the resultant value is assigned to the variable **c**.

Line 13
cout<<c<<endl;
This line will display the following on the screen:
Value of the variable **c**

The output of the program is as follows:
Enter a number
3

The multiplication table is as follows:
3
6
9
12
15
18
21
24
27
30

The output will be displayed on the screen as follows:

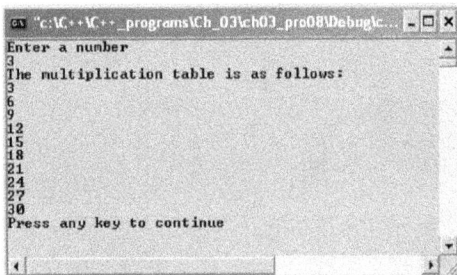

The flowchart in Figure 3-11 gives a diagrammatic representation of the program described in Example 8.

Multiple Initialization

You can specify more than one expression in the initialization part and as well as the increment/decrement part by separating them using the comma operator (,). Also, you can have only one condition expression in the **for** loop.

For example:

```
for(x=0,y=50;x!=y;x++,y--)
{
        body of the loop;
}
```

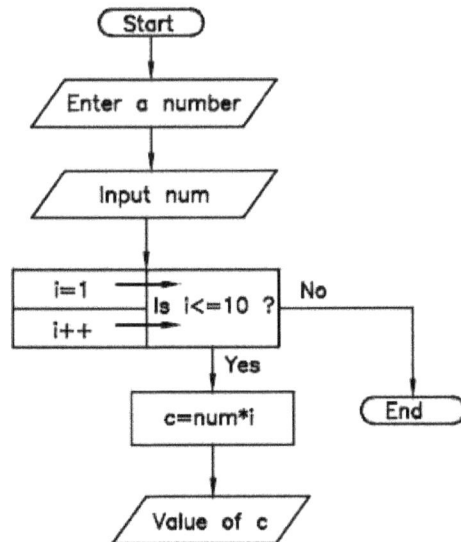

Figure 3-11 *Flowchart of Example 8*

In this example, the variable **x** is initialized to zero and **y** is initialized to fifty. In the increment/decrement part, the variable **x** is incremented by one and **y** is decremented by one. There is only one condition expression **x!=y** (x is not equal to y). The body of the loop will be executed until the given condition becomes false.

You can also skip some or all the expressions of the **for** loop. The syntax is as follows:

```
for( ; ; )
```

If you skip the condition expression, it is assumed to be true. Now, the loop works similar to the infinite loop.

For example:

```
for(i=1; ;i++)
{
        body of the loop;
}
```

In the above example, the variable **i** is initialized to one and the condition part is skipped. So, the condition will always be assumed as true and the body of the loop will be executed indefinitely. The value of the variable **i** is incremented by one after every execution of the loop body.

Nested for Loop

A nested **for** loop is a loop within the body of another loop. In the nested **for** loop, the outer loop takes control over the inner loop. The syntax is as follows:

```
for(i=0;i<5;i++) //Outer loop
{
    for(j=0;j<5;j++) //Inner loop
    {
            body of the loop;
    }
}
```

In the above syntax, when the execution begins, the compiler first encounters the outer loop. If the condition in the outer loop is true, the control will be transferred to the inner loop. When the execution of the inner loop is complete, the control will be transferred back to the increment/decrement part of the outer loop. This process is repeated until the outer loop finishes or the condition in the outer loop becomes false.

The following example illustrates the use of the nested **for** loop.
Write a program to display a right-angled triangle made of star (*) characters.

The following program will display the right-angled triangle of the star characters on the screen.

Example 9

//Write a program to display a right angled triangle of stars (*)   1

```
#include<iostream>                                          2
using namespace std;                                        3
int main()                                                  4
{                                                           5
        int i,j;                                            6
        for(i=0;i<5;i++)//outer loop                        7
        {                                                   8
                for(j=0;j<=i;j++)//inner loop               9
                {                                           10
                        cout<<" * ";                        11
                }//End of inner loop                        12
                cout<<endl;                                 13
        }//End of outer loop                                14
        return 0;                                           15
}                                                           16
```

Explanation

Line 7

for(i=0;i<5;i++)

From this line, the outer **for** loop begins. The variable **i** is initialized to zero. Next, the condition **i<5** is checked whether it is true. If the condition is true, the control will be transferred to the inner loop (line 9). After the completion of the inner loop, the control will be transferred back to the increment/decrement part of the outer loop. If the condition is false, the body of the outer loop will be skipped and the control will be directly transferred to line 15.

Line 8

{

This line indicates the start of the body of the outer **for** loop.

Line 9

for(j=0;j<=i;j++)

From this line, the inner **for** loop begins. This loop is controlled by the outer loop. If the condition in the outer loop is true, the control is transferred to this loop. Otherwise, this loop will be skipped. If the condition in the inner loop is true, the body of the loop will be executed and the control will be directly transferred to line 11. Otherwise, the body of the inner loop will be skipped and the control will be transferred back to the increment/decrement part of the outer loop.

Line 10

{

This line indicates the start of the body of the inner **for** loop.

Line 11

cout<<" * ";

This line will display the following **star character** on the screen:

*

Line 12
}
This line indicates the end of the body of the inner loop.

Line 13
cout<<endl;
This line is used to display the next statement from the new line.

The output of the program is as follows:
```
*
* *
* * *
* * * *
* * * * *
```

The output will be displayed on the screen as follows:

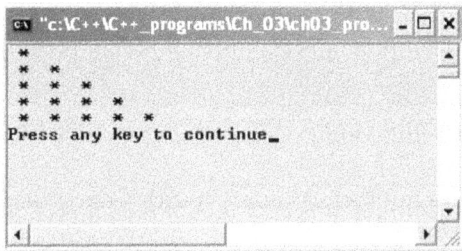

The flowchart in Figure 3-12 gives a diagrammatic representation of the program described in Example 9.

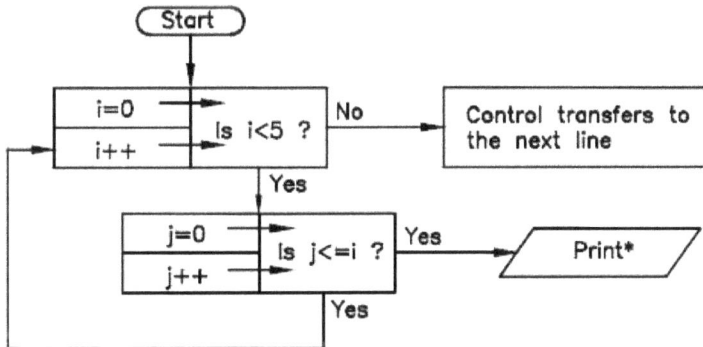

Figure 3-12 *Flowchart of Example 9*

The do-while Loop

The **do-while** loop is similar to the **while** loop, except that in the **do-while** loop, the body of the loop is executed first and the condition is checked at the end. Therefore, the body of the loop must be executed at least once. The **while** statement should be terminated with a semicolon (;). The syntax is as follows:

```
do
{
    body of the loop;
}
while(condition);
```

In the above syntax, the body of the loop is executed first and then the condition is checked. If the condition is true, the body of the loop will be executed again. This process is repeated until the condition becomes false.

The following example illustrates the use of the **do-while** loop.

Example 10

Write a program to illustrate the working of the **do-while** loop.

The following program will prompt the user to enter a number, compare it with a particular condition, and display the resultant value on the screen.

```
//Write a program that will prompt the user to enter a number
//and then repeat the block of code until it is not equal to zero.        1
#include<iostream>                                                         2
using namespace std;                                                       3
int main()                                                                 4
{                                                                          5
    int n;                                                                 6
    do                                                                     7
    {                                                                      8
        cout<<"Enter a value"<<endl;                                       9
        cin>>n;                                                            10
        cout<<"The value entered by you is: "<<n<<endl;                    11
    }                                                                      12
    while(n!=0);                                                           13
    cout<<"Exit from the loop"<<endl;                                      14
    return 0;                                                              15
}                                                                          16
```

Explanation

Line 6
int n;
In this line, **n** is declared as an integer type variable.

Line 7
do
This line is the start point of the **do-while** loop. The statements associated with the **do** statement will be executed first and then the condition within the **while** expression will be checked.

Line 8
{
This line indicates the start of the **do-while** body.

Line 9
cout<<"Enter a value"<<endl;
This line will display the following on the screen.
Enter a value

Line 10
cin>>n;
This line is used to accept the value of a variable **n** from the user.

Line 11
cout<<"The value entered by you is: "<<n<<endl;
This line will display the following on the screen.
The value entered by you is:
This is followed by the value of variable **n**

Line 12
}
This line indicates the end of the **do-while** body.

Line 13
while(n!=0);
The statements associated with the **do** loop must be executed at least once and then the condition given within the **while** statement will be checked. If the condition (n is not equal to zero) is true, the body of the loop will be executed again. Otherwise, the control will be transferred to the next statement following the **while** statement.

The output of the program is as follows:
Enter a value
3
The value entered by you is: 3
Enter a value
0
The value entered by you is: 0
Exit from the loop

The flowchart in Figure 3-13 gives a diagrammatic representation of the program described in Example 10.

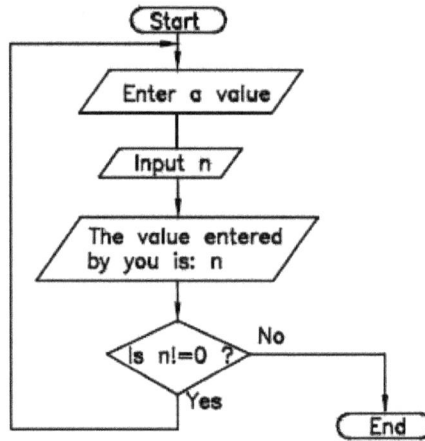

Figure 3-13 *Flowchart of Example 10*

Jump Statements

The **jump statements** transfer the control unconditionally to some other part in a program. In C++, there are four types of jump statements:

1. break
2. continue
3. goto
4. return

The break Statement

The **break** statement is used to exit from any kind of loop such as **for, while,** and **do-while** or the **switch** statement. Alternatively, it is used to transfer the control to the next statement immediately after the loop or the **switch** statement.

The following example illustrates the use of the **break** statement.

Example 11

Write a program to illustrate the working of the **break** statement.

The following program will terminate the execution of the inner loop when the values of the control variables of the outer and the inner loop are equal. This program will also display the values of the variables **i** and **j** on the screen.

```
//Write a program that terminates the execution of the inner loop when the
//values of the control variables of the outer and the inner loop are equal. 1
#include<iostream>                                                        2
```

```
using namespace std;                                                3
int main()                                                          4
{                                                                   5
      int i,j;                                                      6
      for(i=0;i<2;i++)//outer loop                                  7
      {                                                             8
            for(j=2;j>=0;j--)//inner loop                           9
            {                                                      10
                  if(i==j)//Innermost statement                    11
                  {                                                12
                  cout<<"The values of i and j are equal"<<endl;   13
                  break;                                           14
                  }                                                15
                  cout<<"The value of i is: "<<i<<endl;            16
                  cout<<"The value of j is: "<<j<<endl;            17
            }                                                      18
            cout<<"Exit the inner loop"<<endl;                     19
      }                                                            20
      return 0;                                                    21
}                                                                  22
```

Explanation

Line 6
int i,j;
In this line, **i** and **j** are declared as integer type variables.

Line 7
for(i=0;i<=2;i++)
From this line, the outer loop begins. The variable **i** is initialized to zero. Next, the condition **i<=2** is checked whether it is true or false. If the condition is true, the control will be transferred to the inner loop (line 10). After the completion of the inner loop, the control will be transferred back to the increment/decrement part of the outer loop. If the condition is false, the body of the outer loop will be skipped and the control will be directly transferred to line 20.

Line 8
{
This line indicates the start of the body of the outer loop.

Line 9
for(j=2;j>=0;j--)
From this line, the inner loop begins. This loop is controlled by the outer loop. If the condition in the outer loop is true, the compiler encounters this loop. Otherwise, this loop will be skipped. If the condition in the inner loop is true, the body of the loop will be executed and the control will be directly transferred to line 12. Otherwise, the body of the inner loop will be skipped and the control will be transferred back to the increment/decrement part of the outer loop.

Line 10
{
This line indicates the start of the body of the inner loop.

Line 11
if(i==j)
In this line, the **if** statement is used to check whether the value of the variable **i** is equal to the value of the variable **j**. If the condition is true, the statements associated with the **if** statement will be executed. Otherwise, these statements will be skipped.

Line 12
{
This line indicates the start of the body of the **if** statement.

Line 13
cout<<"The values of i and j are equal " <<endl;
This line will display the following on the screen:
The values of i and j are equal

Line 14
break;
The **break** statement will transfer the control outside the innermost statement.

Line 15
}
This line indicates the end of the body of the **if** statement.

Line 16
cout<<"The value of i is: "<<i<<endl;
This line will display the following on the screen:
The value of i is:
This is followed by the value of the variable **i**

Line 17
cout<<"The value of j is: "<<j<<endl;
This line will display the following on the screen:
The value of j is:
This is followed by the value of variable **j**

Line 18
}
This line indicates the end of the body of the inner loop.

Line 19
cout<<"Exit the inner loop"<<endl;
This line will display the following on the screen:
Exit the inner loop

Line 20
}
This line indicates the end of the body of the outer loop.

The output of the program is as follows:
The value of i is: 0
The value of j is: 2
The value of i is: 0
The value of j is: 1
The values of i and j are equal
Exit from the inner loop
The value of i is: 1
The value of j is: 2
The values of i and j are equal
Exit from the inner loop

The continue Statement

The **continue** statement is similar to the **break** statement except that instead of exiting from the loop, the continue statement transfers the control back to the top of the loop for the next iteration. It will skip the remaining part of the body of the loop.

For example:

```
for(i=0;i<=10;i++)
{
    statement 1;
    if(i==5)
    continue;
    statement 2;
}
```

In the above example, when the value of the variable **i** is equal to five, the **continue** statement will be executed. The **statement 2** will be skipped and the control will be transferred back to the increment part of the **for** statement for the next iteration.

The following example illustrates the use of the **continue** statement.

Example 12

Write a program to terminate the execution of the inner loop using the **continue** statement.

The following program will terminate the execution of the inner loop when the values of the control variables of the outer and the inner loop are equal. This program will also display the values of the variables **i** and **j** on the screen.

//Write a program that terminates the execution of the inner loop when the
//values of the control variables of the outer and the inner loop are equal. 1

```
#include<iostream>                                              2
using namespace std;                                            3
int main()                                                      4
{                                                               5
     int i,j;                                                   6
     for(i=0;i<=2;i++)//outer loop                              7
     {                                                          8
          for(j=2;j>=0;j--)//inner loop                         9
          {                                                     10
               if(i==j)//Innermost statement                    11
               {                                                12
                    cout<<"The values of i and j are";          13
                    cout<<" equal"<<endl;                       14
                    continue;                                   15
               }                                                16
               cout<<" The value of i is: " << i <<endl;        17
               cout<<" The value of j is: " << j <<endl;        18
          }                                                     19
          cout<<"Exit the inner loop"<<endl;                    20
     }                                                          21
     return 0;                                                  22
}                                                               23
```

Explanation

The working of Example 12 is the same as Example 11 except that in the former the **continue**
statement is used. When the condition **(i==j)** is true, the statements associated with the **if**
statement will be executed. Next, the **continue** statement will be executed, which ends the
current iteration of the inner loop. Also, the control is transferred back to the decrement part
of the inner loop for the next iteration.

The output of the program is as follows:
The value of i is: 0
The value of j is: 2
The value of i is: 0
The value of j is: 1
The values of i and j are equal
Exit from the inner loop
The value of i is: 1
The value of j is: 2
The values of i and j are equal
The value of i is: 1
The value of j is: 0
Exit from the inner loop

The values of i and j are equal
The value of i is: 2
The value of j is: 1
The value of i is: 2
The value of j is: 0
Exit from the inner loop

The goto Statement

The **goto** statement allows the program control to jump unconditionally to another part of the program, which is associated with the named label. A label is an identifier followed by a colon (:). The syntax is as follows:

    goto label;

The following example illustrates the use of the **goto** statement.

Example 13

Write a program to illustrate the working of the **goto** statement.

The following program will terminate the execution of the loop when the value of the control variable is equal to five. It will then display a message on the screen.

```
//Write a program that terminates the loop
//when the value of the control variable is equal to five    1
#include<iostream>                                            2
using namespace std;                                          3
int main()                                                    4
{                                                             5
        int i;//Control variable                             6
        for(i=1;i<=10;i++)                                    7
        {                                                     8
                if(i==5)                                      9
                goto stop;                                    10
                cout<<"The value of i is: "<<i<<endl;         11
        }                                                     12
        stop:                                                 13
        cout<<"Label is encountered";                        14
        return 0;                                             15
}                                                             16
```

Explanation
Line 7
for(i=1;i<=10;i++)
When the compiler executes this line, the variable **i** is initialized to one and the condition **i<=10** is checked. If the condition is true, the body of the loop will be executed and the control will be transferred to line 9. Otherwise, the body of the loop will be skipped.

Line 9
if(i==5)
In this line, the value of variable **i** is checked to see if it is equal to five. If this condition is true, the control is transferred to the next line, which is a **goto** statement.

Line 10
goto stop;
In this statement, **stop** is used as a label. When this statement is executed, the control will be transferred to the statement (line 14) associated with the label.

Line 11
cout<<"The value of i is: "<<i<<endl;
This line will display the following on the screen:
The value of i is: value of the variable i

Line 14
cout<<"Label is encountered";
This line will display the following on the screen:
Label is encountered

The output of the program is as follows:
The value of i is: 1
The value of i is: 2
The value of i is: 3
The value of i is: 4
Label is encountered

The return Statement

The **return** statement stops the execution of a function and the control returns to the calling function. Now, the execution will begin from the next statement that immediately follows the call in the calling function. The syntax is as discussed next.

```
return expression;
```

In the above syntax, the expression represents the value that is returned to the calling function.

The return statement is of two types, one returns some value and the other returns (nothing).

The functions whose return type is **void** does not have any return statement. For example:

```
void sum()//Calling function
{
    int c= a+b;
    cout<<c;
    return;//Optional because of the void function
}
```

In this example, the **void** specifies to the compiler that no value is returned to the calling function by the **return** statement. You can also use the **return** statement without specifying any value or expression.

The functions whose return type is not **void**, must have the **return** statement that returns some value or expression. For example:

```
int main()
{
    body of the program;
    return 0;
}
```

In the above example, the return type of the **main** function is **int** (Integer). So, the **return** statement returns some integer value to the **main** function.

LOGICAL OPERATORS

You have already learned about the **logical operators** in the earlier chapters. In this section, you will learn about the usage of **logical operators** with the help of a programming example. The syntax for the logical **AND** operator is as follows:

expression1 && expression2

In the above syntax, if both the expressions, **expression1** and **expression2**, are true the operator will return true, otherwise false.

The syntax for the logical **OR** operator is as follows:

expression1 || expression2

In the above syntax, if either of the expression1 or expression2 is true, the operator will return true, otherwise false.

The syntax for the logical **NOT** operator is as follows:

! expression

In the above syntax, if the expression is true, the operator will return false. If the expression is false, the operator will return true. This operator reverses the resultant value of the expression.

The following example illustrates the use of the logical operators.

Example 14

Write a program to find the greatest of the three numbers.

The following program will prompt the user to enter three numbers, compare them, and display the greatest number on the screen.

```
//Write a program to find the greatest among the three numbers    1
#include<iostream>                                                 2
using namespace std;                                               3
int main()                                                         4
{                                                                  5
        int a,b,c;                                                 6
        cout<<"Enter three numbers"<<endl;                         7
        cin>>a>>b>>c;                                              8
        if( a>b && a>c)                                            9
        cout<<"a is the greatest number"<<endl;                    10
        else if(b>c)                                               11
        cout<<"b is the greatest number"<<endl;                    12
        else                                                       13
        cout<<"c is the greatest number"<<endl;                    14
        return 0;                                                  15
}                                                                  16
```

Explanation

Line 9

if(a>b && a>c)

In this statement, the logical **AND** operator is used. If both the conditions **a>b** and **a>c** given in the statement are true, the control will be transferred to line 10. Otherwise, line 10 will be skipped and the control will be transferred to line 11.

The output of the program is as follows:

Enter three numbers

23

34

45

c is the greatest number

Self-Evaluation Test

Answer the following questions and then compare them to the answers given at the end of this chapter:

1. A _____ is a graphical representation of the steps that constitute a program.

2. The _____ control the flow of execution in a program.

3. The _____ statement is a case control statement.

4. The _____ is used to repeat a particular block of code for a specific number of times.

5. The _____ statement is used to exit from any kind of loop or **switch** statement.

Review Questions

Answer the following questions:

1. The control structures specify the order of the execution of the statement. (T/F)

2. The **if** statement is a single path statement. (T/F)

3. In the **switch** statement, the flow of execution is controlled by a variable or an expression. (T/F)

4. In the **do-while** loop, the body of the loop must be executed atleast once. (T/F)

5. The **continue** statement transfers the control outside the loop. (T/F)

Exercises

Exercise 1

Using the **if-else** statement, write a program to find whether the number is even or odd.

Exercise 2

Write a program to find the square of the first ten natural numbers using the **for** loop.

Exercise 3

Write a program to display the day of a week according to the value entered by the user, using the **switch** statement.

Answers to Self-Evaluation Test

1. flowchart, **2.** control structures, **3. switch**, **4. for** loop, **5. break**

Chapter 4

Functions and Arrays

Learning Objectives

After completing this chapter, you will be able to:
- *Understand functions and function types.*
- *Understand function overloading.*
- *Understand recursion.*
- *Understand arrays and array types.*
- *Understand the concept of passing arrays to functions.*

INTRODUCTION

All the programs that you have studied until now consisted of a small number of statements. If there are hundreds of statements in a program, it will become complex and difficult to understand them. C++ provides certain statements known as functions to remove such complexity.

An array is a collection of data elements of the same type.

In this chapter, you will learn more about the functions and arrays.

FUNCTIONS

A function is a group of statements that perform a specific task. A function has a name and a return type. It also has a list of arguments and their respective data types passed to it. A program can be divided into small functions such that each function performs a specific task.

Declaring a Function

A function must be declared before being used in the program. The syntax for declaring a function is as follows:

    ret_type fun_name (data_type argument 1,......., data_type argument n);

In the above syntax, the **ret_type** specifies the type of data returned by the function. The **fun_name** specifies the name of the function, which is used as a reference in the program. The argument list receives the values that are passed when a function call is made in the program. The function declaration must be terminated by a semicolon (;).

Defining the Body of a Function

The function body contains the statements that are executed when a function call is made in the program. The function body specifies the behavior of the function. The syntax is as follows:

    ret_type fun_name (data_type argument_1,........, data_type argument_n)
    {
        body of the function;
    }

In the above syntax, the first line is the same as the declaration of a function except that it is not terminated by a semicolon. The curly braces {} represent the start and the end of the body of a function. The body of the function contains the statements that are executed when a function call is made in the program.

Calling a Function

A function call is made in a program by specifying the function name followed by a pair of parentheses and terminated with a semicolon. The syntax is as follows:

    fun_name();

If a function has a return type, it must return a value when the function call is made in the program. The syntax is as follows:

    data_type var_name = fun_name ( );

In the above syntax, the returning value of the function is assigned to the variable **var_name**.

The following example illustrates the use of function declaration, function definition, and function call.

Write a program to calculate the factorial of a number.

Example 1

The following program will prompt the user to enter a number, calculate its factorial, and display the resultant value on the screen. The line numbers on the right are not a part of the program and are for reference only.

```
//Write a program to calculate the factorial of a number    1
#include<iostream>                                           2
using namespace std;                                         3
int fact(int a);//Declaration of the function               4
int main()                                                   5
{                                                            6
        int n, val;                                          7
        cout<<"Enter a number"<<endl;                        8
        cin>>n;                                              9
        val = fact(n);//Function call                        10
        cout<<"Factorial of ";                               11
        cout<<n;                                             12
        cout<<" is: ";                                       13
        cout<<val<<endl;                                     14
        return 0;                                            15
}                                                            16
int fact(int a)//Definition of the function body             17
{                                                            18
        int i=1, fac;//Local to this function                19
        fac=a;                                               20
        while(fac!=0)                                        21
        {                                                    22
                i=fac*i;                                     23
                fac--;                                       24
        }                                                    25
        return i;                                            26
}                                                            27
```

Explanation

Line 4

int fact(int a);

The line given above represents the declaration of a function. In this line, **int** specifies that the return type of the function is of integer type, **fact** is the name of the function, and **int a** is an argument, which receives an integer value when this function is called in the program.

Line 10

val = fact(n);

In this line, a function call is made and the value of the variable **n** is passed as an argument. The value will be received by the variable **a** in the function definition. Next, the resultant value, which is returned by the function will be assigned back to the variable **val**.

Line 17

int fact(int a)

The definition of the function **int fact(int a)** starts from this line. This line is the same as the function declaration, except that it is not terminated by a semicolon.

Line 18

{

This line indicates the start of the body of the function.

Line 19

int i=1, fac;

In this line, **i** and **fac** are declared as integer type variables and 1 is assigned as an initial valueto the variable **i**. The scope of these variables is local to the function **fact** and cannot be used outside this function.

Line 20

fac=a;

In line 10, a function call is made in the program. The value of the variable **n** is passed as an argument, which is received by the variable **a** in the definition of the function. In this line, the value of variable **a** is assigned to the variable **fac**.

Line 21

while(fac!=0)

In this line, the **while** statement is used to verify a given condition. If the condition **fac!=0** (value of variable fac is not equal to zero) is true, the control will be transferred to line 23. Otherwise, the control will be transferred to line 26. The body of the **while** loop will be executed repeatedly until the given condition is false.

Line 23

i=fac*i;

In this line, the value of variable **fac** is multiplied by the value of variable **i** and the resultant value is assigned back to the variable **i**.

Line 24
fac--;
In this line, the value of variable **fac** decreases by one.

Line 26
return i;
When the condition given in line 20 is false, the control is passed to this line. In this line, the value of variable **i** will be returned back to line 10, where the function call is made.

The output of the program is as follows:
Enter a number
5
Factorial of 5 is: 120

The output will be displayed on the screen as follows:

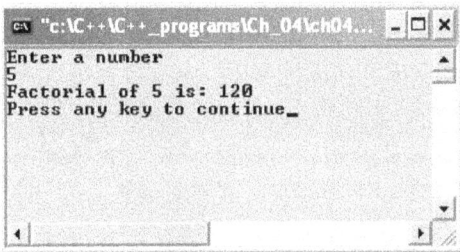

```
c:\C++\C++_programs\Ch_04\ch04...  _ □ ×
Enter a number
5
Factorial of 5 is: 120
Press any key to continue_
```

Passing Default Values to Arguments

In a function declaration, you can also pass default values to some or all of its arguments.

The following example illustrates the concept of passing default values to arguments.

Example 2

Write a program to calculate the factorial of a number by using the default value as an argument.

The following program will prompt the user to enter a number, calculate its factorial, and display the resultant value on the screen.

```
//Write a program to calculate the factorial of a number    1
#include<iostream>                                           2
using namespace std;                                         3
int fact (int a=5)                                           4
{                                                            5
        int i=1,fac;                                         6
        fac=a;                                               7
        while(fac!=0)                                        8
        {                                                    9
                i=fac*i;                                     10
```

```
            fac--;                                              11
    }                                                           12
        return i;                                               13
}                                                               14
int main()                                                      15
{                                                               16
        int value;                                              17
        value= fact ( );                                        18
        cout<<"The factorial is: ";                             19
        cout<<value<<endl;                                      20
        return 0;                                               21
}                                                               22
```

Explanation
Line 4
int fact (int a=5)
In this line, **5** is the default value assigned to the variable **a**.

Line 18
value= fact ( );
In this line, the function **fact()** is called. No argument is passed in this function call because the default value **5** is already assigned to variable **a** in the declaration. If you pass any value when the function call is made, then that value will be assigned to the variable **a**.

The output of the program is as follows:
The factorial is: 120

Function with no Return Type and without Arguments
In this section, you will learn about the functions that do not have a return type and an argument list. In these types of functions, no value is returned back by the function. Also, no argument is passed when a function call is made in the program. The syntax for declaring a function with no return type and without arguments is as follows:

```
    void fun_name()
```

In the above syntax, **void** specifies that this function has no return type. The **fun_name** specifies the function name and the empty parentheses () specify that this function does not have any argument list.

The following example illustrates the use of a function that does not have a return type and an argument list.

Write a program to calculate the fibonacci series of numbers.

Example 3

The following program will prompt the user to enter a number, which is treated as the limit of the series. It will also calculate the fibonacci series upto the given limit and display the resultant series on the screen.

```
//Write a program to calculate the fibonacci series of numbers          1
#include<iostream>                                                      2
using namespace std;                                                    3
void fib();//Function declaration                                       4
int limit;//Global variable                                            5
int main()                                                              6
{                                                                       7
        cout<<"Enter the limit of the fibonacci series: "<<endl;        8
        cin>>limit;                                                     9
        cout<<"The fibonacci series is as follows: "<<endl;            10
        fib ( );                                                       11
        return 0;                                                      12
}                                                                      13
void fib()//Function definition                                        14
{                                                                      15
        int a=0,b=1,c;//Local scope                                    16
        for(c=0;c<=limit;c=a+b)                                        17
        {                                                              18
                cout<<c<<endl;                                         19
                a=b;                                                   20
                b=c;                                                   21
        }                                                              22
}                                                                      23
```

Explanation

Line 4
void fib( );
In this line, the **fib( )** function, which has no return type and no argument list is declared.

Line 5
int limit;
In this line, **limit** is declared as an integer type variable. This variable has a global scope and can be used anywhere in the program.

Line 11
fib( );
In this line, a function call is made to the function **fib( )**.

Line 14
void fib( )
The function definition starts from this line. In this line, the keyword **void** is used because the function **fib( )** has no return type.

Line 15
{
This line indicates the start of the body of the function **fib( )**.

Line 16
int a=0,b=1,c;
In this line, **a**, **b**, and **c** are declared as integer type variables. The variable **a** is initialized to 0 and the variable **b** is initialized to 1. These variables have a local scope and can be used only inside the **fib( )** function.

Line 17
for(c=0;c<=limit;c=a+b)
The line given above is a **for** loop. In this **for** loop, variable **c** (loop control variable) will be initialized to 0. Next, the given condition will be checked. If the condition is true, the control will be transferred to line 19. Otherwise, the control will be transferred outside the body of the loop. After each execution of the body of the loop, the control will be transferred back to the increment part (c=a+b). After the increment, the given condition will be checked again. This process will be repeated until the given condition is false.

Line 19
cout<<c<<endl;
This line displays the following on the screen:
value of the variable **c**

Line 20
a=b;
In this line, the value of the variable **b** is assigned to the variable **a**.

Line 21
b=c;
In this line, the value of the variable **c** is assigned to the variable **b**.

The output of the program is as follows:
Enter the limit of the fibonacci series:
55
The fibonacci series is as follows:
0
1
1
2
3
5
8
13
21
34
55

The output will be displayed on the screen as follows:

> **Note**
> *In the fibonacci series, the next number is always the sum of the last two numbers.*

Function with Return Type and without Arguments

In this section, you will learn about the functions that have a return type but do not have an argument list. In these types of functions, a value must be returned by the function and no argument can be passed when a function call is made in the program.

The syntax for declaring a function with a return type and without arguments is as follows:

    ret_type fun_name()

In the above syntax, the **ret_type** specifies the type of value, which is returned by the function. The **fun_name** represents the function name and the empty parentheses () specify that no argument is passed during the function call.

The following example illustrates the use of a function that has a return type but does not have an argument list.

Example 4

Write a program to calculate the factorial of a number.

The following program will prompt the user to enter a number, calculate its factorial, and display the resultant value on the screen.

```
//Write a program to calculate the factorial of a number        1
#include<iostream>                                               2
using namespace std;                                             3
int n;//Global scope                                            4
int fact();//Function declaration                                5
int main()                                                       6
{                                                                7
        int val;                                                 8
```

```
        cout<<"Enter a number"<<endl;                              9
        cin>>n;                                                    10
        val=fact();//Function call                                 11
        cout<<"The factorial is: "<<val<<endl;                     12
        return 0;                                                  13
}                                                                  14
int fact()                                                         15
{                                                                  16
        int i=1;                                                   17
        while(n!=0)                                                18
        {                                                          19
                i=n*i;                                             20
                n--;                                               21
        }                                                          22
        return i;                                                  23
}                                                                  24
```

Explanation
Line 5
int fact();
Line 5 shows the declaration of the function **fact()**. The return type of this function is an integer type.

Line 11
val=fact();
In this line, a function call is made to the function **fact( )**. After the execution of this statement, the control will be directly transferred to the definition of the function(line 15). Next, the function body will be executed and the resultant value will be returned back to line 11. This resultant value will be assigned to the variable **val**.

The working of Example 4 is the same as of Example 2.

The output of the program is as follows:
Enter a number
4
The factorial is: 24

Function with Return Type and with Arguments
In this section, you will learn about the functions that have a return type and also contain an argument list. In these types of functions, a value must be returned by the function. Also, the arguments can be passed when a function call is made in the program. The syntax for declaring a function with a return type and also with arguments is as follows:

    ret_type fun_name (data_type arg1,......., data_type argn)

Refer to Example 2, which illustrates the use of the functions that have a return type and contain an argument list.

Function Overloading

The term function overloading means that more than one function can have the same name in a program. These functions are differentiated on the basis of number of arguments, their sequence, return types, or data types. For example:

```
void area(int a, int b)
void area(int c)
```

In the above example, both functions have the same name. The first function contains two integer arguments, while the second contains one integer argument. These functions are differentiated by the compiler on the basis of the number of arguments when a function call is made. If two arguments are passed during a function call, the first function will be executed. If one argument is passed, the second function will be executed.

The following example illustrates the use of function overloading.

Example 5

Write a program to calculate the area of a rectangle and a square.

The following program will calculate the area of a rectangle and a square and display the resultant values on the screen.

```
//Write a program to find the area of a rectangle and a square        1
#include<iostream>                                                     2
using namespace std;                                                   3
int area(int l, int b);                                                4
int area(int a);                                                       5
int main()                                                             6
{                                                                      7
        int i,j;                                                       8
        i=area(10,20);                                                 9
        cout<<"The area of the rectangle is: "<< i<<endl;             10
        j=area(5);                                                    11
        cout<<"The area of the square is: "<< j<<endl;               12
        return 0;                                                    13
}                                                                     14
int area(int l, int b)                                               15
{                                                                     16
        int k;                                                       17
        k=l*b;                                                       18
        return k;                                                    19
}                                                                     20
int area(int a)                                                      21
{                                                                     22
        int c;                                                       23
```

```
        c=a*a;                                              24
        return c;                                           25
}                                                           26
```

Explanation
Line 9
i=area(10,20);
In this line, a call is made to the function **area()** and two arguments 10 and 20 are passed. The compiler will differentiate by the number of arguments and the control will be directly transferred to line 15. The value 10 will be assigned to the variable **l** and value 20 will be assigned to the variable **b**. After the execution of the function body, the resultant value 200 will be returned back to line 9. Next, this resultant value will be assigned to the variable **i**.

Line 11
j=area(5);
In this line, the function **area()** is called and only one argument 5 is passed. Now, the control will be directly transferred to line 21. The value 5 will be assigned to the variable **a**. After the execution of the function body, the resultant value 25 will be returned back to line 11. Next, this resultant value will be assigned to the variable **j**.

Line 18
k=l*b;
In this line, the value of the variable **l** (10) is multiplied by the value of the variable **b** (20) and the resultant value (200) is assigned to the variable **k**.

Line 19
return k;
In the line given above, the value of the variable **k** will be returned back to line 9.

The output of the program is as follows:
The area of the rectangle is: 200
The area of the square is: 25

RECURSION
Recursion is a technique in which a function calls itself one or more times. Recursion is useful for calculating the factorial of a number, displaying the fibonacci series, and so on. In recursion, the function call statement is a part of the function body. For example:

```
    void average()      //Function definition
    {                   //Start of the function body
        statement_1;
        average();      //Function calls itself
        statement_2;
    }                   //End of the function body
    int main()
    {
        statement_3;
```

```
        average();        //Function call
    }
```

In the above example, after the execution of **statement_3**, a call is made to the function **average()**. The control is transferred to the definition and the body of the function is executed. In the body of the function, the function **average()** calls itself and again the control is transferred to the definition of the function. This process is repeated until a particular condition is false.

The following example illustrates the use of recursion.
..
..

Example 6

Write a program to calculate the factorial of a number using recursion.
The following program will prompt the user to enter a number, calculate its factorial, and display the resultant value on the screen.

```
//Write a program to calculate the factorial of a number    1
#include<iostream>                                           2
using namespace std;                                         3
int num;                                                     4
long fact(int num);                                          5
int main()                                                   6
{                                                            7
        long int a;                                          8
        cout<<"Enter a number: "<<endl;                      9
        cin>>num;                                            10
        a=fact(num);                                         11
        cout<<"The factorial is: "<<a<<endl;                 12
        return 0;                                            13
}                                                            14
long fact(int i)                                             15
{                                                            16
        if(i==1)                                             17
        {                                                    18
                return 1;                                    19
        }                                                    20
        else                                                 21
        {                                                    22
                return i * fact(i-1);                        23
        }                                                    24
}                                                            25
```

Explanation

Line 11
a=fact(num);
In this line, a call is made to the function **fact()**. The value of the variable **num** will be passed as an argument. After the execution of this statement, the control will be directly transferred to line 15.

Line 15
long fact(int i)
Here, the value of the variable **num** (passed as an argument) will be assigned to the variable **i**. Now, the control will be transferred to line 17.

Line 17
if(i==1)
In this line, the given condition is checked to see if the value of variable **i** is equal to 1. If the condition is true, value 1 will be returned (because the factorial of value 1 is 1) to line 11. Otherwise, the control will be transferred to line 21.

Line 19
return 1;
If the condition given in line 17 is true, this line will be executed. Otherwise, this line will be skipped. In this line, value 1 is returned back to line 11.

Line 23
return i * fact(i-1);
If the condition given in line 17 is false, the line given above will be executed. In this line, the function **fact()** calls itself again and again until the value of variable **i** is not equal to 1 and the resultant value is returned back to line 11.

For example, if you want to calculate the factorial of number 5, it can be calculated as follows:

     5 * 4 * 3 * 2 * 1

The resultant value 120 is returned back to the line where the function call is made.

The output of the program is as follows:
Enter a number:
6
The factorial is: 720

ARRAYS

An array is a collection of data elements of the same type. These elements are referred by a common name. The array elements are stored in contiguous memory locations. You can refer to a particular data element by using the index. The index starts from the lowest address (**0**) and ends at the highest address (n-1, here n specifies the total number of elements).

Declaring an Array

An array must be declared before it can be used in a program. The syntax for declaring an array is as discussed next.

    data_type arr_name [size of array];

The above syntax shows the declaration of a single dimension array. The **data_type** specifies the type of data elements to be stored in an array. The **arr_name** specifies the name of the array and the **[size of array]** specifies the total number of elements that the array can hold. For example, the code for declaring a single dimensional array of integers, called **pin_code**, which can store a maximum of 6 integer values is as follows:

    int pin_code [6];

When the above code is executed, the compiler reserves 12 contiguous bytes for the array **pin_code**. This is because each integer element requires 2 bytes of memory space. Figure 4-1 shows the memory allocation of the **pin_code** array.

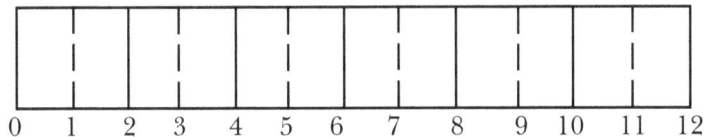

Figure 4-1 *Memory allocation of the array*

Initializing an Array

Initialization means to assign initial values to an array. An array can be initialized in many ways, which are as follows:

a. You can initialize an array during its declaration. For example:

    int pin_code [6] = {1,5,2,1,0,7};

In the above example, the values inside the curly braces and separated by a comma are assigned to the **pin_code** array, as follows:

    1 is assigned to pin_code[0]
    5 is assigned to pin_code[1]
    2 is assigned to pin_code[2]
    1 is assigned to pin_code[3]
    0 is assigned to pin_code[4]
    7 is assigned to pin_code[5]

Figure 4-2 shows the storage of the **pin_code** array

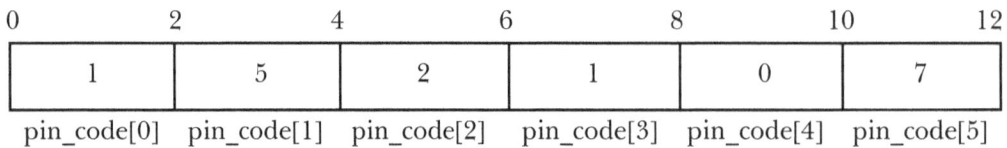

0	2	4	6	8	10	12

1	5	2	1	0	7
pin_code[0]	pin_code[1]	pin_code[2]	pin_code[3]	pin_code[4]	pin_code[5]

Figure 4-2 *Memory allocation*

b. You can also initialize an array without specifying its size. For example:

    char designation[ ] = {'M', 'A', 'N', 'A', 'G', 'E', 'R', '\0'};

In the above example, the array **designation** is a character type array. The size of the array is not specified in the square brackets. So, the size of the array is equal to the total number of characters given in the curly braces, which is 8 in this case. The character values assigned to the array are as follows:

    designation[0] = 'M'
    designation[1] = 'A'
    ----
    designation[6] = 'R'
    designation[7] = '\0' \\Null character

In this example, the last character specifies the **NULL** character. Every character array contains the **NULL** character at the last location.

You can also assign a string (group of more than one characters) to an array of characters. For example:

    char designation[ ] = "MANAGER";

c. You can also assign initial values to each of the array elements with the help of a loop. For example:

```
int pin_code [6];//Array declaration
for(int i=0; i<=5;i++)
{
    pin_code[i]=i;
}
```

Accessing the Elements of an Array

You can access each element of an array by placing its index value in the square brackets. The syntax for accessing the elements of an array is as follows:

    arr_name [index value];

In this syntax, the **arr_name** specifies the name of the array and the index value specifies the element to be accessed.

For example, if you want to access the fourth element of the **pin_code** array, use the following code:

    pin_code [3];

In the above code, the index value **3** is placed in the square brackets because the index starts from zero.

The following example illustrates the concept of accessing the elements of an array.

Example 7

Write a program to add two integer type arrays.

The following program will prompt the user to enter values for two integer type arrays, add them, store the resultant values in the third array, and then display the resultant array on the screen.

```
//Write a program to add two integer type arrays                                1
#include<iostream>                                                              2
using namespace std;                                                            3
int main()                                                                      4
{                                                                               5
      int a[3], b[3], c[3];//Array declaration                                  6
      int i;                                                                    7
      cout<<"Enter three values for the first array:"<<endl;                    8
      for(i=0; i<=2; i++)                                                       9
      {                                                                        10
            cin>>a[i];                                                         11
      }                                                                        12
      cout<<"Enter three values for the second array:"<<endl;                  13
      for(i=0;i<=2;i++)                                                        14
      {                                                                        15
            cin>>b[i];                                                         16
      }                                                                        17
      cout<<"After addition, the third array contains:"<<endl;                 18
      for(i=0;i<=2;i++)                                                        19
      {                                                                        20
            c[i] = a[i] + b[i];                                                21
            cout<<"At "<<i<<" location "<<c[i]<<" is stored"<<endl;            22
      }                                                                        23
      return 0;                                                                24
}                                                                              25
```

Explanation
Line 6
int a[3], b[3], c[3];
In this line, **a**, **b**, and **c** are declared as integer type arrays. The size of each array is 3, which means each array can store a maximum of three integer values.

Line 11
cin>>a[i];
This statement is associated with the **for** loop (line 9) and is used to read the values of the array **a[ ]**. The **for** loop is executed three times. Also, this statement (line 11) will be executed three times to read the values of **a[0]**, **a[1]**, and **a[2]**.

Line 16
cin>>b[i];
This statement is also associated with the **for** loop (line 14) and is used to read the values of the array **b[ ]**. The **for** loop is executed three times. Also, this statement (line 16) will be executed three times to read the values of **b[0]**, **b[1]**, and **b[2]**.

Line 21
c[i] = a[i] + b[i];
This statement is also associated with the **for** loop (line 19). In this line, the values stored in the array **a[ ]** will be added to the values stored in the array **b[ ]** and the resultant values will be assigned to the array **c[ ]**. When the loop is executed for the first time, the value stored in the location **a[0]** and the value stored in the location **b[0]** will be added and the resultant value will be stored in the location **c[0]**. This process will be repeated three times.

The output of the program is as follows:
Enter three values for the first array:
12
23
26
Enter three values for the second array:
25
26
27
After addition, the third array contains:
At 0 location 37 is stored
At 1 location 49 is stored
At 2 location 53 is stored

The output will be displayed on the screen as follows:

```
Enter three values for the first array:
12
23
26
Enter three values for the second array:
25
26
27
After addition, the third array contains:
At 0 location 37 is stored
At 1 location 49 is stored
At 2 location 53 is stored
Press any key to continue_
```

Bounds Checking

In C++, no bounds checking is performed on an array. So, you must use a valid range of index values (from the lowest address to the highest address) to access the data elements of an array. If you are using an index value that is not in the valid range, then you are overrunning the bounds of an array. In this case, the value stored at that particular location is read or overwritten.

For example:

```
int a[5];
for(int i=0; i<=5; i++)
{
    cin>>a[i];
}
```

In the above example, an integer type array **a[ ]** is declared and the size of this array is 5. The **for** loop is used to read the values of the array **a[ ]**. The **for** loop executes six times and reads six values but the size of the array **a[ ]** is 5. Here, the array bounds are overrun and the value that is stored earlier at the sixth place is overwritten.

Multidimensional Array

A multidimensional array is also known as an array of arrays, or in other words, an array within another array. The multidimensional array can have more than one dimension such as 2, 3, 4, upto n. A two-dimensional array is the simplest type of multidimensional array. The syntax for declaring a two-dimensional array is as follows:

data_type arr_name [size] [size];

The above syntax contains two square brackets, which represent that this is a two-dimensional array. The value given in the first square bracket specifies the number of rows in an array and the value given in the second square bracket specifies the number of columns in an array. The number of bytes occupied by a two-dimensional array can be calculated as follows:

Total number of bytes= number of rows * number of columns * size of data type

For example, to create a two-dimensional array of an integer type that has three rows and three columns in each row, the code will be as follows:

    int a[3] [3];

In the above example, the total number of bytes occupied by array **a[ ] [ ]** is equal to 18 (**3 * 3 * 2**).

Figure 4-3 represents a two-dimensional array.

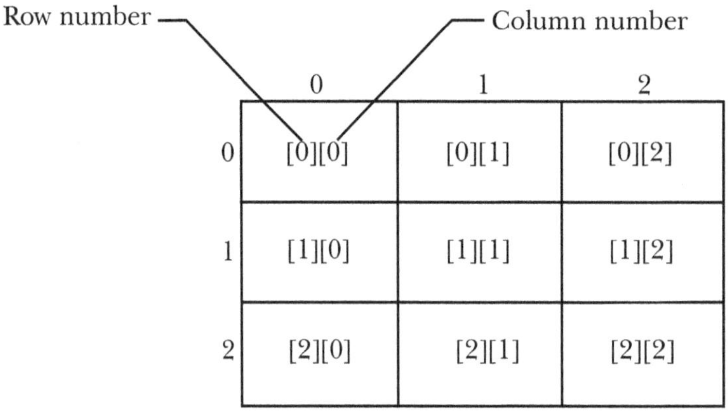

Figure 4-3 *Two-dimensional array*

In a two-dimensional array, the index value consists of two values. One specifies the row number and the other specifies the column number in that particular row. For example, you may want to access the data element, which is stored in the second column of row one in array **a[ ] [ ]**. You can access the given element by specifying the following index value:

    a[1] [2];

The following example illustrates the use of two-dimensional arrays.

Example 8

Write a program to display a two-dimensional array of integer type on the screen.

The following program will load the values from 0 to 8 in a two-dimensional array and then display the resultant array on the screen.

```
//Write a program to illustrate the use of a two-dimensional array        1
#include<iostream>                                                        2
using namespace std;                                                      3
int main()                                                                4
```

```
{                                                                          5
       int i, j, k=0;                                                      6
       int a[3][3];                                                        7
       for(i=0;i<3;i++)//Loop for rows                                     8
       {                                                                   9
              for(j=0;j<3;j++)//Loop for columns                          10
              {                                                           11
                     a[i][j]=k;                                           12
                     k++;                                                 13
              }                                                           14
       }                                                                  15
       for(i=0;i<3;i++)//Loop for rows                                    16
       {                                                                  17
              for(j=0;j<3;j++)//Loop for columns                          18
              {                                                           19
                     cout<<a[i][j]<<" ";                                  20
              }                                                           21
              cout<<endl;                                                 22
       }                                                                  23
       return 0;                                                          24
}                                                                         25
```

Explanation

Line 7
int a[3][3];
In this line, a two-dimensional array with the dimensions 3, 3 is declared as an integer type array.

Line 8
for(i=0;i<3;i++)
The loop given above is used for the rows. The number of iterations of this loop is equal to the number of rows. In this program, the number of rows is equal to 3. So this loop will be executed 3 times. In each iteration, it will load the values for each row. In the first iteration, it will load for row 0, in the second iteration for row 1, and in the third iteration for row 2.

Line 10
for(j=0;j<3;j++)
When the condition given in line 8 is true, the control will be transferred to this line. This loop is used for the columns and is repeated three times because the number of columns in a row is equal to three. In each iteration, it will load one value in one column.

Line 12
a[i][j]=k;
When the condition given in line 10 is true, the control will be transferred to this line. In this line, the value of the variable **k** is assigned to the array **a[i][j]**. Here, the variable **i** represents the row number and the variable **j** represents the column number. Whenever this statement is executed, it will load one value in a particular column, which in turn is in a particular row.

For example, in the first iteration of the loop (line 10), this statement will load value 0 in the location **a[0][0]**, in the second iteration load value 1 in **a[0][1]**, and in the third iteration load value 2 in **a[0][2]**, and so on.

The output of the program is as follows:
0 1 2
3 4 5
6 7 8

The output will be displayed on the screen as follows:

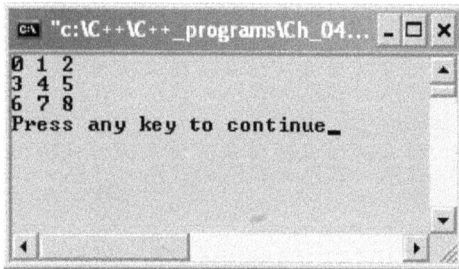

```
c:\C++\C++_programs\Ch_04...  _ □ ×
0 1 2
3 4 5
6 7 8
Press any key to continue_
```

Figure 4-4 shows the values stored in the array **a[3][3]**.

[j]	0	1	2
[i]			
0	0	1	2
1	3	4	5
2	6	7	8

Figure 4-4 *Storage Representation*

Passing Arrays to Functions as Arguments

In C++, a one dimensional array can be passed as an argument. You can pass only the array name but not the entire array. The array name provides the reference to the starting address of the array. The syntax for passing an array to a function as an argument is as follows:

Return_type fun_name(data_type arr_name[size])

For example:

    void demo(int a[ ]);//Function declaration

In the above example, an integer type array **a[ ]** is passed as an argument to the function **demo**. When this function is called in the program, the array name **a** will be passed without any index value. The code for calling the function **demo( )** is as follows:

    demo(a);//Function call

The following program illustrates the concept of passing an array as an argument to a function.

Example 9

Write a program to add two integer type arrays.

The following program will prompt the user to enter six values for two integer type arrays, add them, store the resultant values into the third integer type array, and display the resultant array on the screen.

```
//Write a program to add two integer type arrays              1
#include<iostream>                                            2
using namespace std;                                          3
void sum(int a[ ], int b[ ], int c[ ]);                       4
int main()                                                    5
{                                                             6
        int d[3], e[3], f[3], i;                              7
        cout<<"Enter three values for the first array:"<<endl;   8
        for(i=0; i<3; i++)                                    9
        {                                                     10
              cin>>d[i];                                      11
        }                                                     12
        cout<<"Enter three values for the second array:"<<endl;  13
        for(i=0; i<3; i++)                                    14
        {                                                     15
              cin>>e[i];                                      16
        }                                                     17
        sum(d, e, f);//Function call                          18
        return 0;                                             19
}                                                             20
void sum(int a[ ], int b[ ], int c[ ])                        21
{                                                             22
        cout<<"After addition, the third array contains:"<<endl;  23
        for(int j=0; j<3; j++)                                24
        {                                                     25
              c[j]= a[j] + b[j];                              26
```

```
            cout<<"At "<<j<<" location "<<c[j]<<" is stored"<<endl;   27
    }                                                                  28
}                                                                      29
```

Explanation

Line 4
void sum(int a[ ], int b[ ], int c[ ]);
In this line, the function **sum( )** is declared whose return type is **void**. In this declaration, three single dimensional arrays **a[ ]**, **b[ ]**, and **c[ ]** are passed as arguments.

Line 18
sum(d, e, f);
In this line, a function call is made to the function **sum( )** in the program and three array names **d**, **e**, and **f** are passed as arguments. Here, only the names are passed, not the entire arrays. These names refer to the starting addresses of these three arrays.

Line 21
void sum(int a[ ], int b[ ], int c[ ])
After the function call is made, the control will be transferred to this statement. Here, the starting addresses of the arrays **d**, **e**, and **f** are assigned to the arrays **a[ ]**, **b[ ]**, and **c[ ]**, respectively.

The output of the program is as follows:
Enter three value for the first array:
12
13
14
Enter three values for the second array:
12
13
14
After addition, the third array contains:
At 0 location 24 is stored
At 1 location 26 is stored
At 2 location 27 is stored

Self-Evaluation Test

Answer the following questions and then compare them to the answers given at the end of this chapter:

1. A function has a _____, a _____, and a _____.

2. In function overloading, two functions can have the same _____ in a program.

3. When a function calls itself again and again, it is called _____.

4. An array is a collection of data elements of the same _____.

5. The _____ value is used to access the data element of an array.

Review Questions

Answer the following questions:

1. Define a function.

2. Define function overloading.

3. Define recursion.

4. Define an array.

5. Differentiate between single dimensional and multidimensional arrays.

Exercises

Exercise 1

Write a program to prompt the user to enter a name and display it on the screen using a character array.

Exercise 2

Write a program to display the first ten elements of the fibonacci series using recursion.

Exercise 3

Write a program to prompt the user to enter a number and calculate its square, using a function.

Answers to Self-Evaluation Test

1. name, data type, and list of arguments, **2.** name, **3.** recursion, **4.** type, **5.** index

Chapter 5

Strings, Pointers, and Structures

In this chapter, you will learn about strings, pointers, and structures.

A string is a group of characters that are enclosed in double quotes.

A pointer is a variable that points to another variable in a program.

A structure is a group of data elements with the same or different data types, grouped together under the same name.

STRINGS

A string is a group of characters that are enclosed in double quotes. C++ does not provide a string data type. Therefore, an array of characters is used to store a string. In C++, each string is terminated by a null character '\0'. While declaring an array of characters, you must include an extra space for a null character. For example, you can declare an array that can hold 7 characters, as follows:

    char name[8];

This array can hold 7 characters. It also has an extra space for the null character at the end of the string.

You can assign a string constant to an array of characters by using the following code:

    char name [8] = "America" ;

Figure 5-1 represents the way in which the above string (America) is stored in an array of characters (name).

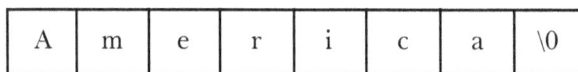

A	m	e	r	i	c	a	\0

Figure 5-1 *Storage representation of a string*

In the above figure, observe that the null character '\0' is automatically added at the end of the string by the compiler.

String Manipulated Functions

C++ provides some functions, which are used for string manipulation. To use these functions, you must include the **string.h** header file in your program.

The list of the string manipulated functions is as follows:

a.   strcpy( )

b.   strcat( )

c.   strlen( )

d.   strcmp( )

e.   strchr( )

The strcpy( ) Function

The **strcpy( )** function is used to copy one string into another string. The syntax is as follows:

    strcpy(str1,str2)

In the above syntax, the string **str2** will be copied into the string **str1**.

For example:

    char a[8]= "America";
    char b[8];
    strcpy (b,a);

In the above example, the string copy function copies the string **America** into the character array **b**.

The strcat( ) Function

The **strcat( )** function is used to concatenate one string to the end of another string. The syntax is as follows:

    strcat(str1,str2)

In the above syntax, **str2** is concatenated to the end of the string **str1**.

For example:

    char a[ ] = "John";
    char b[ ] = "Smith";
    strcat (a,b);

In the above example, the string **Smith** is concatenated to the end of the string **John**. Now, the character array **a[ ]** contains the string **JohnSmith**.

The strlen( ) Function

The **strlen( )** (string length) function is used to find the length of a string. This function returns an integer value that specifies the number of characters held by a string.

The syntax is as follows:

    strlen(str1);

In this syntax, the function **strlen( )** returns the length of the string **str1**, which is passed to it as an argument.

For example:

```
char a[ ]= "Williams";
int i;
i= strlen(a);
```

In the above example, the function **strlen( )** returns an integer value 8 and this value is assigned to the integer variable **i**.

The strcmp( ) Function

The **strcmp( )** (string compare) function is used to compare two strings, character by character such that the first character of the first string is compared to the first character of the second string, and so on. The syntax is as follows:

```
strcmp(str1,str2);
```

In the above syntax, the function **strcmp( )** returns 0 if the string **str1** and string **str2** are identical, less than 0 if **str1** is less than **str2**, and greater than 0 if **str1** is greater than **str2**.

For example, if **str1** is greater than **str2**:

```
char a[ ]= "Billy";//str1
char b[ ]=  "Bill";//str2
int i;
i=strcmp(a,b);
```

In the above example, the function **strcmp( )** returns 1 because the first four characters of both the strings are identical but the character array **a[ ]** contains one extra character **'y'**.

Consider another example where **str1** and **str2** are identical:

```
char a[ ]= "Bill";
char b[ ]= "Bill";
int i;
i=strcmp( );
```

In the above example, the function **strcmp( )** returns 0, because all the four characters in these two strings are identical.

In the other case, **str1** is less than **str2**:

```
char a[ ]= "Bill";
char b[ ]= "Billy";
```

```
int i;
i=strcmp(a,b);
```

In the above example, the function **strcmp( )** returns -1, because the first four characters of both the strings are identical, but the character array **b[ ]** contains one extra character **y**.

The strchr( ) Function

The **strchr( )** function returns a pointer to the first occurrence of a particular character in the string. The syntax is as follows:

```
strchr(str1,ch);
```

For example:

```
char a[ ]= "Billy";
char ch= 'l';
cout<< strchr(a,ch);
```

In this example, the function returns **lly**, because the function **strchr( )** returns a pointer to the first occurrence of character **l** and also returns all the characters following this character.

The following program illustrates the use of the string manipulated functions.

Example 1

Write a program to illustrate the working of the string manipulated functions.

The following program will prompt the user to enter two strings, use the string manipulated functions, and display the resultant values and strings on the screen. The line numbers on the right are not a part of the program and are for reference only.

```
//Write a program to illustrate the use of the string manipulated functions      1
#include<iostream>                                                                2
#include<string>                                                                  3
using namespace std;                                                              4
int main( )                                                                       5
{                                                                                 6
        char a[10] = "John";                                                      7
        char b[10]= "Smith";                                                      8
        int i=strlen(a);                                                          9
        cout<<"The length of the first string is: "<<i<<endl;                     10
        int j=strlen(b);                                                          11
        cout<<"The length of the second string is: "<<j<<endl;                    12
        cout<<"After concatenation: "<<strcat(a,b)<<endl;                         13
        cout<<"After copying, the first string contains: "<<strcpy(a,b)<<endl;    14
        cout<<"The value returned by the function is: "<<strcmp(a,b)<<endl;       15
```

```
        return 0;                                                    16
}                                                                    17
```

Explanation

Line 7
char a[10] = "John";
In this line, the string **John** is assigned to an array of characters **a[ ]**.

Line 8
char b[10] = "Smith";
In this line, the string **Smith** is assigned to an array of characters (**b[ ]**).

Line 9
int i=strlen(a);
The **strlen( )** function returns the number of characters (4) held by the character array **a[ ]** and the resultant value is assigned to the variable **i**.

Line 10
cout<<"The length of the first string is: "<<i<<endl;
This line will display the following on the screen:
The length of the first string is: 4

Line 11
int j=strlen(b);
The **strlen( )** function returns the number of characters (5) held by the character array **b[ ]** and the resultant value is assigned to the variable **j**.

Line 12
cout<<"The length of the second string is: "<<j<<endl;
This line will display the following on the screen:
The length of the second string is: 5

Line 13
cout<<"After concatenation: "<<strcat(a,b)<<endl;
In this line, the function **strcat(a,b)** appends the contents of the second string (b) at the end of the contents of the first string (a) and the resultant string is displayed on the screen as follows:
After concatenation: JohnSmith

Line 14
cout<<"After copying, the first string contains: "<<strcpy(a,b)<<endl;
In this line, the **strcpy(a,b)** function copies the contents of the second string (b) into the first string (a) and the resultant string is assigned back to the first string (a). Next, this line displays the following on the screen:
After copying, the first string contains: Smith

Line 16

cout< <"The value returned by the function is: "< <strcmp(a,b)< <endl;
In this line, the function **strcmp(a,b)** is used to compare the contents of both the strings. This function will return zero because both the strings contain the same value **(Smith)** and are identical. Next, this line will display the following on the screen:
The value returned by the function is: 0

The output of the program is as follows:
The length of the first string is: 4
The length of the second string is: 5
After concatenation: JohnSmith
After copying, the first string contains: Smith
The value returned by the function is: 0

The output will be displayed on the screen as follows:

POINTERS

In this section, you will learn about pointer definition, pointer declaration and initialization, pointer arithmetic, pointers and arrays, and pointers and functions.

Defining a Pointer

A pointer is a variable that can hold the memory address of another variable. In other words, a pointer variable is used to access the value stored in another variable. Figure 5-2 shows the pictorial representation of a pointer.

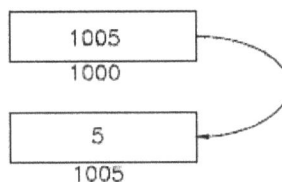

Figure 5-2 Pictorial representation of a pointer

In the above figure, the values **1000** and **1005** represent the memory addresses. In this figure, the memory address **1000** points to another memory address **1005** and can access the value **5** stored in it.

Declaring a Pointer

A pointer variable must be declared before being used in the program. The syntax for declaring a pointer variable is as follows:

    data_type * var_name;

In the above syntax, the **data_type** specifies the type of variables that can be pointed by a pointer variable. The * (asterisk) is a unary operator and the **var_name** refers to the name of the pointer variable.

Initializing a Pointer Variable

In the initialization process, an initial value is assigned to the pointer variable with the help of an assignment operator. The syntax is as discussed next.

    data_type * var_name1 = &var_name2;

In the above syntax, the **&** (ampersand) symbol is used as the address operator, which returns the memory address of the variable **var_name2.** Next, the memory address is assigned to the **var_name1**.

For example:

    int i=22;
    int *p =&i;

In the above example, the address operator (&) returns the address of the variable **i**, which is assigned to the pointer variable **p**. The * (asterisk) operator is used to access the value (22) that is stored in the variable **i**.

The following example illustrates the use of pointers.

Example 2

Write a program to illustrate the working of pointers.

The following program will display the memory address pointed by a pointer variable and also the values stored in it.

```
//Write a program to illustrate the working of pointers        1
#include<iostream>                                             2
using namespace std;                                          3
int main( )                                                   4
{                                                             5
        int *p;//Pointer declaration                         6
        int i = 12;                                          7
```

```
        p=&i;//Pointer initialization                                    8
        cout<<"The memory address assigned to the pointer variable is: ";  9
        cout<<p<<endl;                                                  10
        cout<<"The value accessed by the pointer variable is: ";        11
        cout<<*p<<endl;                                                 12
        return 0;                                                       13
}                                                                       14
```

Explanation

Line 6
int *p;
In this line, an integer type pointer variable **p** is declared. This pointer variable can only point to the integer variable.

Line 7
int i = 12;
In this line, **i** is declared as an integer type variable and **12** is assigned as its initial value.

Line 8
p=&i;
In this line, the **&** operator returns the memory address of the variable **i** and this memory address is assigned to the pointer variable **p**.

Line 9
cout<<"The memory address assigned to the pointer variable is: ";
This line will display the following on the screen:
The memory address assigned to the pointer variable is:

Line 10
cout<<p<<endl;
This line will display the memory address, which is assigned to the pointer variable **p** in line 8.

Line 11
cout<<"The value accessed by the pointer variable is: ";
This line will display the following on the screen:
The value accessed by the pointer variable is:

Line 12
cout<<*p<<endl;
In this line, the ***** symbol is used with the pointer variable **p** to access the value **12**, which is stored in the memory address of the variable i.

The output of the program is as follows:
The memory address assigned to the pointer variable is: 0012FEC8
The value accessed by the pointer variable is: 12

Note

The memory address in the resulting output can vary from compiler to compiler.

Assigning a Pointer Variable

Alongwith initializing a pointer variable, you can also assign a pointer variable to another pointer variable. This variable is assigned as an initial value and is discussed in the next example.

For example:

```
int i=22;
int *p, *p1;
p=&i;
p1=p;
```

In the above example, there are two integer pointer variables **p** and **p1**. The memory address of the variable **i** is assigned to the pointer variable **p** as an initial value. After that, the pointer variable **p** is assigned to the second pointer variable **p1**. Now, **p1** points to the same memory address, which was earlier pointed by the pointer variable **p**. So, both the pointer variables point to the same memory location.

Figure 5-3 shows the pictorial representation of the above exam

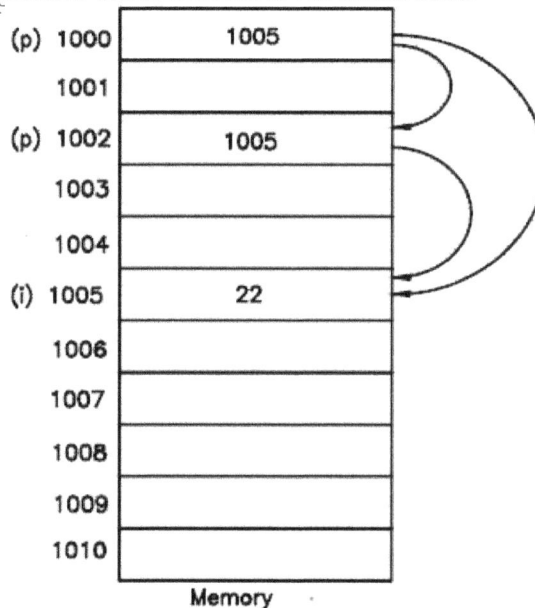

Figure 5-3 Pointer assignment

Pointer Arithmetic

You cannot perform all kinds of arithmetic operations with pointers. The addition and subtraction is possible but you cannot perform multiplication and division with them. You can perform these operations only on integer and character type pointers but not on the float and double type pointers.

For example, assume there is an integer type pointer variable **i**, which is two bytes long. The variable currently points to the memory address **1000**. After the execution of the statement given below, the pointer variable **i** will point to the next location **1002**. This is because after the increment, it will point to the next integer value.

    i++;

You can also perform subtraction in the same way as addition. For example, assume there is an integer type pointer variable **i**, which is two bytes long. The variable currently points to the memory address **1000**. After the execution of the statement given below, the pointer variable **i** will point to the preceding value **998**. This is because after the decrement, it will point to the preceding integer value.

    i--;

You can also add or subtract an integer value to or from the pointer variables.

For example, assume there is an integer type pointer variable **i**, which is two bytes long. The variable currently points to the memory address **1000.** After the execution of the statement given below, the pointer variable **i** will point to the fourth element, which is stored at a memory address **1008**.

    i= i+4;

You can also compare two pointer variables with the help of relational operators.

For example:

```
int i=10;
int j=20;
int *p, *p1;
p=&i;//Assigning memory address of i
p1=&j;//Assigning memory address of j
if(p>p1)
{
    statements;
}
```

In the above example, the **if** statement is used to compare the memory addresses, which are pointed   by the pointer variable **p** and the pointer variable **p1**.

The following example illustrates the concept of pointer arithmetic.

Example 3

Write a program to perform arithmetic operations on pointers.

The following program will display the memory addresses and also the values stored in them.

```
//Write a program to perform the arithmetic operations on pointers        1
#include<iostream>                                                         2
using namespace std;                                                       3
int main( )                                                                4
{                                                                          5
        int i=10;                                                          6
        int j=20;                                                          7
        int *p, *p1;                                                       8
        p=&i;                                                              9
        p1=&j;                                                             10
        cout<<"The pointer p points to the memory address: "<<p<<endl;    11
        cout<<"The pointer p1 points to the memory address: "<<p1<<endl;  12
        cout<<"The value accessed by the pointer p is: "<<*p<<endl;       13
        cout<<"The value accessed by the pointer p1 is: "<<*p1<<endl;     14
        p++;                                                               15
        cout<<"After the increment, the pointer p points to: "<<p<<endl; 16
        p1--;                                                              17
        cout<<"After the decrement, the pointer p1 points to: "<<p1<<endl; 18
        if(p>p1)                                                           19
        {                                                                  20
                cout<<"The pointer p points to "
                        "a higher address than p1"<<endl;                 21
        }                                                                  22
        return 0;                                                          23
}                                                                          24
```

Explanation
Line 9
p=&i;
In this line, the memory address of the variable **i** is assigned to the pointer variable **p**.

Line 10
p1=&j;
In this line, the memory address of the variable **j** is assigned to the pointer variable **p1**.

Line 11
cout<<"The pointer p points to the memory address: "<<p<<endl;
This line will display the following on the screen:

The pointer p points to the memory address:
This line will also display the address, which is pointed by the pointer variable **p**.

Line 12
cout<<"The pointer p1 points to the memory address: "<<p1<<endl;
This line will display the following on the screen:
The pointer p1 points to the memory address:
It will also display the address, which is pointed by the pointer variable **p1**.

Line 13
cout<<"The value accessed by the pointer p is: "<<*p<<endl;
This line will display the following on the screen:
The value accessed by the pointer p is:
It will also display the value stored in the variable **i**, which is pointed by the pointer variable **p**.

Line 14
cout<<"The value accessed by the pointer p1 is: "<<*p1<<endl;
This line will display the following on the screen:
The value accessed by the pointer p1 is:
It will also display the value stored in the variable **j**, which is pointed by the pointer variable **p1**.

Line 15
p++;
When this line is executed by the compiler, the pointer variable will point to the next memory address.

Line 16
cout<<"After the increment, the pointer p points to: "<<p<<endl;
This line will display the following on the screen:
After the increment, the pointer p points to:
It will also display the address, which is pointed by the pointer variable **p**.

Line 17
p1--;
When this line is executed by the compiler, the pointer variable will point to the preceding memory address.

Line 18
cout<<"After the decrement, the pointer p1 points to: "<<p1<<endl;
This line will display the following on the screen:
After the decrement, the pointer p1 points to:
It will also display the address, which is pointed by the pointer variable **p1**.

Line 19
if(p>p1)
In this line, the memory address, which is pointed by the pointer variable **p** and the memory address, which is pointed by the pointer variable **p1** are compared with the help of a relational

operator (greater than). If the memory address pointed by **p** is higher than the memory address pointed by **p1,** the control will be transferred to line 21. Otherwise, the control will be transferred to line 23.

Line 20
{
This line indicates the start of the body of the **if** statement.

Line 21
cout<<"The pointer p points to a higher address than p1"<<endl;
This line will display the following on the screen:
The pointer p points to a higher address than p1

Line 22
}
This line indicates the end of the body of the **if** statement.

The output of the program is as follows:
The pointer p points to the memory address: 0012FED4
The pointer p1 points to the memory address: 0012FEC8
The value accessed by the pointer p is: 10
The value accessed by the pointer p1 is: 20
After the increment, the pointer p points to: 0012FED8
After the decrement, the pointer p1 points to: 0012FEC4
The pointer p points to a higher address than p1

Pointers and Arrays

A pointer can also hold the memory address of an array. But, the pointer can only hold the starting address (address of the first element) of an array. The syntax is as follows:

```
data_type * pntr_name =  arr_name;
```

For example:

```
int *p;
int num [ ]={2, 4, 6, 7, 8};
p=num;
```

In the above example, the starting address of the array **num** is assigned to the pointer variable **p**. You can access the third element of the array **num** by any of the following two ways:

a.   By using the array index, as given below:

```
num[2];
```

b.   By using the pointer arithmetic, as given below:

   *(p+2);

Here, the pointer **p** points to the starting memory address of the array **num** and the integer value **2** is added to it. Now, the pointer **p** points to the third element of the array **num**. The asterisk (*) is used to access the value of the third element.

The following example illustrates the use of pointers to access the array elements.

Example 4

Write a program to access the elements of an integer type array using pointers.

The following program will access the array elements and display them on the screen.

```
//Write a program to access the array elements using pointers          1
#include<iostream>                                                     2
using namespace std;                                                   3
int main( )                                                            4
{                                                                      5
       int num[6] ={10, 20, 30, 40, 50, 60};                          6
       int *p;                                                         7
       cout<<"The array elements are as follows:"<<endl;              8
       for(p=num; p<&num[6]; p++)                                     9
       {                                                              10
              cout<<*p<<endl;                                         11
       }                                                              12
       return 0;                                                      13
}                                                                     14
```

Explanation
Line 9
for(p=num; p<&num[6]; p++)
In the initialization part of this **for** loop, the starting address of the array **num[ ]** is assigned to the pointer variable **p**. In the conditional expression **p<&num[6]**, the memory address, which is pointed by the pointer variable **p**, is compared to the highest memory address (address of the last element) of the array. If the address pointed by **p** is less than the highest memory address, the control is transferred to line 11. Otherwise, the control is transferred to line 13. After the completion of each iteration, the control is transferred back to the increment part (p++) of the **for** loop. In this part, the value of the pointer variable **p** is incremented. After each increment, the pointer **p** points to the next memory address of the array.

Line 10
{
This line indicates the start of the body of the **for** loop.

Line 11
cout<<*p<<endl;
This statement is used to display the data elements of the array **num[ ]** on the screen.

Line 12
}
This line indicates the end of the body of the **for** loop.

The output of the program is as follows:
The array elements are as follows:
10
20
30
40
50
60

Pointers to Pointers
In C++, you can also create a pointer that points to another pointer, which in turn points to some data. A pointer to a pointer variable is declared as follows:

    data_type **var_name;

In the above declaration, the pointer to a pointer variable **var_name** is preceded by two asterisk (*****) symbols rather than one.

For example:

    int i=10;
    int *p, **p1;
    p=&i;
    p1=&p;

In the above example, the memory address of the variable **i** is assigned to the pointer variable **p** and the memory address of the pointer variable **p** is assigned to the pointer to a pointer variable **p1**. Now, **p1** can access the value **(10)** of the variable **i**. Figure 5-4 illustrates the concept of the pointer to a pointer.

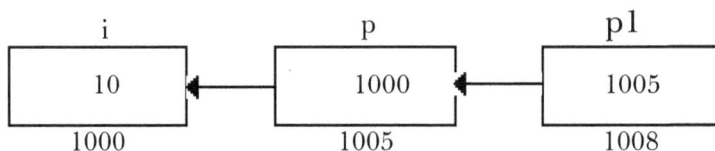

Figure 5-4 *Pointers to Pointers*

The following example illustrates the concept of pointers to pointers.

Write a program to illustrate the working of a pointer to a pointer variable.

Example 5

The following program will access the value of a variable and display the resultant value on the screen.

```
//Write a program to access the value of a variable by using
//a pointer to a pointer variable                              1
#include<iostream>                                             2
using namespace std;                                           3
int main( )                                                    4
{                                                              5
        int j=20;                                              6
        int *k;                                                7
        int **l;                                               8
        k=&j;                                                  9
        l=&k;                                                  10
        cout<<"The value of j is: ";                           11
        cout<<**l<<endl;                                       12
        return 0;                                              13
}                                                              14
```

Explanation
Line 7
int *k;
In this line, **k** is declared as a pointer to an integer variable and it can hold the address of another integer variable.

Line 8
int **l;
In this line, **l** is declared as an integer type pointer to a pointer variable. This variable can point to another pointer variable of an integer type.

Line 9
k=&j;
In this line, the **&** operator returns the memory address of the variable **j**, which is assigned to the pointer variable **k**.

Line 10
l=&k;
Here, the **&** operator returns the memory address of the pointer variable **k**, which is assigned to the variable **l**.

Line 11
cout<<"The value of j is: ";

This line will display the following on the screen:
The value of j is:

Line 12
cout<<l<<endl;**
This line will display the value of the variable **j**.

The output of the program is:
The value of j is: 20

Pointers to Functions

In C++, a pointer can also point to a function, which means a pointer can also hold the starting address of a function. You can use this pointer when a function is passed to another function as an argument or a function call is made in the program. The syntax for declaring a pointer to a function is as follows:

data_type (*fun_name) ( );

In the above syntax, the **data_type** specifies the type of value returned by the pointer. The **fun_name** represents the pointer name, which must be enclosed in parenthesis while declaring a pointer to a function. If the pointer name is not enclosed in parenthesis, then the compiler interprets it as a simple function statement. The ( ) is used to carry the number of arguments and its types. The number of arguments and its types should be the same as the function, which has been pointed by the pointer.

The syntax for initializing a pointer to a function is as follows:

data_type (*fun_name) ( ) = fun_name1;

In the above syntax, the **fun_name1** represents the function name that is assigned to the pointer **fun_name**. Now, the pointer **fun_name** points to the starting address of the function **fun_name1**.

For example:

int multiply (int a, int b); //Function declaration
int (* mult) (int a, int b) = multiply; //Pointer to a function

In the above example, **multiply** is declared as an integer type function that contains two integer type arguments. In the next line, a pointer to a function **mult** is declared and the starting address of the multiply is assigned to it with the help of the assignment operator.

The following example illustrates the use of a pointer to a function.

Write a program to illustrate the working of a pointer to a function.

Example 6

The program given next will prompt the user to enter two numbers, perform multiplication and division operations, and display the resultant values on the screen.

```
//Write a program to pass a function to another function as an argument    1
#include<iostream>                                                         2
using namespace std;                                                       3
int mult(int a, int b)                                                     4
{                                                                          5
        return a*b;                                                        6
}                                                                          7
int remain(int a, int b)                                                   8
{                                                                          9
        return a%b;                                                       10
}                                                                         11
int (*multiply) (int,int) = mult;                                         12
int (*remainder) (int,int) = remain;                                      13
int calculation(int a, int b, int (*fun_call) (int, int))                 14
{                                                                         15
        int k;                                                            16
        k= (*fun_call) (a,b);                                             17
        return k;                                                         18
}                                                                         19
int main()                                                                20
{                                                                         21
        int m, n, o, p;                                                   22
        cout<<"Enter two values:"<<endl;                                  23
        cin>>m>>n;                                                        24
        o =calculation (m, n, multiply);                                  25
        p =calculation (m, n, remainder);                                 26
        cout<<"The multiplication is equal to: "<<o<<endl;                27
        cout<<"The remainder after division is: "<<p<<endl;              28
        return 0;                                                         29
}                                                                         30
```

Explanation
Line 12
int (*multiply) (int,int) = mult;
In this line, a pointer to a function ***multiply** is declared and the starting address of the function **mult** is assigned to it.

Line 13
int (*remainder) (int,int) = remain;

In this line, a pointer to a function ***remainder** is declared and the starting address of the function **remain** is assigned to it.

Line 14
int calculation(int a, int b, (*fun_call) (int, int))
In this line, **calculation** is declared as a function with an integer return type. Three arguments are passed into this function, **int a**, **int b**, and a pointer to a function **(*fun_call)**.

Line 25
o =calculation (m, n, multiply);
Here, a function call is made to the function **calculation.** The values of variables **m** and **n** and pointer to a function **multiply** are passed as an argument. After the execution of this statement, the control will be transferred to line 14. In line 14, the values of variables **m** and **n** are assigned to the variables **a** and **b**, respectively. The memory address held by **multiply** is assigned to the pointer to a function ***fun_call**.

The functionality of line 26 is the same as line 25.

The output of the program is:
Enter two values:
45
5
The multiplication is equal to: 225
The remainder after division is: 0

The output will be displayed on the screen as follows:

Passing Arguments by Reference
In all the earlier programs, you passed the values directly as arguments when a function call was made in the program and these values were assigned to the variables in the function definition. You can interchange the values of these arguments directly. For this purpose, you need to use pointer variables in the function definition and pass the address of the variables when a function call is made.

The following example illustrates the use of passing arguments by reference.

Write a program to swap two integer type values.

Example 7

The following program will prompt the user to enter two values, swap them, and display the resultant values on the screen.

```
//Write a program to swap two integer type values          1
#include<iostream>                                          2
using namespace std;                                        3
void swap( int *a, int *b);//Function declaration           4
int main( )                                                 5
{                                                           6
      int i,j;                                              7
      cout<<"Enter two values:"<<endl;                      8
      cin>>i>>j;                                             9
      swap(&i,&j);                                          10
      cout<<"After swapping, the value of the variable i is: " <<i<<endl;   11
      cout<<"After swapping, the value of the variable j is: " <<j<<endl;   12
      return 0;                                             13
}                                                           14
void swap(int *a, int *b)//Function definition              15
{                                                           16
      int c;                                                17
      c=*a;                                                 18
      *a=*b;                                                19
      *b=c;                                                 20
}                                                           21
```

Explanation
Line 10
swap(&i,&j);
In this line, a function call is made to the function **swap** and the memory addresses of variables **i** and **j** are passed as arguments. After the execution of this line, the control will be transferred to line 15.

Line 15
void swap(int *a, int*b)
In this line, the addresses of variables **i** and **j** are assigned to the pointer variables **a** and **b**, respectively.

Line 16
{
This line indicates the start of the function body.

Line 18

c=*a
In this line, the * symbol returns the value, which is stored in the memory address pointed by the pointer variable **a**. The resultant value is assigned to the variable **c**.

Line 19
*a=*b;
In this line, the * symbol returns the value, which is stored in the memory address pointed by the pointer variable **b**. The resultant value is assigned to the pointer variable ***a**.

Line 20
*b=c;
Here, the value of the variable **c** is assigned to the pointer variable ***b**.

The output of the program is:
Enter two values:
45
56
After swapping,   the value of the variable i is: 56
After swapping, the value of the variable j is: 45

The output will be displayed on the screen as follows:

STRUCTURES

A structure is a group of data elements that may have different data types, but these elements are grouped together under the same name. A structure consists of certain variables, known as members. These members are logically related to each other.

Declaring a Structure

The syntax for declaring a structure is as follows:

```
struct structure_name
{
    data_type member_name;
    data_type member_name;
    data_type member_name;
    data_type member_name;
};
```

In this syntax, the **struct** keyword is used to specify to the compiler that a structure is being declared. A structure must be terminated with a semicolon.

For example:

```
struct student
{
    char name[30];
    int stu_id;
    char address[50];
    char city[20];
};
```

A structure is a user-defined data type. You can create structure objects in the following way:

```
struct student
{
    char name[30];
    int stu_id;
    char address[50];
    char city[20];
}s1,s2,s3;
```

or

```
struct student
{
    char name[30];
    int stu_id;
    char address[50];
    char city[20];
};
student s1, s2, s3;
```

Whenever an object of a structure is created, a sufficient amount of memory is allocated to it. As shown in the given example, there are three objects **s1**, **s2**, and **s3** of the structure **student** and an equal amount of memory space (30+2+50+20=102 bytes) is allocated to each of the three objects. Each structure object has its own copies of the structure members.

Initializing Structure Members

You can assign an initial value to each of the structure members by using the dot operator (**.**). The syntax is as follows:

```
structure_name.member_name = value;
```

For example:

```
s1.name= "John";
```

```
        s1.stu_id=101;
        s2.name= "William";
        s2.roll_number=102;
```

As discussed before, each structure object has its own copies of the structure members. Therefore, in the above example, the **name** field of **s1** is different from the **name** field of **s2**.

Accessing Structure Members

You can access individual members of a structure by using the dot operator (**.**). The syntax is as follows:

```
        structure_name.member_name
```

To access the **name** member of the **s1** object of **student** structure, you can write the following code:

```
        s1.name;
```

The following example illustrates the use of structures.
Write a program to display the values of the members of a structure.

Example 8

The following program will prompt the user to enter some values, assign them to the copy of the members of the objects of a structure, and then display the resultant values on the screen.

```
//Write a program to display the values of the members of a structure       1
#include<iostream>                                                          2
using namespace std;                                                        3
int main( )                                                                 4
{                                                                           5
        struct student                                                     6
        {                                                                   7
                char name[30];                                              8
                int stu_id;                                                 9
                char city[20];                                             10
                char state[20];                                            11
        };                                                                 12
        student s1,s2;                                                     13
        cout<<"Enter the information of the first student:"<<endl;         14
        cout<<"Enter the name:"<<endl;                                     15
        cin>>s1.name;                                                      16
        cout<<"Enter the student ID:"<<endl;                              17
        cin>>s1.stu_id;                                                    18
        cout<<"Enter the city:"<<endl;                                    19
        cin>>s1.city;                                                     20
```

```
        cout<<"Enter the state:"<<endl;                              21
        cin>>s1.state;                                               22
        cout<<"Enter the information of the second student:"<<endl;  23
        cout<<"Enter the name:"<<endl;                               24
        cin>>s2.name;                                                25
        cout<<"Enter the student ID:"<<endl;                         26
        cin>>s2.stu_id;                                              27
        cout<<"Enter the city:"<<endl;                               28
        cin>>s2.city;                                                29
        cout<<"Enter the state:"<<endl;                              30
        cin>>s2.state;                                               31
        cout<<"The information of the first student is:"<<endl;      32
        cout<<"Name:"<<s1.name<<endl;                                33
        cout<<"Student ID:"<<s1.stu_id<<endl;                        34
        cout<<"City:"<<s1.city<<endl;                                35
        cout<<"State:"<<s1.state<<endl;                              36
        cout<<"The information of the second student is:"<<endl;     37
        cout<<"Name:"<<s2.name<<endl;                                38
        cout<<"Student ID:"<<s2.stu_id<<endl;                        39
        cout<<"City:"<<s2.city<<endl;                                40
        cout<<"State:"<<s2.state<<endl;                              41
        return 0;                                                    42
}                                                                    43
```

Explanation
Lines 6 to 12
struct student
{
**   char name[30];**
**   int stu_id;**
**   char city[20];**
**   char state[20];**
};
Lines 6 to 12 show the declaration of the structure **student**. The **name**, **stu_id**, **city**, and **state** are the members of the structure **student**. The declaration must be terminated with a semicolon.

Line 13
student s1,s2;
In this line, **s1**, **s2** are the variables (objects) of the structure type. Each of these variables has its own copy of the structure's members.

Line 16
cin>>s1.name;
This line is used to read a value from the user for the member **name** of the object **s1**.

Line 25
cin> >s2.name;
This line is used to read a value from the user for the member **name** of the object **s2**. Each object contains its own copy of the structure's members. So, the **name** field of **s1** is different from the name field of **s2**.

Line 33
cout< <"Name:"< <s1.name< <endl;
This line will display the following on the screen:
Name:
and also the value of the field **name** of the object **s1**.

The output of the program is as follows:
Enter the information of the first student:
Enter the name:
John
Enter the student ID:
101
Enter the city:
NewYork
Enter the state:
NewYork
Enter the information of the second student:
Enter the name:
William
Enter the student ID:
102
Enter the city:
Schererville
Enter the state:
Indiana
The information of the first student is:
Name: John
Student ID: 101
City: New York
State: New York
The information of the second student is:
Name: William
Student ID: 102
City: Schererville
State: Indiana

Assigning Structures
You can assign the values stored in one structure variable to another with the help of the assignment operator. The syntax is as follows:

structure_var1=structure_var2;

In the above syntax, the **structure_var1** and **structure_var2** are the objects of the same structure. Both the structure objects contain their own copies of the structure's members. The information stored in **structure_var2** is assigned to **structure_var1**.

The following example illustrates the concept of assigning structures.
Write a program to assign the values of one structure object to another and then display them on the screen.

The following program will prompt the user to enter the values for an object of a structure, assign them to another object, and display the resultant values on the screen.

Example 9

```
//Write a program to assign the information of one structure object
//to another and display it                                        1
#include<iostream>                                                  2
using namespace std;                                                3
int main( )                                                         4
{                                                                   5
        struct demo                                                 6
        {                                                           7
                int acc_number;                                     8
                char name[20];                                      9
        }d1,d2;                                                     10
        cout<<"Please enter the following information:"<<endl;     11
        cout<<"Enter the account number:"<<endl;                   12
        cin>>d1.acc_number;                                        13
        cout<<"Enter the name:"<<endl;                             14
        cin>>d1.name;                                              15
        d2=d1;                                                     16
        cout<<"After assignment:"<<endl;                          17
        cout<<"Account Number: "<<d2.acc_number<<endl;            18
        cout<<"Name: "<<d2.name<<endl;                            19
        return 0;                                                 20
}                                                                  21
```

Explanation
Lines 6 to 10
struct demo
{
        int acc_number;
        char name[20];
}d1,d2;

Lines 6 to 10 show the declaration of the structure **demo**. In line 10, the variables **d1** and **d2** are declared as the variables of the structure type.

Line 16
d2=d1;
Here, the information (acc_number and name) stored in the object **d1** is assigned to another object **d2**. Now, both **d1** and **d2** contain the same information.

The output of the program is as follows:
Please enter the following information:
Enter the account number:
101
Enter the name:
Smith
After assignment:
Account Number: 101
Name: Smith

Array of Structures

The array of a structure is used when you want to store a large amount of information such as the details about the employees of an organization. You cannot declare an array before the declaration of a structure.

The syntax is as follows:

    str_name var1[size];

In the above syntax, **str_name** specifies the structure name. The variable **var1** represents the variable or object of the structure type and the **size** represents the maximum number of elements that the array **var1** can hold.

For example, for declaring a 50 elements array of structures of the type **demo** (declared in the example 9), you will write the code given next.

    struct demo d[50];
        or
    demo d[50];

The following example illustrates the use of the array of a structure.
Write a program to illustrate the working of an array of a structure.

The following program will prompt the user to enter the values, assign them to the copy of the members of the objects of a structure, and display the resultant values on the screen.

Example 10

```
//Write a program to read the information of some of the account holders
//and display it on the screen                                          1
#include<iostream>                                                      2
using namespace std;                                                    3
int main( )                                                             4
{                                                                       5
        struct demo                                                     6
        {                                                               7
                int acc_number;                                         8
                char name[5];                                           9
        };                                                             10
        demo user[5];                                                  11
        cout<<"Please enter the following information:"<<endl;         12
        for(int i=0;i<5;i++)                                           13
        {                                                              14
                cout<<"Enter the account number:"<<endl;               15
                cin>>user[i].acc_number;                               16
                cout<<"Enter the name:"<<endl;                         17
                cin>>user[i].name;                                     18
        }                                                              19
        cout<<"The information entered by you is:"<<endl;              20
        for(int i=0;i<5;i++)                                           21
        {                                                              22
                cout<<"Account Number: "<<d[i].acc_number<<endl;       23
                cout<<"Name: "<<d[i].name<<endl;                       24
        }                                                              25
        return 0;                                                      26
}                                                                      27
```

The output of the program is as follows:
Please enter the following information:
Enter the account number:
101
Enter the name:
John
Enter the account number:
102
Enter the name:
William
Enter the account number:
103
Enter the name:
Smith
Enter the account number:
104

Enter the name:
Michael
Enter the account number:
105
Enter the name:
Olsen
The information entered by you is:
Account Number: 101
Name: John
Account Number: 102
Name: William
Account Number: 103
Name: Smith
Account Number: 104
Name: Michael
Account Number: 105
Name: Olsen

Passing Structures to Functions

A structure can also be passed as an argument to a function.

For example:

```
struct demo
{
    int acc_number;
    char name[20];
}d1,d2;
d1.acc_number =101;
d1.name = "John";
void pass(d1);//Function call
----------
----------
void pass(struct demo d2)
{
    ----------
    ----------
}
```

In the above example, the variables **d1** and **d2** are the objects of the same structure type (demo). The object **d1** is passed as an argument when a function call is made to the function **pass( )** and the information stored in **d1** (argument) is assigned to another object of the same type **d2** (Parameter). When a structure object is passed, the argument and parameter types should be the same.

The following example illustrates the use of passing a structure to a function.
Write a program to pass a structure as an argument to a function.

The following program will prompt the user to enter the values for an object, pass the object as an argument to a function, and display the resultant values on the screen.

Example 11

```
//Write a program to pass a structure as an argument to a function    1
#include<iostream>                                                     2
using namespace std;                                                   3
struct demo                                                            4
{                                                                      5
        int acc_number;                                               6
        char name[20];                                                7
};                                                                     8
void pass(struct demo d2);                                            9
int main()                                                           10
{                                                                     11
        struct demo d1;                                              12
        d1.acc_number =101;                                          13
        d1.name = "William";                                         14
        pass(d1);                                                    15
        return 0;                                                    16
}                                                                    17
void pass(struct demo d2)                                            18
{                                                                    19
    cout<<"Account Number: "<<d2.acc_number<<endl;                  20
    cout<<"Name: "<<d2.name<<endl;                                  21
}                                                                    22
```

Explanation
Lines 4 to 8
struct demo
{
    int acc_number;
    char name[20];
};
Lines 4 to 8 show the declaration of the structure **demo**. Here, the structure is declared globally. Therefore, it can be used anywhere in the program.
Line 12
struct demo d1;
In this line, the variable **d1** is declared as an object of the structure type **demo**.

Line 13 and 14
d1.acc_number =101;
d1.name = "William";
As you know, each structure object contains its own copy of the members. In this line, the values **101** and **William** are assigned to the **acc_number** and **name** members of the object d1 respectively.

Line 15
pass(d1);
In this line, a function call is made to the function **pass( )** and the structure object **d1** is passed as an argument.

Line 18
void pass(struct demo d2)
After the execution of line 15, the control will reach this line (line 18). The information stored in the structure object **d1** (which is passed as an argument) is assigned to the structure object **d2**. Now, both the objects contain the same information.

The output of the program is as follows:
Account Number: 101
Name: William

Pointers to Structures

A pointer can also hold the address of a structure in the same way as a variable. You can declare a pointer to a structure in the same way as a simple pointer declaration. The syntax is as follows:

```
struct struct_name *var1;
```

In the above syntax, **struct** is a keyword, which specifies to the compiler that a structure is being created. The use of the **struct** keyword in the declaration of a pointer to a structure is optional. The **struct_name** represents the name of the structure. Here, the pointer variable ***var1** is declared as a pointer to a structure.

For example, to declare a pointer to a structure of the structure type **demo**, you can write the code, as given next.

```
demo *d3;
```

When you want to access the members of a structure using a pointer, you must use the **arrow operator** (->), which is a combination of a minus sign and a greater than sign with no space in between. The syntax is as given next.

```
var1->member_name;
```

In the above syntax, the variable **var1** represents a pointer to a structure and the **member_name** refers to a specific member of the structure.

The following example illustrates the use of the pointers to the structures.
Write a program to illustrate the working of the pointer to a structure.

The following program will prompt the user to enter the values for an object of a structure, create a pointer to it, and display the resultant values on the screen.

Example 12

```
//Write a program to illustrate the use of pointers to structures        1
#include<iostream>                                                       2
using namespace std;                                                     3
int main( )                                                              4
{                                                                        5
        struct demo                                                      6
        {                                                                7
                int acc_number;                                          8
                        char name[20];                                   9
         };                                                              10
        demo d1, *d2;                                                    11
        cout<<"Enter the following information:"<<endl;                  12
        cout<<"Enter the account number:"<<endl;                        13
        cin>>d1.acc_number;                                              14
        cout<<"Enter the name:"<<endl;                                   15
        cin>>d1.name;                                                    16
        d2=&d1;                                                          17
        cout<<"The information entered by you is:"<<endl;               18
        cout<<"Account Number: ";                                        19
        cout<<d2->acc_number<<endl;                                      20
        cout<<"Name: ";                                                  21
        cout<<d2->name<<endl;                                            22
        return 0;                                                        23
}                                                                        24
```

Explanation
Line 11
demo d1, *d2;
Here, the variable **d1** is declared as a variable or an object of structure type **demo**. The pointer variable ***d2** is declared as a pointer to a structure of structure type **demo**.

Line 17
d2=&d1;
In this line, the **&** operator returns the memory address of the variable **d1** and this memory address is assigned to the pointer to a structure variable **d2**.

Line 20
cout<<d2->acc_number<<endl;
In this line, the value stored in the structure member **acc_number** is accessed by the pointer to the structure **d2** with the help of the **arrow operator** (->).

Line 22

cout<<d2->name<<endl;
In this line, the value stored in the structure member **name** is accessed by the pointer to the structure **d2** with the help of the **arrow operator** (->).

The output of the program is as follows:
Enter the following information:
Enter the account number:
101
Enter the name:
John
The information entered by you is:
Account Number: 101
Name: John

The output will be displayed on the screen as follows:

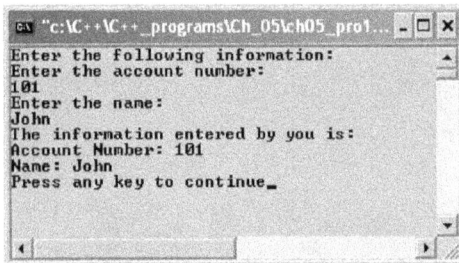

```
"c:\C++\C++_programs\Ch_05\ch05_pro1...
Enter the following information:
Enter the account number:
101
Enter the name:
John
The information entered by you is:
Account Number: 101
Name: John
Press any key to continue_
```

Nested Structures

A nested structure means a structure within another structure.

For example:

```
struct name
{
    char firstname[20];
    char lastname[20];
};
struct address
{
    name n1;//Nested structure
    char city[20];
    char state[20];
};
```

In the given example, the variable **n1** of the structure type **name** is declared within another structure **address**.

The following example illustrates the use of the nested structures.

Write a program to illustrate the working of the nested structures.

Example 13

The following program will prompt the user to enter the values for an object of a structure and display the resultant values on the screen.

```
//Write a program to illustrate the working of the nested structure    1
#include<iostream>                                                      2
using namespace std;                                                    3
int main( )                                                             4
{                                                                       5
        struct name                                                    6
        {                                                              7
                char first_name[20];                                   8
                char last_name[20];                                    9
        };                                                             10
        struct address                                                11
        {                                                             12
                name n1;//Nested structure                            13
                char city[20];                                        14
                char state[20];                                       15
        }a1;                                                          16
        a1.n1.first_name = "John";                                    17
        a1.n1.last_name = "Smith";                                    18
        a1.city= "Washington";                                        19
        a1.state= "Washington";                                       20
        cout<<"First Name: ";                                         21
        cout<<a1.n1.first_name<<endl;                                 22
        cout<<"Last Name: ";                                          23
        cout<<a1.n1.last_name<<endl;                                  24
        cout<<"City: ";                                               25
        cout<<a1.city<<endl;                                          26
        cout<<"State: ";                                              27
        cout<<a1.state<<endl;                                         28
        return 0;                                                     29
}                                                                     30
```

Explanation
Line 13
name n1;
In the given line, the variable **n1** of the structure type **name** is declared within another structure **address**.

Line 17
a1.n1.first_name = "John";

Here, an initial value **John** is assigned to **first_name**, which is a member of the structure type **name**. You cannot assign an initial value directly to the member **first_name** because the variable **n1** of the structure type **name** is declared in the structure **address**.

Line 22
cout<<a1.n1.first_name<<endl;
This line will display the value **John**, which is stored in the **first_name**.

The output of the program is as follows:
First Name: John
Last Name: Smith
City: Washington
State: Washington

Self-Evaluation Test

Answer the following questions and then compare them to the answers given at the end of this chapter:

1. Each string is terminated with a _____ character.

2. The _____ function is used to concatenate one string to the end of another string.

3. A _____ is a variable that can hold the memory address of another variable.

4. A _____ is a group of data elements that may have different data types.

5. A _____ variable points to another pointer.

Review Questions

Answer the following questions:

1. Define pointers.

2. Define pointers to pointers.

3. Explain the concept of passing arguments by reference.

4. Define array of structures.

5. Define pointers to structures.

Exercises

Exercise 1

Write a program to accept a string and check if it is a palindrome.

Exercise 2

Write a program to swap the values 30 and 45, using pass by reference.

Exercise 3

Write a program to create a structure **employee**, which contains the members **emp_name**, **emp_id**, and **city**. The program should save the employee details entered by the user and then display the details of the first 10 employees.

Answers to Self-Evaluation Test

1. null, **2. strcat( )**, **3.** pointer, **4.** structure, **5.** pointer to pointer

Chapter 6

Union,
Enumeration,
and
Preprocessor

Learning Objectives

After completing this chapter, you will be able to:
- *Understand union.*
- *Understand enumeration.*
- *Understand typedef.*
- *Understand preprocessor.*

In this chapter, you will learn about union, enumeration, and preprocessor.

A **union** is a group of data elements that may have different data types but they all share the same memory location.

An enumeration is a user-defined datatype, which consists of a set of named integral constants.

The preprocessor directive is used to include various instructions in the source code of a program. These instructions are transformed before the execution of the program.

UNION

A **union** is a group of data elements that may have different data types. These data elements share the same memory location, which means that the starting address of each data element is the same.

Declaring a Union

The method of declaring a **union** is the same as that of a structure except that the keyword **union** is used in place of the keyword **struct**. The syntax is as follows:

```
union name
{
     data_type member_name1;
     data_type member_name2;
     data_type member_name3;
     data_type member_name4;
}union variables;
```

For example:

```
union demo
{
     int k;
     char m;
}d1, d2;
```

In the above example, **union** is a keyword that specifies to the compiler that a union is being created. The integer variable **k** and character variable **m** are the members of the union **demo**. The variables **d1** and **d2** are the variables of the **union** type. In this, the starting address of the integer member **k** and the character member **m** is the same (**100**), see Figure 6-1. In this figure, the character variable **m** starts

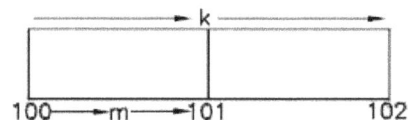

Figure 6-1 *Memory sharing*

from the memory address **100** and reserves one byte. The integer variable **k** also starts from the memory address **100** and reserves two bytes. When a **union** is declared, the compiler automatically allocates enough memory space to hold the largest member variable (in terms of memory space). As in this example, the compiler automatically provides 2 bytes of memory. This is because the largest member is an integer type, which requires 2 bytes of memory space.

Initializing Union Members

You can assign an initial value to each of the union members with the help of the **dot operator** (.) in the same way as in the structures. The syntax for initializing the union members is as follows:

    union_name.member_name = value;

For example:

```
union demo
{
    int k;
    char m;
}d1, d2;

d1.k=10;
d1.m= 'n';
d2.k=20;
d2.m= 'l';
```

In the above example, the union variables **d1** and **d2** have their own copy of members. Here, an integer value 10 is assigned to the member **k** and a character value **n** is assigned to the member **m** of the variable **d1**. Also, an integer value 20 is assigned to the member **k** and a character value l is assigned to the member **m** of the variable **d2**.

Accessing Union Members

You can access the individual members of a union with the use of the dot operator (.) in the same way as in the structures. For example, to access the member **k** of **d1** and the member **m** of **d2** of the union **demo**, you need to write the following code:

```
d1.k;
d2.m;
```

The following example illustrates the use of a **union**.

Example 1

Write a program to display the values of the members of a **union**.

The program given next will prompt the user to enter the values for the members of a union and display the resultant values on the screen. The line numbers on the right are not a part of the program and are for reference only.

```
//Write a program to display the values of the members of a union        1
#include<iostream>                                                        2
using namespace std;                                                      3
int main( )                                                               4
{                                                                         5
        union demo                                                        6
        {                                                                 7
                char name[20];                                            8
                int stu_id;                                               9
        };                                                               10
        demo d1,d2;                                                      11
        cout<<"Enter the information of the first student:"<<endl;       12
        cout<<"Enter the name:"<<endl;                                   13
        cin>>d1.name;                                                    14
        cout<<"The name of the first student is: "<<d1.name<<endl;       15
        cout<<"Enter the student ID:"<<endl;                             16
        cin>>d1.stu_id;                                                  17
        cout<<"The student ID of the first student is: ";               18
        cout<<d1.stu_id<<endl;                                           19
        cout<<"Enter the information of the second student:"<<endl;      20
        cout<<"Enter the name:"<<endl;                                   21
        cin>>d2.name;                                                    22
        cout<<"The name of the second student is: "<<d2.name<<endl;      23
        cout<<"Enter the student ID:"<<endl;                             24
        cin>>d2.stu_id;                                                  25
        cout<<"The student ID of the second student is: ";              26
        cout<<d2.stu_id<<endl;                                           27
        return 0;                                                        28
}                                                                        29
```

The output of the program is as follows:
Enter the information of the first student:
Enter the name:
John
The name of the first student is: John
Enter the student ID:
101
The student ID of the first student is: 101
Enter the information of the second student:
Enter the name:
Smith
The name of the second student is: Smith
Enter the student ID:
102
The student ID of the second student is: 102

The output will be displayed on the screen as follows:

```
Enter the information of the first student:
Enter the name:
John
The name of the first student is: John
Enter the student ID:
101
The student ID of the first student is: 101
Enter the information of the second student:
Enter the name:
Smith
The name of the second student is: Smith
Enter the student ID:
102
The student ID of the second student is: 102
Press any key to continue_
```

ENUMERATION

An enumeration (**enums**) is a user-defined type, which consists of a set of named integral constants. Enumeration is especially used when you want a variable to take only one value from a set of fixed values. This set of values is also known as the enumerated set. The syntax for declaring an enumeration is as follows:

> enum type_name {enumerated set};

In the above syntax, **enum** is the keyword that specifies to the compiler that an enumeration is being created. The **type_name** is the name of the enumeration given by the user. The enumerated set, which is enclosed in the curly braces { } consists of fixed values separated by commas.

For example:

> enum months {January, February, March, April, May, June, July,
> August, September, October, November};

In the above example, **enum** is a keyword. The name **months** specifies the type name enumeration. The fixed set of values is enclosed in the curly braces.

You can use the **enum** type name to declare the variables of its type. For example, to declare variables of the type **months**, you need to write the following code:

> months m1;

Now, you can assign only one valid value from the set of the fixed values (enumerated set) to the variable **m1** of the type months.

For example:

> m1=September;
> m1=December;

In this example, the first assignment **m1 = September** is valid because **September** is a member of the **months** enumerated type. The second assignment **m1 = December** is not valid because **December** is not a member of the **months** enumerated type.

Each member in the enumerated set is treated as an integer. A default integer value is assigned to each member, starting from zero assigned to the first member, one assigned to the second member, and so on. The value assigned to each member is greater by one than the value assigned to the member that precedes it.

For example, the enumerated set in the type **months** is from **January** to **November**. So, the value 0 is assigned to **January**, 1 is assigned to **February**, and 10 is assigned to **November**.

You can also assign an initial value to the individual members of the enumerated set.

For example:

> enum months {January, February, March, April, May, June, July = 7,
>   August, September, October, November};

In the above example, an initial value 7 is assigned to the member **July**. Now, the value 8, which is assigned to the member **August** is one greater than the value assigned to the member **July** that precedes it, and so on.

The following example illustrates the use of enumeration.

Example 2

Write a program to display the values of the members of an enumeration.

The following program will prompt the user to enter the values for the members of an enumeration and display the resultant values on the screen.

```
//Write a program to display the values of the members of an enumeration      1
#include<iostream>                                                            2
using namespace std;                                                          3
int main( )                                                                   4
{                                                                             5
        enum colors {red, blue, green = 10, orange, pink};                    6
        colors c1;                                                            7
        cout<<"Red      "<<red<<endl;                                         8
        cout<<"Blue     "<<blue<<endl;                                        9
        cout<<"Green    "<<green<<endl;                                       10
        cout<<"Orange "<<orange<<endl;                                        11
        cout<<"Pink     "<<pink<<endl;                                        12
        return 0;                                                             13
}                                                                             14
```

Explanation

Line 6

enum colors {red, blue, green = 10, orange, pink};

In this line, an enumeration named colors is declared and an enumerated set is declared in the curly braces. In the enumerated set, an initial value 10 is assigned to the member **green**.

Line 7

colors c1;

Here, variable **c1** is declared as the type **colors**.

The output of the program is as follows:

Red   0
Blue   1
Green   10
Orange 11
Pink   12

Typedef

You can also define a new name for an existing data type with the help of the **typedef** keyword. You are actually creating a synonym for an existing data type. The syntax is as follows:

    typedef data_type newname;

In the above syntax, **typedef** is a keyword. The **data_type** specifies an existing data type such as an integer, float, and so on. The **newname** specifies the name, which is defined for an existing data type.

For example:

    typedef int books;

In the above example, **int** represents the integer data type and **books** is the name defined for the integer type. Now, this name can be used anywhere in the program at the place of an integer data type.

For example, if you want to declare two integer type variables, you can write the following code:

    books a, b;

In the above example, **books** is used as a synonym for an existing data type **int**.

The following example illustrates the use of **typedef**.
Write a program to define a new name for an integer data type.

Example 3

The following program will define the names for a data type, use them for declaring a variable of that type, and display the value stored in the variable on the screen.

```
//Write a program to illustrate the use of typedef          1
#include<iostream>                                           2
using namespace std;                                         3
int main( )                                                  4
{                                                            5
        typedef int order;                                  6
        typedef order account;                              7
        account a=10;                                        8
        order b=20;                                          9
        cout<<"The value stored in variable a is: "<<a<<endl;   10
        cout<<"The value stored in variable b is: "<<b<<endl;   11
        return 0;                                           12
}                                                            13
```

Explanation
Line 6
typedef int order;
Here, a new name **order** is defined for the integer **(int)** data type. The keyword **typedef** specifies to the compiler to recognize **order** as a synonym for the type **int**.

Line 7
typedef order account;
In this line, the **typedef** statement is used to define another synonym **account** for the type **int**. Now, **order** and **account** both are used in place of the type **int** in the program.

Line 8
account a=10;
In this line, **a** is declared as an **account** type variable and 10 is assigned as its initial value. The **account** is defined as a synonym for the integer **(int)** data type.

Line 9
order b=20;
In this line, **b** is declared as an **order** type variable and 20 is assigned as its initial value. The **order** is defined as a synonym for the integer **(int)** data type.

The output of the program is as follows:
The value stored in variable a is: 10
The value stored in variable b is: 20

THE PREPROCESSOR
A preprocessor is a program that makes some conversions such as macro substitutions, including header files, and so on in the source code before the compiler processes it. The preprocessor may also perform conditional compilation.

The Preprocessor Directives

In the source code, the lines that begin with a pound sign (#) are known as preprocessor directives. These directives can be placed anywhere in the program, but usually they are placed at the beginning of the source code. These directives are not terminated with a semicolon because they are not part of the C++ language. The list of the preprocessor directives is discussed next.

a.   #define
b.   #include
c.   #if
d.   #error
e.   #elif
f.   #else
g.   #ifdef
h.   #line
i.   #endif
j.   #ifndef
k.   #undef

You can place only one preprocessor directive in one line.

The #define Directive

The **#define** directive defines an identifier and a replacement token. Whenever the **#define** directive is encountered in the source code, the replacement token will be substituted for all the subsequent occurrences of the identifier in the source code. The identifier is also known as the macro name and the process of substitution is known as macro replacement. The syntax is as follows:

    #define macro_name replacement_token

For example, to use the word **PI** for the value **3.14159**, you can write the following statement:

    #define PI 3.14159

In the above example, the word **PI** represents the macro name and the value **3.14159** represents the replacement token. The **#define** directive directs the preprocessor to replace the word **PI** with the specified value each time it is encountered in the source code.

In the above example, a single identifier is replaced with a specified replacement token. This process is also known as object-like macros.

The **#define** directive can also be used as function-like macros. In the function-like macros, the **#define** directive defines an identifier that can have an argument list enclosed within the parentheses and the replacement token. Each time the identifier is encountered, the arguments within it are replaced with the actual arguments that are passed in the program. The syntax for the **#define** directive is as follows:

#define macro_name (argument list separated by commas) replacement_token

For example:

```
#define SUM(a,b) (a+b)
int main()
{
    int i= SUM(2,3);
    ----------;
}
```

In the above example, when an identifier **SUM** is encountered in the program, the actual arguments **(2,3)** are assigned to variables **a** and **b**, respectively. This identifier is replaced with the replacement token, which is the resultant value of **(a+b)**.

The following example illustrates the use of the **#define** directive.

Example 4

Write a program to calculate the area of a circle.

The following program will prompt the user to enter the radius of a circle, calculate the area, and display the resultant value on the screen.

```
//Write a program to find the area of a circle.              1
#include<iostream>                                           2
using namespace std;                                         3
#define PI 3.14 //Object-like macro                          4
#define AREA(r) (r*r) //Function-like macro                  5
int main()                                                   6
{                                                            7
        double i;                                            8
        int j;                                               9
        cout<<"Enter the radius:"<<endl;                     10
        cin>>j;                                              11
        i= PI * AREA(j);                                     12
        cout<<"The area of the circle is: "<<i<<endl;        13
        return 0;                                            14
}                                                            15
```

Explanation
Line 4
#define PI 3.14
This line represents the object-like macro **#define PI 3.14**. The **#define** directive in this line directs the preprocessor to substitute the value **3.14** in place of the macro name **PI** in the line 12.

Line 5
#define AREA(r) (r*r)
This line represents the function-like macro. In this line, the macro name **AREA** is followed by an argument **r**, which in turn is followed by a replacement token **r*r**.

Line 12
i= PI * AREA(j);
In this line, the identifier **PI** is replaced with the specified value **3.14** and the value of the variable **j** is assigned to the variable **r** by the preprocessor. Next, the value **3.14** is multiplied with the resultant value returned by the replacement token **r*r**.

The output of the program is as follows:
Enter the radius:
6
The area of the circle is: 113.04

The output will be displayed on the screen as follows:

The #include Directive

The **#include** directive directs the compiler to read a source file called the header file and include it in the C++ program. These header files contain function prototypes, **#define** statements, and so on. The name of the header file must be enclosed in an angular bracket (**<>**) or in double quotes. The syntax is as follows:

    #include<filename.h>
    #include "filename.h"

In the above syntax, the **.h** is used as a file extension.

For example:

    #include<iostream>
        or
    #include<iostream.h>

In the above example, the **#include** directive directs the compiler to read the file named **iostream** and include it in the program. Both statements given above are the same. The use of **.h** in the lower statement is optional.

The Conditional Compilation Directives

Conditional compilation means that a portion of the program's source code will be selectively compiled or ignored depending on certain conditions. There are some directives that control conditional compilation. These are **#if**, **#else**, **#elif**, **#endif**, **#ifdef**, and **#ifndef**.

The #if and #endif Directives

The syntax for the **#if** directive is as follows:

```
#if condition or expression
      statement or block of code
#endif
```

In the above syntax, the statement or block of code between the **#if** and **#endif** will be compiled, if the condition or expression following the **#if** directive is true. Otherwise, it will be ignored. Here, the **#endif** directive refers to the end of the **#if** block.

For example:

```
#define COUNT 10
int main( )
{
    ----------;
    #if COUNT>9
            cout<<"Count is greater";
    #endif
    ----------;
}
```

In the above example, the **#define** directive directs the preprocessor to substitute a value **10** in place of **COUNT**. When the execution begins, the condition **COUNT>9** is checked if it is true. Here, the condition is true because the value **10** is greater than the value **9**. So, the next statement will be executed and it will display the following statement on the screen:
Count is greater

The #else Directive

The working of the **#else** directive is the same as the **else** statement. If the condition or expression specified with the **#if** directive is false, the statement associated with the **#else** directive will be compiled. The syntax is as follows:

```
#if condition or expression
      statement or block of code
#else
      statement or block of code
#endif
```

For example:

```
#define COUNT 10
int main( )
{
    ----------;
    #if COUNT>20
            cout<<"Count is greater";
    #else
            cout<<"Count is smaller";
    #endif
    ----------;
}
```

In the above example, the condition **COUNT>20** is false. So, the statement associated with the **#else** directive will be compiled and it will display the following statement on the screen: Count is smaller

The #elif Directive

The **#elif** directive is also known as the **else if** directive. The working of the **#elif** directive is the same as the **elseif** statement. The syntax is as follows:

```
#if condition or expression
    statement1
#elif condition or expression
    statement2
#elif condition or expression
    statement3
#elif condition or expression
    statement4
#endif
```

In the above syntax, if the condition or expression following the **#if** directive is true, the statement associated with it will be compiled and all the **#elif** directives will be skipped. Otherwise, the next **#elif** will be tested.

For example:

```
#define points_scored 50
int main()
{
    ----------;
    #if points_scored>=90
            cout<<"Grade A";
    #elif points_scored>=70
            cout<<"Grade B";
```

```
        #elif points_scored>=50
                cout<<"Grade C";
        #elif points_scored>=30
                cout<<"Fail";
        #endif
        ----------;
    }
```

In the above example, the **#define** directive substitutes the value **50** in the place of the identifier **points_scored**. Here, the condition given with the **#if** directive is false. So, the condition given with the next **#elif** directive will be checked. If it is true, the statement associated with it will be compiled. Otherwise, the next **#elif** directive will be tested, and so on.

The #ifdef and #ifndef Directives

The **#ifdef** directive and **#ifndef** directives are also known as if defined and if not defined directives, respectively.

The syntax of the **#ifdef** is as follows:

```
        #ifdef macro_name
            statement
        #endif
```

In the above syntax, if **macro_name** has already been defined in a **#define** statement, the statement associated with **#ifdef** will be compiled. Otherwise, it will be skipped.

For example:

```
        #ifdef JOHN
            cout<<"Hi, John";
        #endif
```

In this example, if the macro name **JOHN** has already been defined in a **#define** statement, the next **cout** statement will be compiled.

The syntax of the **#ifndef** is as follows:

```
        #ifndef macro_name
            statement
        #endif
```

In the above syntax, if the **macro_name** is not defined in a **#define** statement, the statement associated with **#ifndef** will be compiled. Otherwise, it will be skipped.

For example:

```
#ifndef JOHN
    cout<<"Hi, John";
#endif
```

In this example, if the macro name **JOHN** has not been defined in a **#define** statement, the next **cout** statement will be compiled.

The #undef Directive

The **#undef** directive is used to remove a macro that has been previously defined in a **#define** statement. The syntax is as follows:

```
#undef macro_name
```

For example:

```
#define COUNT 100
#undef COUNT
```

In the previous example, the **#define** directive defines the macro **COUNT**. The **#undef** directive undefines the macro **COUNT**, which was previously defined in a **#define** statement.

The #line Directive

If you want to change the contents of __LINE__ and __FILE__, you can do it with the help of the **#line** directive. The __LINE__ and __FILE__ identifiers are predefined to a compiler. The __LINE__ identifier contains the value, which is the line number of the currently compiled line of the source code. The __FILE__ identifier contains a string value that specifies the name of the source file being compiled. The syntax of the **#line** directive is as follows:

```
#line value "filename"
```

In the above syntax, the **value** specifies a positive integer value, which is the new value of the __LINE__ identifier. The **filename** is optional. If you specify any valid **filename**, it becomes the new value of the __FILE__ identifier.

For example:

```
#line 10 line_directive
int main( )                        //Line 10
{                                  //Line 11
    cout<<__LINE__;                //Line 12
    cout<<__FILE__;
    return 0;
}
```

In this example, the value 10 resets the line counter and becomes the new value of the __LINE__ identifier and **line_directive** is the file name, which becomes the new value of the __FILE__ identifier. The first **cout** statement displays the line number, which is 12 and the other **cout** statement displays the file name, which is **line_directive** on the screen.

The #error Directive

The **#error** directive is used to stop the compilation of the program. The syntax is as follows:

    #error error_message

The **error_message** specifies the message, which is displayed when the **#error** directive is encountered along with some other information defined by the compiler.

The # Operator

The **#** is known as the **stringize** operator. This operator converts the argument into a quoted string that follows it. The syntax is as follows:

    # argument

The **stringize** operator converts the value that is stored in this argument into a quoted string.

For example:

```
#define demo(a) #a
int main( )
{
    cout<<demo(How are you);
    return 0;
}
```

In the above example, the value **How are you** of the argument **a** will be converted into a quoted string **"How are you"**.

The ## Operator

The **##** is known as the token-pasting operator. This operator is used to concatenate two tokens. The syntax is as follows:

    #define demo(x,y) x##y

For example:

```
#define demo(x,y) x##y
int main( )
{
    int xy=100;
    cout<<demo(x,y);
    return 0;
}
```

In this example, the token-pasting operator concatenates the variables **x** and **y**. After concatenation, it refers to the variable **xy** and displays its value **100** on the screen.

Self-Evaluation Test

Answer the following questions and then compare them to the answers given at the end of this chapter:

1. In a **union**, the _____ address for each data element is the same.

2. Enumeration is a _____ type.

3. Typedef is used to create a _____ for an existing data type.

4. A preprocessor directive begins with a _____ symbol.

5. The _____ directive is used to read a source file called _____ file.

Review Questions

Answer the following questions:

1. Differentiate between a structure and a **union**.

2. Define enumeration.

3. Define **typedef**.

4. Define the **#undef** directive.

5. Define the stringize operator.

Exercises

Exercise 1

Write a program to create a structure **employee**, which contains the members **emp_name**, **emp_id**, and **city**. The program should save the employee details entered by the user and then display the details of the first 10 employees.

Exercise 2

Write a program to define a function-like macro **SQUARE** that contains one integer argument and displays the square of that integer value.

Answers to Self-Evaluation Test

1. starting, **2.** user-defined, **3.** synonym, **4.** #, **5. #include**, header

Chapter 7

Data Structures

After completing this chapter, you will be able to:

- *Understand dynamic memory allocation operators.*
- *Understand data structures.*
- *Understand the concept of linked lists.*
- *Understand the concept of tree.*
- *Understand the concept of stack.*
- *Understand the concept of queue.*
- *Understand the concept of graph.*
- *Understand traversing operations.*
- *Understand searching operations.*
- *Understand inserting operations.*
- *Understand deleting operations.*
- *Understand sorting operations.*
- *Understand merging operations.*

In this chapter, you will learn about dynamic memory allocation operators, data structures, types of data structures and their operations.

DYNAMIC MEMORY ALLOCATION OPERATORS

Dynamic memory allocation means memory is allocated and deallocated (releasing the memory) at runtime when the program is being executed. The main advantage of dynamic memory allocation is that you can increase or decrease the size of the data structure at the execution time. There are two operators that are used for dynamic memory allocation. These are as follows:

a. new
b. delete

The new Operator

The **new** operator is used to allocate the memory dynamically for a specified data type. It returns a pointer that contains the starting address of that memory. The syntax for declaring the **new** operator is as follows:

    pointer_var = new type;

In the above syntax, the **pointer_var** represents a pointer variable. This pointer variable is used to receive a pointer that contains the starting address, which is returned by the **new** operator. The **type** specifies the type of data, which is pointed by the pointer variable.

For example:

    int *p1;
    p1 = new int;

In the above example, **p1** is declared as a pointer to an integer. The **new** operator is used to allocate memory space of 2 bytes for the **integer** data type (**p1**).

Consider a case when you try to allocate memory for a data type with the help of the **new** operator but you find that the available memory is insufficient to fill that allocation request. In such a case, an exception (run-time error) will be generated by the system. This is known as the **bad_alloc** exception. If this exception is not properly handled, your program will be terminated. The concept of exception handling will be described in a later chapter.

The delete Operator

The **delete** operator is used to deallocate or free the memory space, which was earlier allocated by using the **new** operator. The syntax is as follows:

    delete pointer_var;

In the above syntax, the **delete** operator frees the memory space that is pointed by the pointer variable **pointer_var**.

The following example illustrates the use of the **new** and **delete** operators.

Example 1

Write a program to allocate memory space to hold a **float** value.

The following program will allocate the memory space to a **float** value and display the memory address as well as the value stored in it on the screen. The line numbers on the right are not a part of the program and are for reference only.

```
//Write a program to allocate the memory space to hold a float value    1
#include<iostream>                                                      2
using namespace std;                                                    3
int main( )                                                             4
{                                                                       5
        float *p1;                                                      6
        p1=new float;                                                   7
        *p1=10.23;                                                      8
        cout<<"The memory address pointed "
                "by the pointer p1 is: "<<p1<<endl;                     9
        cout<<"The value accessed by the pointer variable is: "<<*p1<<endl; 10
        delete p1;                                                      11
        return 0;                                                       12
}                                                                       13
```

Explanation
Line 6
float *p1;
In this line, the variable **p1** is declared as a **float** type pointer variable.

Line 7
p1=new float;
In this line, the **new** operator allocates enough memory space to store an element of the **float** type and then returns an address, which is assigned to the pointer variable **p1**.

Line 8
*p1=10.23;
Here, a float value **10.23** is assigned to the pointer variable **p1**.

Line 11
delete p1;
In this line, the **delete** operator frees the memory space, which is pointed by the pointer variable **p1**.

The output of the program is as follows:
The memory address pointed by pointer p1 is: 9394936
The value accessed by the pointer variable is: 10.23

> **Note**
>
> *The resulting memory address, given in the previous program, varies from compiler to compiler.*

Initializing Dynamic Allocated Memory

You can also assign an initial value to the memory, using the **new** operator. For this, you need to define the value after the **type** name in the **new** statement. The syntax for dynamically allocating a value to the memory is as follows:

    pointer_var = new type (value);

In the above syntax, the **value** specified in the parentheses is assigned as an initial value to the memory whose address is returned by the **new** operator to the pointer variable **pointer_var**.

For example:

    int *p;
    p= new int(20);

In the above example, an initial value **20** is assigned to the memory, which is allocated using the **new** operator.

You can also allocate memory to an array by using the **new** operator. The syntax is as follows:

    pointer_var = new type[size];

In the above syntax, the **size** specifies the maximum number of elements in the array. The following example will explain the concept of allocating memory to an array.

For example:

    int *p;
    p= new int [10];

You can deallocate the memory space of an array in the following way:

    delete [ ] pointer_var;

For example:

    delete [ ]p;

DATA STRUCTURES

A data structure is a way of organizing and storing the data in a computer so that it can be used efficiently.

Types of Data Structures

The different types of data structures are discussed next.

a. Arrays
b. Linked list
c. Tree
d. Stack
e. Queue
f. Graph

Arrays

You have already learned about arrays in Chapter 4.

Linked List

A linked list is a collection of data elements called nodes and each node contains a pointer that points to the next data element in the list. In a linked list, each node contains two parts: data and pointer part. In the data part, a value is stored and the pointer part points to the next data element in the list. Figure 7-1 represents a single linked list that contains 5 nodes.

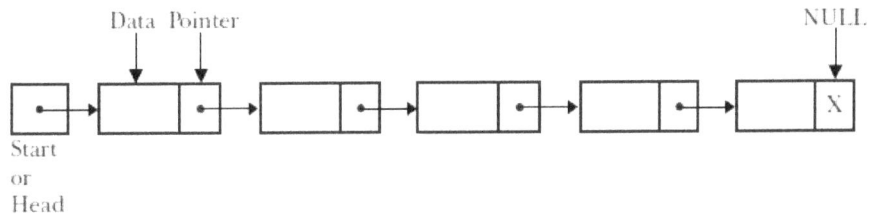

Figure 7-1 *Representation of a linked list*

In the above figure, the first pointer is known as the **Start** or the **Head** pointer. This pointer always points to the first node of the linked list. In the last node, the pointer part contains a cross symbol. This symbol represents the **NULL** pointer, which specifies the end of the linked list.

For example, a linked list that contains a list of names of the students awaiting admission is shown in Figure 7-2. The names are arranged alphabetically and the start pointer points to the name of the student who has the highest marks. In this figure, **Next** represents the pointer part. The **start** pointer points to the **count 7** (Lewis), which has the highest marks among the names of the ten students in the list. The pointer part (Next) of the **count 7** points to the **count 8** (Michael), which has the second highest marks in the list. The pointer part of **count 8** points to the next name (Adams**),** which is at **count 1**. He has the third highest marks in the list. The pointer part of the last student (Harry) in the list contains the **NULL** pointer denoted by a cross sign that represents the end of the list.

Count	Name	Next
1	Adams	4
2	Curt	6
3	Fields	5
4	Green	9
5	Harry	X
6	John	10
7	Lewis	8
8	Michael	1
9	Smith	2
10	Tom	3

Start   7

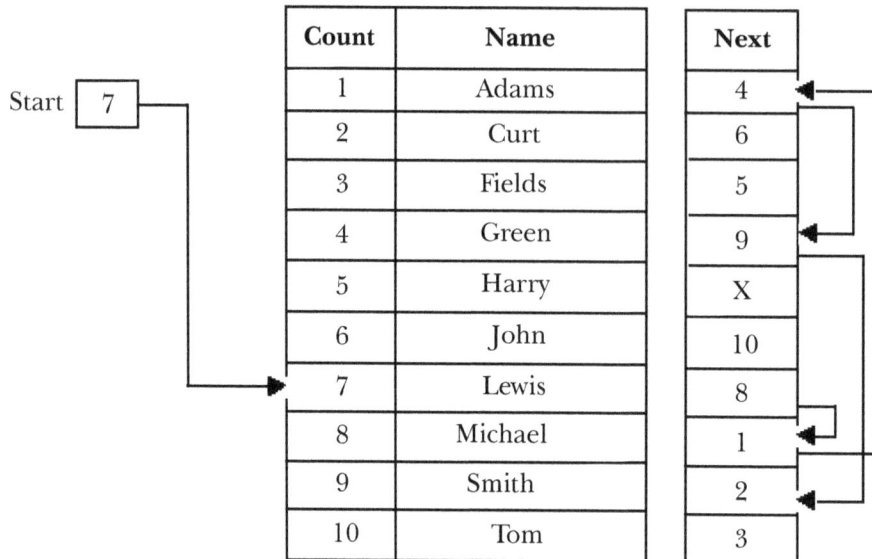

Figure 7-2 *Example of a linked list*

The following program illustrates the use of the linked list.

Example 2

Write a program to create a linked list.

The following program will create a linked list, which contains four nodes. The program will also display the addresses as well as the values that are stored in the nodes.

```
//Write a program to create a linked list           1
#include<iostream>                                   2
using namespace std;                                 3
struct node                                          4
{                                                    5
    char data ;                                      6
    struct node *next ;                              7
};                                                   8
int main( )                                          9
{                                                    10
        node *start=NULL;                            11
        node node1, node2, node3, node4;             12
        start = &node1;                              13
        node1.data = 'A' ;                           14
        node1.next = &node2;                         15
        node2.data = 'B' ;                           16
        node2.next = &node3;                         17
        node3.data = 'C' ;                           18
```

node3.next = &node4;	19
node4.data = 'D' ;	20
node4.next=NULL;	21
for(int i=1;i<=4;i++)	22
{	23
cout<<"Data part of node "<<i	
<<" contains: "<<start->data<<endl;	24
start = start->next;	25
cout<<"Pointer part of node "<<i	
<<" points to: "<<start<<endl;	26
}	27
return 0;	28
}	29

Explanation

Lines 4 to 8

struct node
{
    char data ;
    struct node *next ;
};

Here, a structure named **node** is defined, which has a character variable **data** and a pointer to a structure ***next** as the member elements.

Line 11

node *start=NULL;

In this line, a pointer to a structure ***start** is declared and assigned an initial value **NULL**. The **start** pointer always points to the first node in a single linked list. Here, the **start** pointer contains the **NULL** value, which specifies that the list is empty.

Line 12

node node1, node2, node3, node4;

Here, four variables **node1**, **node2**, **node3**, and **node4** are declared as objects of a structure type **node**.

Line 13

start = &node1;

In this line, the **&** operator returns the memory address of the object **node1**, which is assigned to the **start** pointer. Now, the **start** pointer points to the first node of the linked list.

Line 14

node1.data = 'A' ;

You have already learned that each object of a structure type has its own copy of the structure members. Here, character **A** is assigned to the character variable **data** of the **node1** with the help of the dot (**.**) operator. Now, the data part of **node1** contains **A**.

Line 15

node1.next = &node2;

In this line, the address of **node2** is assigned to the pointer part of **node1**, which points to the next node **node2** in the list.

The working of Lines 16 to 20 is the same as Lines 14 and 15, respectively.

Line 21
node4.next=NULL;
In this line, the **NULL** value is assigned to the pointer part of **node4**, which represents the end of the linked list.

The output of the program is as follows:
Data part of node 1 contains: A
Pointer part of node 1 points to: 0012FEB4
Data part of node 2 contains: B
Pointer part of node 2 points to: 0012FEA4
Data part of node 3 contains: C
Pointer part of node 3 points to: 0012FE94
Data part of node 4 contains: D
Pointer part of node 4 points to: 00000000 //NULL

Tree

A tree is a nonlinear type of data structure that is used to represent the hierarchical relationship between the data elements. These data elements are known as the nodes of the tree. Figure 7-3 represents a simple tree.

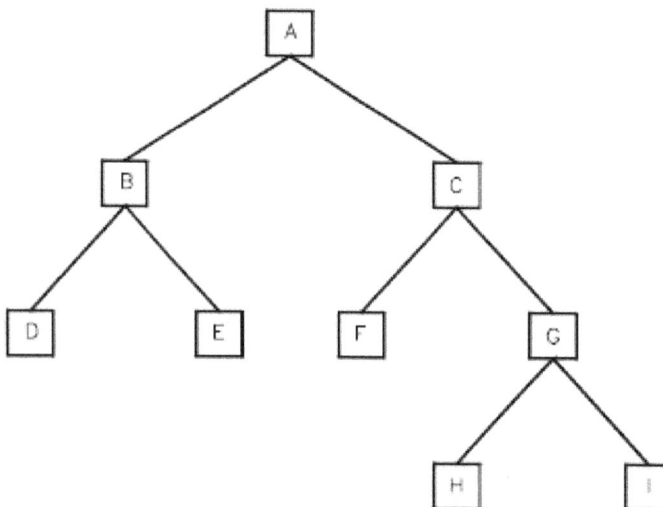

Figure 7-3 Representation of a tree

The tree shown in the above figure is known as the binary tree. The topmost node **A** is called the **root node**. The root node has two subnodes, **node B** and **node C**. These nodes are called the **child nodes** of **node A**. So, **node A** is the parent node of **node B** and **node C**. In a tree, each child node can have at the most one parent node. Here, **B** is called the left successor or the left subtree and **C** is called the right successor or the right subtree of **A**. The left subtree **B** of the root **A** consists of nodes, **D** and **E**. The right subtree **C** of the root **A** consists of nodes, **F**, **G**, **H**, and **I**. Each node in a tree can have 0, 1, or 2 successors. As shown in Figure 7-3, nodes **A**, **B**, **C**, and **G** have two successors and nodes **D**, **E**, **F**, **H**, and **I** do not have any successors.

Stack

A stack is a linear type of data structure, which has a property called last-in-first-out (LIFO). In a stack, the data elements can be inserted or deleted at one end called the top of the stack. Insertion of a data element is referred to as "pushed onto the stack" and the deletion of a data element is referred to as "popped the stack". Figure 7-4 illustrates the working of a stack:

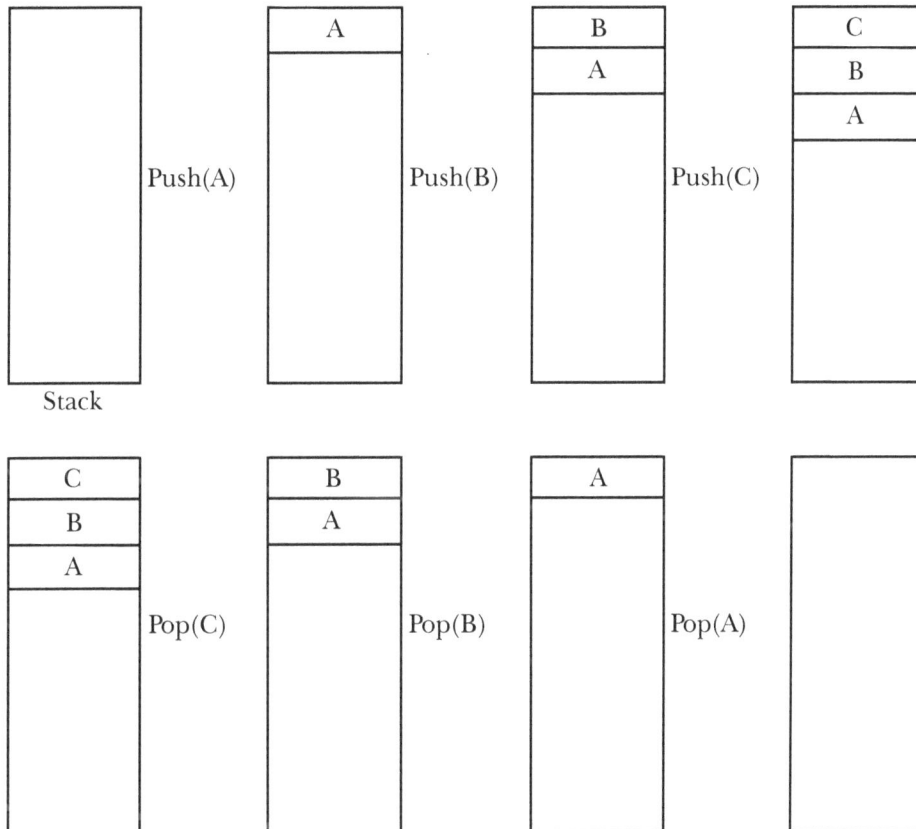

Figure 7-4 *Working of a stack*

In the above figure, the **Push** operation represents a value that is inserted on the top of the Stack. In the beginning, a character value **A** is pushed onto the top of the **Stack**. Next, when another character value **B** is pushed onto the **Stack**, value **A**, which was earlier placed on the top, is moved to the second position in the **Stack**. Now, value **B** is on the top of the **Stack**. Whenever a new value is pushed onto the **Stack**, the value at the top is moved to the next position and the top position is assigned to the currently pushed data element. The **pop** operation represents a value that is removed from the top of the **Stack**. The value or data element, which was inserted or pushed last is the first element to be removed from the **Stack**.

As shown in Figure 7-4, value **C**, which was the last element inserted on the top of the **Stack**, is the first element to be removed from it.

Figure 7-5 represents the implementation of a stack into the memory.

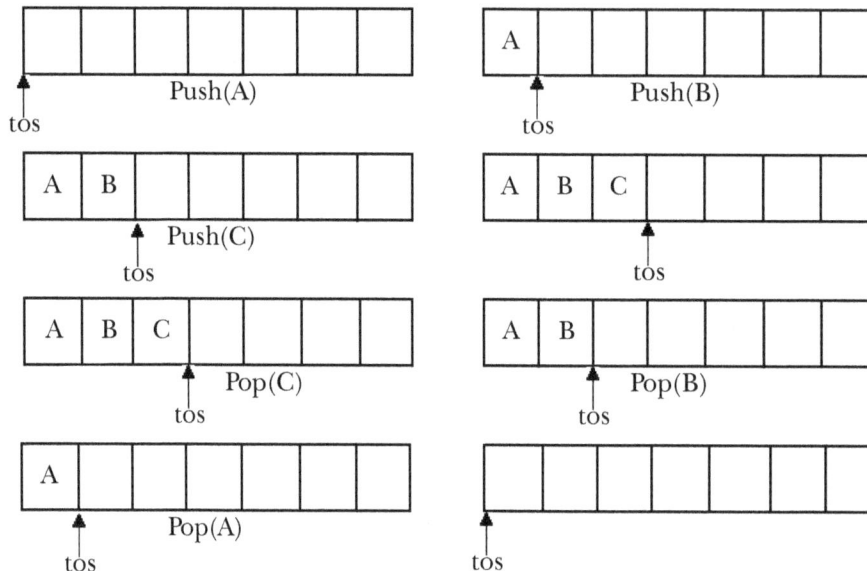

Figure 7-5 Implementation of a stack

In the above figure, the data elements of a stack are stored in an array and **tos** is a pointer variable, which points to the top of the stack. At the beginning, the **tos** points to the starting address of the array. As the data elements are pushed onto the stack, the **tos** pointer moves to the right side and points to the next memory address where the next data element will be inserted. As the data elements are removed from the stack, the **tos** moves to the left side.

Queue

A queue is a linear type of data structure, which is also called first-in-first-out (FIFO). This means that the elements are removed in the same order as they were inserted in the queue. In a queue, all the insertions take place only at one end, which is called 'Rear' and all deletions take place at the other end called 'Front'. A line of people waiting for a security check at the airport is an example of a queue. Figure 7-6 represents of a queue.

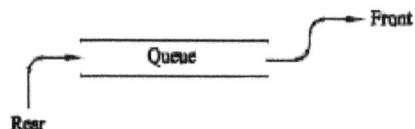

Figure 7-6 Representation of a queue

The **Front** and **Rear** are the pointer variables, which point to the start and the end of the queue. If a queue is empty, the value of both **Front** and **Rear** is 0. Whenever an insertion or deletion takes place in a queue, the values of these pointers are changed. For example, a queue contains four elements **A**, **B**, **C**, and **D**. The data element **A** represents the **Front** and **D** represents the **Rear**, as shown in Figure 7-7.

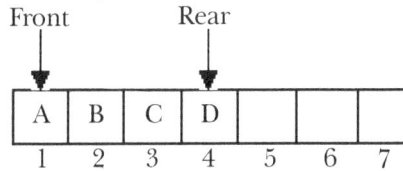

Front   Rear

A	B	C	D			
1	2	3	4	5	6	7

Figure 7-7 *Example of a queue*

In the above figure, the **Front** points to **1** and the **Rear** points to **4**. Now, another element **E** is inserted in the queue, as shown in Figure 7-8.

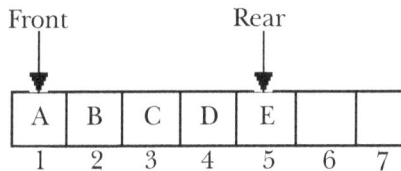

Front   Rear

A	B	C	D	E		
1	2	3	4	5	6	7

Figure 7-8 *After inserting a new element*

After the insertion, the **Front** points to **1** and the **Rear** points to **5**. An element is removed from the queue, as shown in Figure 7-9.

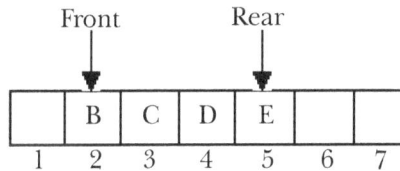

Front   Rear

	B	C	D	E		
1	2	3	4	5	6	7

Figure 7-9 *After removing an element*

In the above figure, element **A** is removed because it is in the **Front** position. Now, **Front** points to **2** and **Rear** points to **5**.

Graph

A graph is a nonlinear type of data structure that consists of a set of nodes that are connected by lines called edges. An edge from one node to another node specifies the relationship between these nodes. A graph or an undirected graph is used in a case where a set of data elements or nodes contain a relationship that cannot be represented in the hierarchical manner. Figure 7-10 represents a simple graph that consists of four nodes **A, B, C,** and **D** and a set of edges that connects them. An example of a graph is a road map in which the names of the cities are represented as nodes and the links between them are represented as edges.

To take an example, a graph consists of two components, a set of nodes, denoted by **V** and a set of edges, denoted by **E**. In this graph, each edge **e** (representing only one edge) in **E** is uniquely identified with an unordered pair [u,v] of nodes in **V**. The nodes **u** and **v** are known as the endpoints of the edge **e**, represented as e=[u, v]. Figure 7-11 represents an undirected graph. In this figure, there are 5 nodes **A, B, C, D,** and **E** and 8 edges: **[A,B]**, **[B,C]**, **[C,D]**, **[D,E]**, **[A,E]**, **[C,E]**, **[B,E]**, and **[C,A]**.

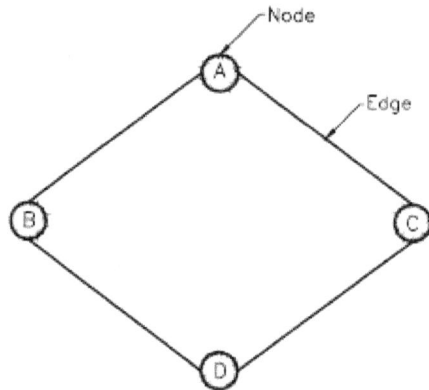

Figure 7-10 *Representation of an undirected graph*

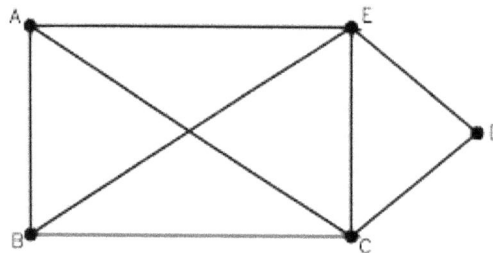

Figure 7-11 *Example of a graph*

You can also measure the degree of a node, which is the number of edges that a node contains. The degree is denoted as **deg[node]**. As shown in the above figure, deg(A) = 3 and deg(D) = 2.

Directed Graph

Until now, you have learned about the undirected graph, in which the directions are not assigned to the edges. There is another type of graph in which each edge is assigned a particular direction. This graph is known as a directed graph. Each edge is uniquely identified from an ordered pair of nodes, which specify the origin and the destination of the edge. Figure 7-12 represents a directed graph. In this figure, there are four nodes **A, B, C,** and **D** and five directed edges: **[A, B]**, **[B, C]**, **[C, D]**, **[A, D]**, **[C, A]**.

You can also measure the indegree and outdegree of a node. The indegree, denoted as **indeg(node)**, is the number of edges that end at a particular node. The outdegree, denoted as **outdeg(node)**, is the number of edges that begin from a particular node. For example, you may have a directed graph G such that e = [u,v], where **e** is an edge starting at node **u** and ending at node **v**. The indegree of the node **u** is the number of edges ending at **u** and the outdegree of the node **u** is the number of edges starting from **u**. As shown in the figure given above, the **indeg(A)** is equal to **1** and **outdeg(A)** is equal to **2**.

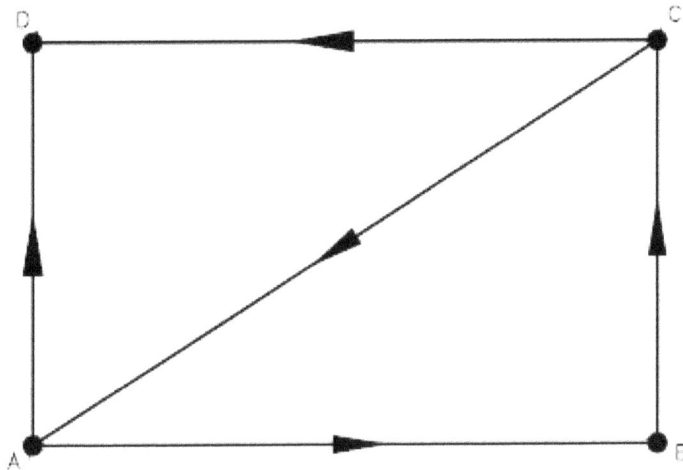

Figure 7-12 *Representation of a directed graph*

Data Structure Operations

You can perform certain operations on the data elements of a data structure. These operations are as follows:

a. Traversing
b. Searching
c. Inserting
d. Deleting
e. Sorting
f. Merging

Traversing

When each data element, node or record of a data structure is accessed at least once, this process is known as traversing. This operation is performed when you want to process certain data items in a record. For example, traversal of a linked list means that you start from the head node of the list and follow the next pointer that points to the next node in the list. This process will repeat until the NULL pointer is accessed. The NULL pointer represents the end of the list.

Searching

Searching means to look for a particular record or a set of records that satisfy a given condition or match a given key value. The search operation is performed in the following two ways:

a. Linear search
b. Binary search

Linear search

The Linear search, also known as the sequential search, is one in which each record or node is searched in a data structure, one at a time. This process starts from the beginning of a particular data structure and continues till a match is found. This search method is applicable when the number of data elements or nodes in a particular data structure are less. This is because the time taken by this method is proportional to the number of comparisons. The complexity is used to measure the time and space used by an algorithm (which means steps to solve a particular problem). The complexity of this search method for a data structure with n elements is n/2. It is also denoted as $C(n)=n/2$. The best case is that in which only one comparison is made. The worst case is one in which no match is found and the search is done for n number of times.

For example, you have an array **DEMO** of 10 elements and you want to search a given value **VALUE** in **DEMO**. In a linear search, **VALUE** is compared with each element of **DEMO** one by one. At first **DEMO[1]** = **VALUE** is tested to see if the first element of the array **DEMO** is equal to the given value **VALUE**. If it is equal, the search will be stopped. Otherwise, the next element **DEMO[2]** = **VALUE** will be tested and so on, until the last element is encountered or a match is found.

Binary search

The **binary** search is a technique to search an element in a sorted array. This technique is used when the number of elements are in a large quantity. In this technique, at first the median of the list is found. Then, the desired value is compared with the value of the median. If the desired value is less than the value at the median, you will find the desired value in the list of elements that comes before the median. The remaining half list of elements is eliminated. If the desired value is greater than the value at the median, you will find the desired value in the list of elements that comes after the median. The first half of the list is eliminated. This process is repeated until a suitable match is found or the list becomes empty. The complexity of this method is denoted as follows:

$$C(n) = \log_2 n$$

For example, if a value is searched in a list of 10,000 elements, not more than 13 comparisons are required.

Consider another example, in which an integer array contains 11 values that are sorted in an ascending order, as shown in Figure 7-13 and you have to find the value 79.

10	15	36	42	56	68	79	85	90	93	96

Figure 7-13 Representation of an array

At first, the median is found, which is the 6th element in the array. The value stored at median location is 68, which is smaller than the desired value 79. It means that the desired value comes after the median. So, the elements from 1 to 6 are eliminated and the remaining list contains only five elements, as shown in Figure 7-14.

79	85	90	93	96

Figure 7-14 *Remaining list of an array*

Now, again the median is found, which is the 3rd element in the remaining array. The value stored at the median location is 90, which is greater than the desired value 79. It means that the desired value comes before the median. So, the last three elements (90, 93, and 96) are eliminated and the remaining list contains only two elements (79 and 85). In the next step, one of the values 79 or 85 is chosen as a median. The value chosen depends on the compiler. Finally, the value 85 is eliminated.

Inserting
This operation is used to add a new data element, a node, or a record to the structure.

Deleting
This operation is used to remove a data element, a node, or a record from the structure.

Sorting
The sorting operation is used to rearrange the data in some logical order. For example, the numeric values are sorted in an ascending or descending order and the character values are sorted in an alphabetical order.

For example, an array **DEMO** contains 5 elements:

55, 67, 11, 34, 25

After sorting, the array **DEMO** contains:

11, 25, 34, 55, 67

You can sort a list of elements by using the following methods:

a. Bubble sort
b. Quick sort
c. Heap sort
d. Insertion sort
e. Selection sort

Bubble sort
The bubble sort is the simplest method of sorting. In the bubble sort, if there are **n** number of elements, then **n-1** comparisons are required to sort the elements in the ascending order. For example, there is a list of numbers A[1], A[2], A[3],........., A[N] in the memory.

The working of the bubble sort is as follows:

Step 1: Firstly, A[1] and A[2] are compared and then these numbers are arranged such that A[1]< A[2]. Next, A[2] is compared with A[3] and then arranged such that A[2]<A[3]. This process is repeated until A[N-1] and A[N] are compared such that A[N-1]<A[N]. After the completion of this step, the largest element is moved to the nth position.

Step 2: In this step, **step1** is repeated but comparisons are made upto A[N-2] and A[N-1], which is one less than **step1**. After the completion of this step, the second largest element is moved to the n-1th position.

Step n-1: In this step, only A[1] and A[2] are compared and arranged such that A[1]<A[2]. After this step, the elements will be sorted in an ascending order.

Quick sort

The quick sort is another sorting method, in which an entire list of elements is divided into two sublists. This is also called the reduction step. The reduction step is repeated for each sublist that contains 2 or more elements. The working of this method is illustrated with the help of the following list of ten elements:

42, 31, 10, 56, 79, 92, 41, 65, 22, 85

At first, the first element 42 is selected and the entire list is scanned from the right to the left by comparing each element with 42 starting from the last element 85. When a number, which is less than 42 is found, the scanning process is terminated. In this case, the number is 22. Now, elements 42 and 22 are interchanged and you will get the following list:

22, 31, 10, 56, 79, 92, 41, 65, 42, 85

Observe that the value on the right of 42 is greater than 42. The next scan begins in the opposite direction from the left to the right, starting from 22. While scanning, each element is compared with 42 and this process is stopped when a number greater than 42 is found. In this case, the number is 56. Now, elements 42 and 56 are interchanged and you will get the following list:

22, 31, 10, 42, 79, 92, 41, 65, 56, 85

Observe that the values on the left of 42 are smaller than 42. The next scan begins from the right to the left, starting from 56. While scanning, each element is compared with 42 and this process is stopped when a number less than 42 is found. In this case, the number is 41. Now, elements 42 and 41 are interchanged and you will get the following list:

22, 31, 10, 41, 79, 92, 42, 65, 56, 85

Next, the scan begins from the left to the right, starting from 41. The number 79 is greater than 42. The elements 42 and 79 are interchanged and you will get the following list:

22, 31, 10, 41, 42, 92, 79, 65, 56, 85
The scan begins from the right to the left, starting from 79. No number smaller than 42 is found. It means that the number 42 is on its final position in the list. The values on the right are greater and on the left are less than 42. The list is divided into the following two sublists:

22, 31, 10, 41, 42, 92, 79, 65, 56, 85
First sublist   Second sublist

The reduction step is repeated for both the sublists until each sublist contains 2 or more elements.

Heap sort

In this section, you will learn about another type of tree structure, which is called a heap. In a heap, the topmost node or the root node contains the largest value. The heap sort method is used to sort the data elements of a heap into a logical order. This sorting process is done using the following steps:

a. Remove the node that contains the largest value from the heap and replace it with the value, which is at the rightmost leaf.
b. Restore the heap.
c. Repeat step 1 and 2 until there is a   right leaf in a heap.

Figures 7-15 through 7-18 represent the working of the heap sort method.

Figure 7-15 represents a heap, in which the root node contains the value 90 and the rightmost node contains the value 21.

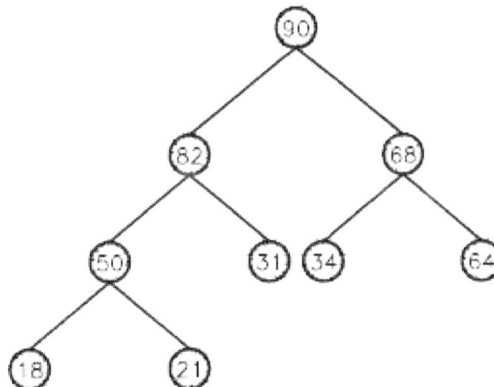

Figure 7-15 Representing a heap

Remove 90 and replace it with 21 and you will get the following tree, as shown in Figure 7-16.

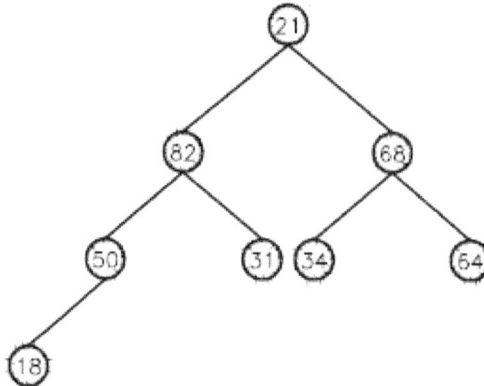

Figure 7-16 *Representing a tree after replacement*

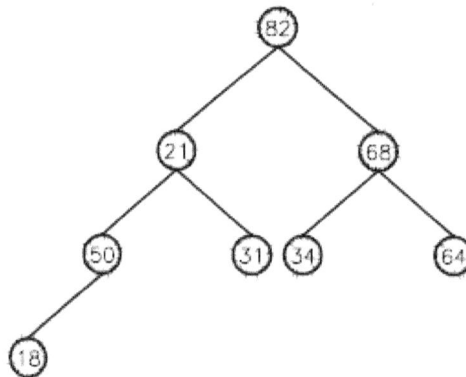

Figure 7-17 *Representation of a tree after the values are interchanged*

Next, compare 21 with its two children 82 and 68. You will see that 21 is less than its left child (82). Now, interchange 21 and 82 and you will get the following tree, as shown in Figure 7-17.

Next, compare 21 with its two children 50 and 31. Again, 21 is less than its left child (50). Interchange 21 and 50. Now, compare 21 with its new child 18. Here, 21 is greater than its left child (18). The value 21 is on its appropriate position in the tree, as shown in Figure 7-18.

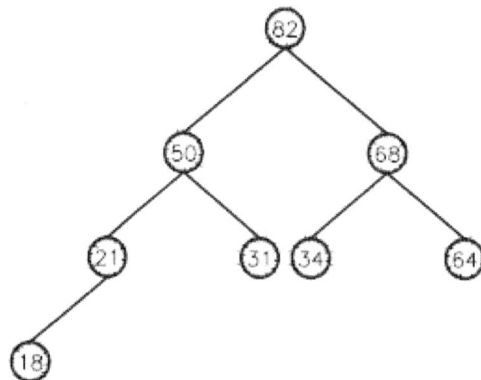

Figure 7-18 *Representation of a tree after the values are interchanged again*

Insertion sort

This is another sorting method, which is used when the data elements in a structure are few in number. The working of this method is illustrated with the help of an example, which is discussed next.

Suppose an array A contains the following 8 elements:

70, 30, 40, 10, 80, 20, 60, 50

In pass1, value 30 is compared with the value 70. Because value 30 is less than value 70, the values will be interchanged. Now, the array contains the elements:

30, 70, 40, 10, 80, 20, 60, 50

In pass2, first the value 40 is compared with the value 70. Because value 40 is less than value 70, the values 40 and 70 are interchanged. Now, value 40 is again compared with value 30, but value 40 is greater than 30. So, there is no change in the positions of value 30 and 40. Now, the array contains the elements:

30, 40, 70, 10, 80, 20, 60, 50

In pass3, value 10 is compared with the value 70. Because value 10 is less than value 70, the values 10 and 70 are interchanged. Now, value 10 is again compared with value 40, which is greater. So, the values 10 and 40 are interchanged. Next, value 10 is compared with value 30, which is greater. Again, the values 10 and 30 are interchanged. Now, the array contains the elements:

10, 30, 40, 70, 80, 20, 60, 50

In pass4, value 80 is compared with value 70. No change takes place in the positions of these values because the value 80 is greater than the value 70. The array now contains the elements:

10, 30, 40, 70, 80, 20, 60, 50

Next, all the values 20, 60, and 50 are compared with the values in the same way as discussed above and they are appropriately positioned in the array. After all the comparisons have been made, the array will contain the elements in the following order:

10, 20, 30, 40, 50, 60, 70, 80

The complexity of this method is $O(n^2)$.

Selection sort

In the selection sort, first find the smallest element and interchange it with the first element in the list. Next, find the second smallest element and interchange it with the second element in the list, and so on until all the elements in the list are placed at their appropriate positions. The following example illustrates the working of the selection sort:

Suppose an array A contains the following 8 elements:

70, 30, 40, 10, 80, 20, 60, 50
In pass1, the smallest element in the list is searched, which is 10. Next, it is interchanged with the first element (70). Now, the array A contains the following list:

10, 30, 40, 70, 80, 20, 60, 50

In pass2, the second smallest element is searched, which is 20. It is interchanged with the second element (30). After this pass, the first two elements are at their appropriate positions and in a sorted order. The array A now contains the following list:

10, 20, 40, 70, 80, 30, 60, 50

This process will be repeated until all the elements in the list are at their appropriate positions. The above list is sorted in 7 passes. Finally, array A contains the following list:

10, 20, 30, 40, 50, 60, 70, 80

The complexity of this method is $O(n^2)$.

Merging

Merging means "to combine". This data structure operation is used when you want to combine or join two sorted lists. You can merge a list with another list in the following two ways:

a.   The first way is to place the elements of a list (sorted) at the end of another list (sorted) and then apply a sorting method to sort the entire list. This method is time consuming.

b.   The second way is to always match the first element of both the lists and place the smaller element in the combined list one by one. When one list is empty, place all the remaining elements of the other list at the end of the combined list.

The following example illustrates the concept of merging:

Suppose there are two arrays. The first array A contains 6 elements, as follows:

21, 45, 56, 78, 85

The second array B contains 4 elements, as follows:

34, 50, 67, 80

Next, the first elements of both the lists (21 and 34) are compared. After that the smaller element (21) is placed at the first position in the third array C. The array C contains the following element:

21

Again, the first elements of both the lists (45 and 34) are compared. Next, the smaller element (34) is placed at the second position in the third array C. The array C contains the following list:

21, 34

In this way, all the elements in both the lists are placed at their appropriate positions in the third array C. After merging, array C will contain the following:

21, 34, 45, 50, 56, 67, 78, 80, 85

Self-Evaluation Test

Answer the following questions and then compare them to the answers given at the end of this chapter:

1. The _____ operator is used to allocate the memory dynamically.

2. The _____ is a way of organizing and storing the data in a computer.

3. The _____ pointer specifies the end of a linked list.

4. _____ is the property of a stack.

5. The _____ operation is used to access the data elements of a particular data structure at least once.

Review Questions

Answer the following questions:

1. Explain the working of the **new** operator.

2. Define a linked list.

3. Define a queue.

4. Explain the working of the linear search.

5. Differentiate between the bubble sort and the quick sort methods.

Exercise

Exercise 1

Write a program to create a single linked list that contains the names of 10 people. The program should also display their names.

Chapter 8

Classes and Objects

INTRODUCTION

In this chapter, you will learn about classes and objects, which are the main features of object-oriented programming (OOP). Classes and objects are used for data hiding.

DEFINING A CLASS

A class is a collection of data members and member functions. These member functions are used to manipulate the data. A class is a user-defined data type, which hides the data members and member functions from external use, if necessary. It works like a protection cover on the data and functions.

Declaring a Class

A class is declared in the same way as a structure except that a class declaration begins with the keyword **class**. The syntax is as follows:

```
class class_name
{
    access specifier:
            data member;
    access specifier:
            member function;
};
```

In the above syntax, the declaration begins with the keyword **class** followed by a **class_name**, which is an identifier given by the programmer to specify the name of the class. The body of the class is enclosed within the curly braces {} and is terminated by a semicolon (;), and it contains the following:

a. Access specifier
b. Data members
c. Member functions

Access Specifier

An access specifier specifies the visibility of a data member or a member function of a class. It should be terminated by a colon (:). The access specifier can be any one of the following three keywords:

Private

By default, the members of a class are **private**. These members can only be accessed by the other members of the same class.

Public

The **public** members of a class can be accessed by the members of the same class and by the members of the other classes.

Protected

The **protected** members of a class can be accessed by the members of the same class, a friend class, and a derived class. The concept of the friend class and derived class will be discussed later in this chapter.

Data Members

The data members are variables of any valid data type. These variables are declared within the class.

Member Functions

A class contains the following member functions:

a. Simple function
b. Constructors
c. Destructors

Simple Function

You have already learned about these functions in the previous chapter. These functions are defined with a return type and a list of arguments, and are used to manipulate the data members of the class.

Constructors

This is a special member function of a class. This function has the following properties:

a. The constructor name is the same as the name of the class.
b. Nob value is returned by the constructor, which means it does not contain any return type, or void.
c. A constructor is used for memory allocation and also for initialization of the members of a class.

Destructors

The name of a destructor is the same as the name of the class but it is preceded by a negation operator (~). This is basically used for memory de-allocation.

The following example illustrates the declaration of a class:

```
class customer
{
    char name[20];//data member1
    int acc_number;//data member2
    public:
            void getdata( );//member function1
            void showdata( );//member function2
};
```

In the above example, the class **customer** contains two data members and two member functions. The data members in this class are **private** by default because here no access specifier is used. The member function **getdata( )** is used to read the values of the data members from the user and the member function **showdata( )** is used to display these values on the screen. In this example, the member functions are only declared but they are not defined. You can also define the body of a function inside the class declaration (this will be discussed later in this chapter).

Note

A good programming skill requires that all the data members should be declared in the private section and all the member functions should be declared in the public section while defining a class.

Creating the Objects of a Class

An object is an instance of a class. Each object of a class is uniquely identified by its name or properties.

After the declaration of a class, you can create the objects of that type by using the class name. The syntax for creating an object is as follows:

    class_name var1;

In the above syntax, the **class_name** represents the name of the class and **var1** represents an object of a class type, which is specified by the **class_name**.

For example, if you want to create an object of the class **customer**, you will write the following code:

    customer c1;

Here, **customer** is the class name and **c1** is an object of the type **customer**.

You can also create more than one object in a single statement as follows:

    class_name var1, var2, var3, ..., varN;

Here, the object names are separated by a comma operator (**,**).

You can also create one or more than one object at the time of definition of a class. The syntax is as follows:

    class class_name
    {
        access specifier:
                data member;
        access specifier:
                member function;
    }var1, var2, var3;

In this syntax, **var1**, **var2**, and **var3** are declared as the objects of class **class_name**.

For example:

```
class customer
{
    char name[20];
    int acc_number;
public:
    void getdata( );
    void showdata( );
}c1, c2, c3;
```

In the above example, **c1**, **c2**, and **c3** are declared as the objects of the class **customer**.

Accessing the Members of a Class

You cannot access the data members and member functions of a class directly in the **main( )** function. For doing so, the data member or member function must be preceded by an object name and the dot operator (**.**). The syntax is as follows:

```
object_name . function_name (list of arguments);
```

For example, if you want to access the member function **showdata( )** of the class **customer**, you will write the following code:

```
c1.showdata( );
```

You can access the **public** data members of a class directly by using the object name and the dot operator but not the **private** data members.

For example:

```
class demo
{
    int a;
public:
    int b;
};
int main( )
{
    ..........;
    demo d1;
    d1.b=20;
    d1.a=10;//error, because a is private
    ..........;
    ..........;
}
```

In this example, you cannot access the member variable **a** in the **main( )** function with the object **d1** of class **demo**. This is because **a** is declared as a private data member of the class **demo**.

DEFINING MEMBER FUNCTIONS

You can define the member functions of a class in two ways:

a.   Inside the class definition
b.   Outside the class definition

Inside the Class Definition

You can define a member function inside a class definition by replacing the function declaration with a function definition. The syntax is as follows:

```
class class_name
{
     access specifier:
             data members:
     access specifier:
             return_type fun_name (list of arguments)
             {
                     body of the function;
             }
};
```

For example:

```
class customer
{
     char name[20];
     int acc_number;
public:
     void getdata( )
     {
             cout<<"Enter the name of the customer:"<<endl;
             cin>>name;
             cout<<"Enter the account number:"<<endl;
             cin>>acc_number;
     }
     void showdata()
     {
             cout<<"The name entered by you is:";
             cout<<name<<endl;
             cout<<"The account number entered by you is:";
```

```
                        cout<<acc_number<<endl;
              }
      };
```

In this example, the functions **getdata( )** and **showdata( )** are defined inside the class **customer**.

Outside the Class Definition

You can also define a member function of a class outside the class definition. The member function definition is very much similar to the normal function definition. The function definition and member function definition both have a return type, an argument list, and a function body. But a member function also has an identity label that specifies to the compiler the class to which the function belongs. The syntax for defining a function outside the class definition is as follows:

```
      return_type class_name :: fun_name (argument list)
      {
              function body
      }
```

In the above syntax, the identity label **class_name ::** specifies to the compiler that the function specified by **fun_name** belongs to the class specified by **class_name**. The operator **(::)** used in the syntax is called the scope resolution operator, which specifies the scope of the function. The scope of the function means that the function specified by **fun_name** is restricted to the class specified by **class_name**.

For example:

```
      class customer
      {
              char name[20];
              int acc_number;
      public:
              void getdata( );
              void showdata( );
      };
      void customer::getdata()
      {
              cout<<"Enter the name of the customer:"<<endl;
              cin>>name;
              cout<<"Enter the account number:"<<endl;
              cin>>acc_number;
      }
      void customer::showdata()
      {
              cout<<"The name is:";
              cout<<name<<endl;
```

```
        cout<<"The account number is:";
        cout<<acc_number<<endl;
}
```

The following example illustrates the use of a class.

Example 1

Write a program to create a class.

The following program will create a class, which contains the member functions that prompt the user to enter the name and account number. It will also display the resultant values on the screen. The line numbers on the right are not a part of the program and are for reference only.

```
//Write a program to illustrate the use of a class          1
#include<iostream>                                           2
using namespace std;                                         3
class customer                                               4
{                                                            5
        char name[20];                                       6
        int acc_number;                                      7
        public:                                              8
                void getdata( );                             9
                void showdata( );                            10
};                                                           11
void customer::getdata( )                                    12
{                                                            13
        cout<<"Enter the name of the customer:"<<endl;       14
        cin>>name;                                           15
        cout<<"Enter the account number:"<<endl;             16
        cin>>acc_number;                                     17
}                                                            18
void customer::showdata( )                                   19
{                                                            20
        cout<<"The name is: ";                               21
        cout<<name<<endl;                                    22
        cout<<"The account number is:   ";                   23
        cout<<acc_number<<endl;                              24
}                                                            25
int main( )                                                  26
{                                                            27
        customer c1, c2, c3;                                 28
        c1.getdata( );                                       29
        c1.showdata( );                                      30
        c2.getdata( );                                       31
        c2.showdata( );                                      32
        c3.getdata( );                                       33
```

c3.showdata( );	34
return 0;	35
}	36

Explanation

Line 4
class customer
In this line, **class** is the keyword and **customer** is the name of the class.

Line 5
{
This line indicates the start of the definition of the class **customer**.

Line 6 and 7
char name[20];
int acc_number;
These lines contain two data members of the class **customer**. Here, no access specifier is specified with these data members. So, they are considered as **private** data members and can be accessed only within the same class **customer**.

Lines 8 to 10
public:
    void getdata( );
    void showdata( );
Lines 9 and 10 contain two member functions of the class **customer**, **getdata( )** and **showdata( )**. Line 8 contains an access specifier **public**, which specifies that both the member functions can be accessed in the same class and also from outside the class **customer**.

Line 11
};
This line indicates the end of the definition of the class **customer** and is terminated by a semicolon.

Line 12
void customer::getdata( )
Here, the member function **getdata( )** is defined outside the class **customer** definition.

Line 19
void customer::showdata( )
Here, the member function **showdata( )** is defined outside the class **customer** definition.

Line 28
customer c1, c2, c3;
In this line, three objects **c1**, **c2**, and **c3** are declared as **customer** type and each of them has its own copy of data members of the class **customer**.

Line 29
c1.getdata( );

In this line, a function call is made to the member function **getdata( )**, which is used to read the value of data members of the class from the end user. Here, the values entered by the user are assigned to the copy of the data members of the object **c1**.

Line 30
c1.showdata( );
In this line, a function call is made to the member function **showdata( )**, which is used to display the values of data members of the object **c1** on the screen.

Line 31
c2.getdata( );
In this line, a function call is made to the member function **getdata( )**, which is used to read the values of data members of the class from the end user. Here, the values entered by the user are assigned to the copy of the data members of the object **c2**.

Line 32
c2.showdata();
In this line, a function call is made to the member function **showdata()**, which is used to display the values of data members of the object **c2** on the screen.

The output of the program is as follows:
Enter the name of the customer:
John
Enter the account number
102
The name is: John
The account number is: 102
Enter the name of the customer:
Smith
Enter the account number
110
The name is: Smith
The account number is: 110
Enter the name of the customer:
Michael
Enter the account number
145
The name is: Michael
The account number is: 145

The output will be displayed on the screen as follows:

```
c:\C++\C++_programs\Ch_08\ch08_pro01\...  _ □ ×
Enter the name of the customer:
John
Enter the account number:
102
The name is: John
The account number is: 102
Enter the name of the customer:
Smith
Enter the account number:
110
The name is: Smith
The account number is: 110
Enter the name of the customer:
Michael
Enter the account number:
145
The name is: Michael
The account number is: 145
Press any key to continue
```

MEMORY ALLOCATION FOR OBJECTS

When an object of a class is created, some amount of memory is allocated to it. The amount of memory allocated to an object is equal to the amount of memory required by the data members of that class. This is because each object member of a class has its own copy of the data members. All the objects of a class share the same copy of the member functions of a class, as shown in Figure 8-1.

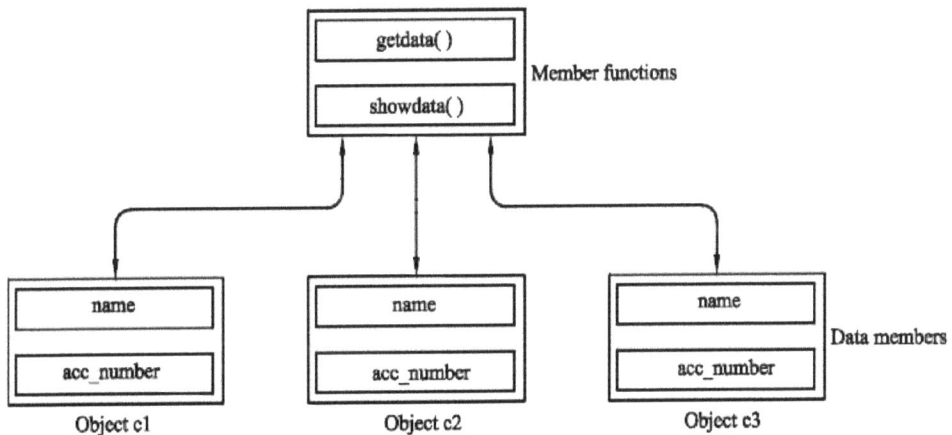

Figure 8-1 *Memory allocation*

In the above figure, the member functions of a class are shared by all the three objects **c1, c2,** and **c3** and each object has its own copy of data members of a class.

NESTED MEMBER FUNCTIONS

Until now, you have observed that a member function of a class is called with the help of an object of that class and a dot operator. You can also make a call to a member function of a class by using its name inside another member function of the same class. These type of functions are called nested member functions.

The following example illustrates the use of the nested member functions.

Example 2

Write a program to find the average of three numbers.

The following program will prompt the user to enter three numbers, calculate their average, and display the resultant value on the screen.

```
//Write a program to calculate the average of three numbers    1
#include<iostream>                                             2
using namespace std;                                           3
class average                                                  4
{                                                              5
        int a, b, c, d;                                        6
        public:                                                7
                void input( );                                 8
                void show( );                                  9
                int avrg( );                                   10
};                                                             11
void average :: input(void)                                    12
{                                                              13
        cout<<"Enter three values"<<endl;                     14
        cin>>a>>b>>c;                                          15
}                                                              16
int average::avrg(void)                                        17
{                                                              18
        d=(a+b+c)/3;                                           19
        return d;                                              20
}                                                              21
void average::show(void)                                       22
{                                                              23
        cout<<"The average of three numbers is: "<< avrg( )<<endl;   24
}                                                              25
int main( )                                                    26
{                                                              27
        average a1;                                            28
        a1.input( );                                           29
        a1.show( );                                            30
        return 0;                                              31
}                                                              32
```

Explanation
Lines 22 to 25
void average::show(void)
{
      cout<<"The average of three numbers is:"<< avrg()<<endl;

}

These lines contain the definition of the member function **show( )**. In the body of this function, another member function **avrg( )** is called, which returns the resultant value after calculating the average of three numbers.

The output of the program is as follows:
Enter three values
26
25
24
The average of three numbers is: 25

FRIEND FUNCTIONS

You can also access the **private** and **protected** data members of a class by using the **friend** function. The syntax for declaring a **friend** function is as follows:

    friend ret_type fun_name (argument list)

The **friend** function is not a member of a class. A **friend** function declared in the **public** or the **private** section in the definition of a class is not affected like the other member functions of the class. You can define a **friend** function outside the class definition without using the class name and scope resolution operator (**::**). You can also make a call to a **friend** function in the main program without the help of any object. A **friend** function always contains an object as an argument.

The following example illustrates the use of the **friend** function.

Example 3

Write a program to calculate the average of three numbers.

The following program will prompt the user to enter three numbers, calculate their average, and display the resultant value on the screen.

```
//Write a program to calculate the average of three numbers          1
#include<iostream>                                                    2
using namespace std;                                                  3
class average                                                         4
{                                                                     5
      int a, b, c;                                                    6
      public:                                                         7
              friend int avrg(average a1);                            8
              void input();                                           9
};                                                                    10
void average::input(void)                                            11
{                                                                     12
      cout<<"Enter three values"<<endl;                              13
```

```
        cin>>a>>b>>c;                                           14
}                                                               15
int avrg(average a1)                                            16
{                                                               17
        return (a1.a+a1.b+a1.c)/3;                              18
}                                                               19
int main( )                                                     20
{                                                               21
        average n;                                              22
        n.input();                                              23
        cout<<"The average of three numbers is: "<<avrg(n)<<endl;  24
        return 0;                                               25
}                                                               26
```

Explanation

Line 8

friend int avrg(average a1);

In this line, the function **avrg** is declared as a **friend** function and it takes an object **a1** of the class **average** as an argument.

Lines 16 to 19

int avrg(average a1)

{

    return (a1.a+a1.b+a1.c)/3;

}

Lines 16 to 19 contain the definition of the function **avrg**, which is a **friend** of the class **average**. This function is not the member of the class. So, it is defined outside the class definition as a normal function without using the class name and the scope resolution operator.

Line 22

average n;

In this line, the variable **n** is declared as an object of type **average**.

Line 23

n.input();

In this line, a call is made to the member function **input( )** with the help of an object **n** and a dot operator.

Line 24

cout<<avrg(n);

In this line, a call is made to the **friend** function **avrg(n)** and an object of the class **average** is passed as an argument.

The output of the program is as follows:

Enter three numbers
26
25
24
The average of three numbers is: 25

ARRAY OF OBJECTS

As you already know that an array is a collection of data elements of the same type. Similarly, an array can also contain a collection of objects that are of the same class type. These types of arrays are known as array of objects. The syntax for declaring an array of objects is the same as for an array of any type.

For example:

```
class demo
{
    int a, b;
    public:
            void input( );
            void show( );
};
int main( )
{
    demo d[3];
    ..........;
    ..........;
}
```

In the above example, array **d** represents an array of objects that contains three objects **d[0]**, **d[1]**, and **d[2]** of type **demo**.

The following example illustrates the use of an array of objects.

Example 4

Write a program to create an array of objects.

The following program will prompt the user to enter a name and employee ID, create an array of objects, and display the resultant array on the screen.

```
//Write a program to create an array of objects          1
#include<iostream>                                        2
using namespace std;                                      3
class employee                                            4
{                                                         5
        char name[30];                                   6
        int emp_id;                                       7
```

```
        public:                                              8
                void input( );                               9
                void show( );                                10
};                                                           11
void employee :: input( )                                    12
{                                                            13
        cout<<"Enter the name:"<<endl;                       14
        cin>>name;                                           15
        cout<<"Enter employee ID:"<<endl;                    16
        cin>>emp_id;                                         17
}                                                            18
void employee :: show( )                                     19
{                                                            20
        cout<<"The name entered by you is: "<<name<<endl;    21
        cout<<"The employee ID is: "<<emp_id<<endl;          22
}                                                            23
int main( )                                                  24
{                                                            25
        employee e[3];//Array of objects                     26
        int i;                                               27
        for (i=0;i<3;i++)                                    28
                e[i].input( );                               29
        for(i=0;i<3;i++)                                     30
                e[i].show( );                                31
        return 0;                                            32
}                                                            33
```

The output of the program is as follows:
Enter the name:
John
Enter employee ID:
110
Enter the name:
Smith
Enter employee ID:
130
Enter the name:
Michael
Enter employee ID:
125
The name entered by you is: John
The employee ID is: 110
The name entered by you is: Smith
The employee ID is: 130
The name entered by you is: Michael
The employee ID is: 125

PASSING OBJECTS TO FUNCTIONS

An object can be passed to a function as an argument in the same way as the variables of any other data type. In this process, a copy of the object is passed to a function. If any change is made to the given object inside the function, it will not be reflected in the actual object. This process is similar to the concept of pass by value. Another way of passing an object is to pass the starting address of the object to a function. If any change is made to the object inside the function, it will be reflected in the actual object. This process is similar to the concept of pass by reference.

The following example illustrates the use of passing objects to functions.

Example 5

Write a program to multiply the values of two objects.

The program given next will multiply the values of two objects that are passed as arguments to a function, assign the resultant value to the third object, and display the resultant value on the screen.

```
//Write a program to multiply the values of two objects        1
#include<iostream>                                             2
using namespace std;                                           3
class multiply                                                 4
{                                                              5
    int a;                                                     6
    public:                                                    7
       void getvalue(int x)                                    8
       {                                                       9
            a=x;                                               10
       }                                                       11
       void showvalue( )                                       12
       {                                                       13
            cout<<a;                                           14
       }                                                       15
       void mul(multiply m1, multiply m2);                     16
};                                                             17
void multiply :: mul(multiply m1, multiply m2)                 18
{                                                              19
    a= m1.a * m2.a;                                            20
}                                                              21
int main( )                                                    22
{                                                              23
       multiply M1, M2, M3;                                    24
       M1.getvalue(10);                                        25
       M2.getvalue(20);                                        26
       M3.mul(M1, M2);                                         27
       cout<<"M1= ";M1.showvalue();cout<<endl;                 28
```

```
    cout<<"M2= ",M2.showvalue();cout<<endl;                    29
    cout<<"M3= ";M3.showvalue();cout<<endl;                    30
    return 0;                                                  31
}                                                              32
```

Explanation

Line 16
void mul(multiply m1, multiply m2);
In this line, the function **mul** is declared inside the definition of the class **multiply**. Also the argument list contains two arguments **m1** and **m2**, which are objects of the class **multiply**.

Line 25
M1.getvalue(10);
In this line, a function call is made to the **getvalue( )** function and value 10 is passed as an argument. Here, value 10 is assigned to the variable **a**, which is the copy of object **M1**.

Line 26
M2.getvalue(20);
In this line, a function call is made to the **getvalue( )** function and value 20 is passed as an argument. Here, value 20 is assigned to variable **a**, which is the copy of object **M2**.

Line 27
M3.mul(M1, M2);
Here, a function call is made to function **mul( )**, and two objects **M1** and **M2** of class **multiply** are passed as arguments. The copies of these objects are assigned to **m1** and **m2** respectively, in line 18, respectively. After this assignment, value 10 stored in variable **a** of object **M1** and value 20 stored in variable **a** of object **M2** are multiplied and the resultant value 200 is assigned to object **M3**.

The output of the program is as follows:
M1= 10
M2= 20
M3= 200

ASSIGNING AN OBJECT

You can also assign an object to another object but both the objects should be of the same type. This means both the objects should belong to the same class. The syntax for assigning an object to another object is given next.

    obj1=obj2;

In the above syntax, **obj1** and **obj2** belong to the same class. The data of the object **obj2** is copied to the data of the object **obj1**.

The following example illustrates the use of assignment of an object.

Example 6

Write a program to assign the data of an object to another object of a class.

The following program will assign the data of an object to another object and display the resultant values on the screen.

```
//Write a program to assign the data of an object to another object    1
#include<iostream>                                                      2
using namespace std;                                                    3
class assign                                                            4
{                                                                       5
        float x;                                                        6
        public:                                                         7
                void input(float a)                                     8
                {                                                       9
                        x=a;                                            10
                }                                                       11
                float show( )                                          12
                {                                                       13
                        return x;                                       14
                }                                                       15
};                                                                      16
int main( )                                                             17
{                                                                       18
        assign a1,a2;                                                   19
        a1.input(10.23);                                                20
        a2=a1;                                                          21
        cout<<"The value assigned to object a2 is: "<<a2.show( )<<endl; 22
        return 0;                                                       23
}                                                                       24
```

Explanation
Line 19
assign a1,a2;
In this line, variables **a1** and **a2** are declared as objects of the class **assign**.

Line 20
a1.input(10.23);
Here, a call is made to the **input( )** function and a float value 10.23 is passed as an argument. This value is assigned to the variable **a** in line 8. The function call is made with the object **a1**. So, the value 10.23 is assigned to the copy of the data member **x** of object **a1**.

Line 21
a2=a1;

In this line, the value 10.23 stored in the copy of the data member **x** of object **a1** is assigned to the copy of the data member **x** of object **a2**.

The output of the program is as follows:
The value assigned to object a2 is: 10.23

POINTERS TO OBJECTS

Like the pointer to a variable, you can also create pointers to objects. The starting address of the object is assigned to the pointer. After that, you can access the members of a class with the help of the arrow operator (**->**) rather than the dot operator (**.**). The syntax is as follows:

    pointer_var =&obj_name;

In the above syntax, the **&** operator returns the starting address of the object specified by the **obj_name**. Next, the resultant address is assigned to the pointer variable specified by the **pointer_var**.

For example:

```
class demo
{
    int i;
    public:
            void input(int a)
            {
                    i=a;
            }
            int show( )
            {
                    return i;
            }
};
int main( )
{
    demo d1, *p;
    p=&d1;
    p->input(10);
    p->show( );
    ----------;
    ----------;
}
```

In the above example, variable **d1** is declared as an object of the class **demo**. A pointer variable **p** is declared as a pointer to the object. The **&** operator returns the starting address of object **d1**, which is assigned to **p**. Now, the member functions **input( )** and **show( )** of class **demo** can be accessed with the help of the pointer to the object **p.**

You can also assign an array of objects to the pointer to an object variable. The syntax for assigning an array of objects to the pointer to an object is as follows:

    pointer_var = obj_name[number of objects];

In the above syntax, the address of the first object of the **array of objects** is assigned to the pointer variable. If the pointer variable is incremented, it will point to the next object in the array.

For example:

```
class demo
{
    int i;
    public:
            void input(int a)
            {
                    i=a;
            }
            int show( )
            {
                    return i;
            }
};
int main( )
{
    demo d1[5], *p;
    int j;
    p=d1;
    for(j=0; j<5; j++)
    {
            p->input(10);
            p++;
    }
    for(j=0; j<5; j++)
            p->show( );
    ----------;
    ----------;
}
```

In the above example, an array of objects **d1** of class **demo** is declared and the size of the array is 5. A pointer variable **p** is declared as a pointer to an object. In the statement **p=d1;**, by default, the address of the first object of the array **d1** is assigned to the pointer to an object **p**. When **p** is incremented in statement **p++;**, it will point to the next object of the array.

If the data members of a class are **public**, you can assign the address of the copy of data member of an object to a pointer variable.

The syntax is as follows:

    pointer_var = &obj_name.data_member;

In the above syntax, the **&** operator returns the address of the copy of the data member **data_member** of the object **obj_name**. This address is then assigned to the pointer variable specified by the **pointer_var**.

For example:

```
class demo
{
    public:
            int i;
            void input(int a)
            {
                    i=a;
            }
};
int main( )
{
    demo d1;
    int *p;
    d1.input(10);
    p=&d1.i;
    cout<<*p;
    ----------;
    ----------;
}
```

In the above example, the data member **i** of class **demo** is declared as **public** and **d1** is declared as an object of type **demo**. In the statement **p=&d1.i;**, the address of the copy of data member **i** of object **d1** is assigned to the pointer variable **p**. Now, you can directly access the value 10, which is stored in the variable **i**, by using the ***p** statement.

STATIC DATA MEMBERS

Until now, you have learned that each object of a class has its own copy of data members. To make a data member common to all the objects, you need to declare the data member as **static** by using the **static** keyword in the declaration statement. The characteristic of a static data member is that only one copy is created for the entire class and all the objects share the same copy. All the **static** data members are initialized to zero before the creation of the first object. The syntax for declaring a **static** data member is as follows:

```
class class_name
{
    static data_type var_name;//declaration
    ----------;
```

```
        ----------;
    };
    data_type class_name :: var_name;//definition
```

In the above syntax, the declaration part contains a keyword **static**, which directs the compiler that only one copy of the data member, specified by **var_name**, is created for the entire class. When a **static** variable is declared inside the definition of a class, no memory space is allocated to it and it cannot be used for the entire class. So, to make it global and to provide enough memory space to it, it must be defined outside the definition of a class with the help of the scope resolution operator (**::**). The **static** data member is defined outside the class in the same way as a function is declared outside the definition of a class.

You can also assign an initial value to a **static** data member in the definition. The syntax is as follows:

```
    data_type class_name :: var_name=value;
```

In this syntax, an initial value specified by **value** is assigned to the variable specified by **var_name**.

For example:

```
    class demo
    {
        static int i;//declaration
        ----------;
        ----------;
    }d1, d2;
    int demo :: i;//definition
```

In the above example, **d1** and **d2** are the objects of the class **demo** and the data member **i** is declared as a **static** data member. So both the objects **d1** and **d2** will share the same copy of data member **i**, as shown in Figure 8-2.

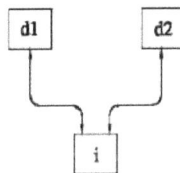

Figure 8-2 *Representation of a static data member*

The following example illustrates the use of the **static** data members.

Example 7

Write a program to illustrate the working of a **static** data member.

The following program will assign the values to a static data member, pass it as an argument to the member functions, and display the resultant values on the screen.

```
//Write a program to illustrate the working of the static data members    1
#include<iostream>                                                          2
using namespace std;                                                        3
class static_demo                                                           4
{                                                                           5
    static int a;//declaration                                             6
    public:                                                                7
        void input(int x)                                                  8
        {                                                                  9
            a=x;                                                          10
        }                                                                 11
        void show()                                                       12
        {                                                                 13
            cout<<"The value stored in a is: "<<a;                        14
        }                                                                 15
};                                                                        16
int static_demo::a;//definition                                           17
int main( )                                                               18
{                                                                         19
        static_demo d1, d2, d3;                                           20
        d1.input(10);                                                     21
        d1.show( );                                                       22
        d2.show( );                                                       23
        d3.show( );                                                       24
        d2.input(20);                                                     25
        d1.show( );                                                       26
        d2.show( );                                                       27
        d3.show( );                                                       28
        return 0;                                                         29
}                                                                         30
```

Explanation
Line 6
static int a;
Here, the integer type variable **a** is declared as a **static** data member of the class **static_demo**. It means that only one copy of the variable **a** exists for the entire class and all the objects will share the same copy.

Line 17
int demo::a;
Here, variable **a** is defined outside the class **static_demo**. This definition makes the variable **a** global and also initializes it with the value 0.

Line 21
d1.input(10);
Here, a function call is made to the member function **input( )** and value 10 is passed as an argument. This value is then assigned to the variable **a** in the body of the function. Now, the variable **a** contains value 10.

Line 22 to Line 24
d1.show();
d2.show();
d3.show();
In these lines, a call is made to the member function **show( )** with three different objects **d1, d2,** and **d3**. This function will display the same value 10 for all the three objects because only one copy of the variable **a** exists and it is shared by all the three objects, as shown in Figure 8-3.

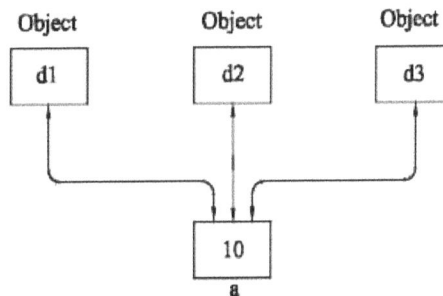

Figure 8-3 *Representation of variable sharing*

Line 25
d2.input(20);
In this line, the member function **input( )** is called with the object **d2** and the value 20 is passed as an argument. This value is then assigned to the variable **a** in the body of the function. Now, the previous value 10 in the variable **a** is overwritten with the new value 20. Now, the variable **a** contains the value 20.

The output of the program is as follows:
The value stored in a is: 10
The value stored in a is: 10
The value stored in a is: 10
The value stored in a is: 20
The value stored in a is: 20
The value stored in a is: 20

STATIC MEMBER FUNCTIONS

You can also declare the member functions of a class as **static** member functions. A member function is declared **static** in the same way as a data member is declared **static** by using the **static** keyword. The syntax is as follows:

    static return_type fun_name (arguments list);

When a function is declared as a **static** member function in a class, it can only access the **static** data members and **static** member functions of that particular class. You can make a call to a **static** member function of a class by using a class name and a scope resolution operator (**::**), as follows:

    class_name :: fun_name( );

For example:

```
class demo
{
    int a;
    static int b;
    public:
            void input( );
            static void show( );
};
----------;
int main( )
{
    demo d1, d2;
    d1.input( );
    demo :: show( );
    ----------;
    ----------;
}
```

In the above example, the member function **show( )** is declared as **static**. So, it can only access the **static** data member **b**. In the statement **demo :: show( );**, a call is made to the **static** member function by using the class name **demo** and the scope resolution operator (**::**).

The following example illustrates the use of the **static** member functions.

Example 8

Write a program to illustrate the working of a **static** member function.

The following program will assign the values to a static data member, pass it as an argument to a static member function, and display the resultant values on the screen.

```
//Write a program to illustrate the use of static member functions    1
#include<iostream>                                                     2
using namespace std;                                                   3
class static_demo                                                      4
{                                                                      5
        static int a;                                                 6
        public:                                                       7
                void input(int x)                                     8
                {                                                     9
                        a=x;                                          10
                }                                                     11
                static void show( )                                   12
                {                                                     13
                        cout<<"Value stored in a is: "<<a<<endl;      14
                }                                                     15
};                                                                    16
int static_demo :: a;                                                 17
int main( )                                                           18
{                                                                     19
        static_demo d1, d2;                                           20
        d1.input(10);                                                 21
        d2.input(20);                                                 22
        d1.display( );                                                23
        static_demo :: show();                                        24
        return 0;                                                     25
}                                                                     26
```

Explanation

Lines 12 to 15
static void show( )
{
        cout<<"Value stored in a is: "<<a<<endl;
}
In these lines, the **static** member function **show( )** is defined. This function can only access the static data member **a** of the class **static_demo**.

Line 24
static_demo :: show();
Here, a call is made to the **static** member function **show( )**.

The output of the program is as follows:
Value stored in a is: 20

LOCAL CLASSES

You can also define a class within the body of a function or inside a block of code. These classes are known as local classes. In a local class, you cannot define a **static** data member or a **static** member function. The enclosing function or the block of code in which a local class is defined cannot access the **private** data member of that class. The syntax for the local class is as follows:

```
return_type
{
    ----------;
    class class_name
    {
            data members;
            access_specifier:
                    member functions;
    };
    ----------;
    class_name obj1;//object creation
    ----------;
}
```

The following example illustrates the use of local classes.

Example 9

Write a program to illustrate the working of a local class.

The following program will multiply two numbers. These numbers are passed as arguments to a member function in a local class. The program will display the resultant value on the screen.

```
//Write a program to illustrate the use of local classes        1
#include<iostream>                                               2
using namespace std;                                             3
void mul();//function declaration                                4
int main()                                                       5
{                                                                6
    mul( );                                                      7
    return 0;                                                    8
}                                                                9
void mul( )//function definition                                10
{                                                               11
        class multiply//definition of local class              12
        {                                                       13
                int a, b, c;                                    14
                public:                                         15
                        void input(int x, int y)                16
                        {                                       17
                                a=x;                            18
```

```
                    b=y;                                      19
               }                                              20
               int show()                                    21
               {                                              22
                    c=a*b;                                    23
                    return c;                                 24
               }                                              25
          };                                                 26
          multiply m1;                                       27
          m1.input(10,20);                                   28
          cout<<"After multiplication, c contains: "<<m1.show()<<endl;  29
     }                                                       30
```

The output of the program is as follows:
After multiplication, c contains: 200

The this pointer

When a function call is made to the member function of a class with an object, an implicit argument is passed automatically by the compiler. This argument is a pointer, which points to the invoking object (the object on which the function is called). The pointer is known as the **this** pointer.

For example, a call is made to the member function **demo( )** with an object **obj1** in the following way:

    obj1.demo( );

Here, the **this** pointer will contain the address of object **obj1**.

In a member function, you can directly access the private data member of a class without using any object. You can also do so by using the **this** pointer.

For example:

```
class demo
{
    int a;
    ----------;
    public:
            void show( )
            {
                    this->a;//accessing variable a
            }
            ----------;
};
```

In this example, the **private** data member **a** will be directly accessed by using the **this** pointer.

The following example illustrates the use of the pointer **this**.

Example 10

Write a program to multiply two numbers using the pointer **this**.

The following program will multiply two numbers, assign the resultant value to another variable, and display it on the screen.

```
//Write a program to multiply two numbers          1
#include<iostream>                                  2
using namespace std;                                3
class multiply                                      4
{                                                   5
        int a, b, c;                                6
        public:                                     7
                void input(int x, int y)            8
                {                                   9
                        this->a=x;                  10
                        this->b=y;                  11
                }                                   12
                int show( )                         13
                {                                   14
                        this->c=this->a*this->b;    15
                        return this->c;             16
                }                                   17
};                                                  18
int main( )                                         19
{                                                   20
        multiply m1, m2;                            21
        m1.input(10,20);                            22
        cout<<"After multiplication c contains: "<<m1.show( )<<endl;    23
        m2.input(20,30);                            24
        cout<<"After multiplication c contains: "<<m2.show( )<<endl;    25
        return 0;                                   26
}                                                   27
```

Explanation
Line 22
m1.input(10,20);
In this line, the member function **input(10,20)** is invoked with the object **m1**. In the function definition (Lines 8 to 12), the **this** pointer points to the object **m1**.

Line 23
cout<<"After multiplication c contains: "<<m1.show( )<<endl;
In this line, the member function **show( )** is invoked with the object **m1**. In the function definition (Lines 13 to 17), the **this** pointer points to the object **m1**.

Line 24
m2.input(20,30);
In this line, the member function **input(10,20)** is invoked with the object **m2**. In the function definition (Lines 8 to 12), the **this** pointer points to the object **m2**.

Line 25
cout<<"After multiplication c contains: "<<m1.show( )<<endl;
In this line, the member function **show( )** is invoked with the object **m2**. In the function definition (Lines 13 to 17), the **this** pointer points to the object **m2**.

The output of the program is as follows:
After multiplication c contains: 200
After multiplication c contains: 600

INLINE FUNCTIONS

The **inline** functions are the small functions that may have one or two statements in the function body. The main characteristic of the **inline** functions is that when they are invoked, they expand in a line. This means in the inline functions, the function call is replaced with the corresponding function code by the compiler. You can create an **inline** function by using the **inline** keyword in the function definition. The syntax for **inline** functions is as follows:

```
inline return_type fun_name
{
    function code;
}
```

For example:

```
inline int mul(int a, int b)
{
    return (a*b);
}
int main( )
{
    cout<<mul(10,20);
    return 0;
}
```

In the above example, when **mul(int a, int b)** is invoked at some point in the main program, the entire code of function definition is replaced with the function call.

The **inline** functions are mainly used to increase the speed of execution. The **inline** functions have an advantage when the function body contains one or two statements. As the number of statements increase, the benefits of the **inline** functions get reduced.

Self-Evaluation Test

Answer the following questions and then compare them to the answers given at the end of this chapter:

1. A class is a collection of _____ and _____.

2. The _____ member of a class cannot be accessed from outside the class.

3. An _____ is an instance of a class.

4. A _____ function is not a member of a class.

5. The entire class has only one copy of a _____ data member.

Review Questions

Answer the following questions:

1. Define a class.

2. Define an object and also its creation.

3. Explain a **friend** function.

4. How does a **static** data member differ from a simple data member of a class?

5. Explain **inline** function.

Exercise

Exercise 1

Write a program to define a class **Area** that uses the member functions to input the dimensions (length and breadth) of a rectangle, calculates the area, and also displays the result.

Answers to Self-Evaluation Test
1. data members and member functions, **2. private**, **3.** object, **4. friend**, **5. static**

Chapter 9

Constructors, Destructors, and Operator Overloading

Learning Objectives

After completing this chapter, you will be able to:

- *Understand constructors.*
- *Understand constructor overloading.*
- *Understand copy constructors.*
- *Understand destructors.*
- *Understand operator overloading.*

INTRODUCTION

In the examples given in the previous chapter, you must have observed that the **private** data members of a class were initialized with some initial value by using certain member functions such as **getdata( )**, **input( )**, and so on. These member functions assign a user-defined initial value to the **private** data members of a class. But these functions cannot initialize the data members automatically at the time of creation of the objects. So, a special member function is used for the automatic initialization of an object at the time of its creation. This member function is known as the constructor. C++ also provides a member function whose purpose is to destroy those objects of a class, which were initialized earlier but are no longer required. This member function is known as destructor.

CONSTRUCTORS

A constructor is a special member function, which is used to initialize the objects of a class. The name of a constructor is the same as the name of a class. The constructors cannot return any value because they do not have any return type, not even **void**. The syntax for initializing the objects of a class is as follows:

```
class class_name
{
    data members:
    public:
            class_name( );//Constructor declaration
            member_function( );
};
class_name :: class_name( )//Constructor definition
{
    statements;
}
```

Whenever an object of a class is created, the constructor associated with that particular class is invoked automatically.

For example:

```
class demo
{
    int a, b;
    public:
            demo( );//Constructor declaration
            ..........;
};
demo :: demo( )//Constructor definition
{
    a=0;
    b=0;
}
```

```
int main( )
{
    demo d1;//Object creation
    ..........;
    ..........;
    return 0;
}
```

In this example, when the statement **demo d1;** is executed, constructor **demo( )** will be invoked automatically. The constructor **demo( )** will initialize the object **d1** and also the data members **a** and **b** with zero.

You do not need to write any statement to invoke a constructor because it is automatically called whenever an object is created. When a constructor does not contain an argument list, it is known as the default constructor. As discussed in the above example, the default constructor of the class **demo** is **demo :: demo( )**. If a constructor is not defined in a class, a default constructor is provided by the compiler.

There are certain characteristics that differentiate constructors from the other member functions. These characteristics are as follows:

1. The name of a constructor is the same as the class name.
2. A constructor should be declared in the **public** section in a class definition.
3. A constructor cannot return any value because it does not have any return type, not even **void**.
4. A constructor is invoked automatically whenever an object of a class is created.

Parameterized Constructors

In the previous section, you have learned about the default constructor, which initializes the copy of data members of each object of a class with an initial value zero. If you want to assign different values to the copy of data members of each object, you can do so with the help of parameterized constructors, which contain an argument list. The syntax for passing the arguments using parameterized constructors is as follows:

```
class_name (data_type arg1, data_type arg2, ......., data_type argN);
```

In the above syntax, the **class_name** specifies the name of the constructor and the parentheses contain the arguments with their data types. The following example will explain the concept of parameterized constructors.

For example:

```
class demo
{
    int a, b;
    public:
            demo (int x, int y);
```

```
          ..........;
    },
    demo ::demo(int x, int y)
    {
        a=x;
        b=y;
    }
```

Now, you can pass the arguments to the constructor **demo( )** in the following two ways:

1. demo d1= demo(10,20);

This is the first method for passing arguments to the constructor **demo( )**. After the execution of the above statement, an object **d1** is created and the values 10 and 20 are assigned to the copy of the data members **a** and **b** of object **d1,** respectively.

2. demo d1(10,20);

This is another method for passing arguments to the constructor **demo( )**.

The following example illustrates the use of parameterized constructors.

Example 1

Write a program to calculate the area of a rectangle.

The following program will calculate the area of a rectangle and display the resultant value on the screen. The line numbers on the right are not a part of the program and are for reference only.

```
//Write a program to calculate the area of a rectangle          1
#include<iostream>                                               2
using namespace std;                                            3
class rectangle                                                 4
{                                                               5
        int length, width;                                      6
        public:                                                 7
                rectangle(int l, int w);//Constructor declaration  8
                int area();                                     9
                void display();                                 10
};                                                              11
rectangle :: rectangle(int l, int w)//Constructor definition    12
{                                                               13
    length=l;                                                  14
    width=w;                                                   15
}                                                               16
```

```
int rectangle :: area( )                                              17
{                                                                     18
    return length * width;                                           19
}                                                                     20
void rectangle :: display( )                                         21
{                                                                     22
    cout<<"The area of the rectangle is: "<<area( )<<endl;           23
}                                                                     24
int main( )                                                          25
{                                                                     26
        rectangle r1(10,20);                                         27
        r1.area();                                                   28
        r1.display();                                                29
        rectangle r2= rectangle(20,20);                              30
        r2.area();                                                   31
        r2.display();                                                32
        return 0;                                                    33
}                                                                    34
```

Explanation

Line 8

rectangle(int l, int w);

In this line, the constructor **rectangle( )** is declared and two integer type variables **l** and **w** are passed as arguments.

The output of the program is as follows:

The area of the rectangle is: 200

The area of the rectangle is: 400

Constructor Overloading

When more than one constructor is defined in a class, it is called constructor overloading. These constructors are differentiated on the basis of the number of arguments and their data types.

For example:

```
class rectangle
{
    int length, width;
    public:
            rectangle( )//First constructor
            {
                    length=1;
                    width=1;
            }
            rectangle(int l)//Second constructor
            {
                    length=l;
```

```
                width=l;
        }
        rectangle(int l, int w)//Third constructor
        {
                length=l;
                width=w;
        }
        rectangle(rectangle &r)//Fourth constructor
        {
                length=r.length;
                width=r.width;
        }
};
```

In the above example, there are four constructors defined in the class **rectangle**. The first does not contain any argument, the second contains only one integer type argument, the third contains two integer type arguments, and the fourth contains an object of the class **rectangle** as an argument. When the statement

        rectangle r1;

is executed, the compiler will invoke the first constructor because values are not passed in the above statement. It will initialize the data members, **length** and **width** of the object **r1** with an initial value 1. When the statement

        rectangle r2(10);

is executed, the compiler will invoke the second constructor because only one value is passed. It will initialize the data members, **length** and **width** of the object **r2** with an initial value 10. When the statement

        rectangle r3(10,20);

is executed, the compiler will invoke the third constructor and initialize both the data members, **length** and **width** of the object **r3** with the initial values 10 and 20, respectively. When the statement
        rectangle r4(r3);

is executed, the compiler will invoke the fourth constructor, which copies the values of the data members of the object **r3** into the data members of the object **r4**. Whenever a constructor is used to copy the values of data members of an object to another object, it is known as a copy constructor. The copy constructors have been discussed in detail later in this chapter.

The following example illustrates the use of constructor overloading.

Example 2

Write a program to find the area of a square.

The following is the program that will calculate the area of a square and display the resultant value on the screen.

```
//Write a program to find the area of a square          1
#include<iostream>                                       2
using namespace std;                                     3
class sqr_area                                           4
{                                                        5
    int a;                                               6
    public:                                              7
        sqr_area( )                                      8
        {                                                9
                a=1;                                     10
        }                                                11
        sqr_area(int x)                                  12
        {                                                13
                a=x;                                     14
        }                                                15
        int area( )                                      16
        {                                                17
                return a*a;                              18
        }                                                19
        void show( )                                     20
        {                                                21
                cout<<"Area of the square is: "<<area( )<<endl;   22
        }                                                23
};                                                       24
int main( )                                              25
{                                                        26
        sqr_area s1;                                     27
        s1.area( );                                      28
        s1.show( );                                      29
        sqr_area s2(10);                                 30
        s2.area();                                       31
        s2.show();                                       32
        return 0;                                        33
}                                                        34
```

Explanation
Lines 8 to 11
sqr_area( )
{

```
        a=1;
}
```

These lines contain the definition of the constructor **sqr_area( )**. Here, the argument list does not contain any argument. A call is made to this constructor when no value is passed at the time of the object creation.

Lines 12 to 15
sqr_area(int x)
```
{
        a=x;
}
```

These lines also contain the definition of the constructor **sqr_area( )**. But here, the argument list contains one integer type argument. A call is made to this constructor when one integer value is passed at the time of object creation.

Line 27
sqr_area s1;
In this line, **s1** is declared as an object of the class **sqr_area**. Here, no value is passed as an argument. So, the constructor defined in line 8 is invoked, which initializes the copy of the data member **a** of object **s1** with an initial value 1.

Line 30
sqr_area s2(10);
In this line, **s2** is declared as an object of the class **sqr_area**. Here, one integer value is passed as an argument. So, the constructor defined in line 12 is invoked, which initializes the copy of data member **a** of object **s1** with an initial value 10.

The output of the program is as follows:
Area of the square is: 1
Area of the square is: 100

Copy Constructors

As discussed in the earlier section, a copy constructor is used to copy the values of data members of an object into another object of the same class. Basically, it is used to declare and initialize an object from another object. The syntax for declaring a copy constructor is as follows:

```
    class_name (class_name &obj1);
```

In the above syntax, a reference to an object **&obj1** is passed as an argument.

For example, in class **sqr_area**, there are two objects **s1** and **s2** and you want to declare and initialize object **s2** from the object **s1**. You can do so by using the following statement:

```
    sqr_area s2(s1);
```

In this statement, the copy of data members of object **s2** is initialized with the values of the copy of data members of object **s1**.

You can also declare and initialize an object from another object of the same class, as shown in the following statement:

    class_name obj2=obj1;

For example:

    sqr_area s2=s1;

The following example illustrates the use of the copy constructor.

Example 3

Write a program to calculate the area of a square.

The following program will calculate the area of a square and display the resultant value on the screen.

```
//Write a program to calculate the area of a square       1
#include<iostream>                                         2
using namespace std;                                       3
class sqr_area                                             4
{                                                          5
    int a;                                                6
    public:                                               7
        sqr_area( )                                       8
        {                                                 9
            a=1;                                          10
        }                                                11
        sqr_area(int x)                                  12
        {                                                13
            a=x;                                         14
        }                                                15
        sqr_area(sqr_area &s)//Definition of copy constructor  16
        {                                                17
            a=s.a;                                       18
        }                                                19
        int area( )                                      20
        {                                                21
            return a*a;                                  22
        }                                                23
        void show( )                                     24
        {                                                25
            cout<<"Area of the square is: "<<area( )<<endl;  26
        }                                                27
};                                                       28
int main( )                                               29
```

```
{                                                                    30
        sqr_area s1;                                                 31
        s1.area( );                                                  32
        s1.show( );                                                  33
        sqr_area s2(10);                                             34
        s2.area();                                                   35
        s2.show();                                                   36
        sqr_area s3(s2);                                             37
        return 0;                                                    38
}                                                                    39
```

Explanation

Lines 16 to 19
sqr_area(sqr_area &s)
{
        a=s.a;
}

These lines contain the definition of the copy constructor **sqr_area( )**. Here, the reference of an object **s** of the same class **sqr_area** is passed as an argument. A call is made to this constructor, when an object is passed as an argument at the time of the object creation.

Line 37
sqr_area s3(s2);
In this line, a call is made to the copy constructor **sqr_area( )** and an object **s2** is passed as an argument. Now, the copy constructor initializes the copy of the data member of object **s3** with an initial value 10 (value of copy of data member **a** of object **s2**).

The output of the program is as follows:
Area of the square is: 1
Area of the square is: 100
Area of the square is: 100

DESTRUCTORS

Like a constructor, a destructor is also a member function. But it is used to destroy the objects that have been created by a constructor and are no longer required. The name of a destructor is the same as the name of a class but it is preceded by a **tlide** (~) symbol. The syntax for declaring a destructor is as follows:

```
~ class_name( )
{
    statements;
}
```

For example:

```
~ rectangle( );
```

In the above example, a destructor of the class **rectangle** is declared.

The most important property of a destructor is that it does not take any argument and also does not have a return type. The main task of a destructor is to free the memory space that is no longer accessible. If a destructor is not already defined in a class, the compiler will generate one. This destructor is known as the default destructor.

The following example illustrates the use of destructors.

Example 4

Write a program to illustrate the working of destructors.

The following program will create and destroy two objects of a class and display some messages at the time of creation and destruction on the screen.

```
//Write a program to create and destroy the objects of a class        1
#include<iostream>                                                     2
using namespace std;                                                   3
class demo                                                             4
{                                                                      5
        public:                                                        6
                demo( )                                                7
                {                                                      8
                        cout<<"Object created"<<endl;                  9
                }                                                      10
                ~demo( )                                              11
                {                                                     12
                        cout<<"Object destroyed"<<endl;              13
                }                                                     14
};                                                                    15
int main( )                                                           16
{                                                                     17
        demo d1;                                                     18
        {                                                            19
                demo d2;                                             20
        }                                                            21
        return 0;                                                   22
}                                                                    23
```

Explanation
Lines 11 to 14
~demo( )
{
        cout<<"Object destroyed"<<endl;
}
These lines contain the definition of a destructor **~demo( )** of the class **demo**. A call is made to the destructor **~demo( )** when an object of a class is out of scope or is no longer required.

The destructor **~demo( )** display the following on the screen:
Object destroyed

Line 18
demo d1;
In this line, **d1** is declared as an object of the class **demo**. While executing this statement, the compiler makes a call to the default constructor **demo( )**. This constructor will create an object **d1** and also display the following statement on the screen:
Object created

Line 19
{
This line indicates the start of a new block of statements.

Line 20
demo d2;
In this line, **d2** is declared as another object of the class **demo**. Object **d2** is declared in a new block. So, the scope of object **d2** is local to this block.

Line 21
}
This line indicates the end of a new block of statements. Here, the destructor is invoked by the compiler because object **d2** is out of scope and is no longer required.

Before the termination of the entire program, the destructor will be invoked again by the compiler to clean up the memory space occupied by the object **d1**.

The output of the program is as follows:
Object created
Object created
Object destroyed
Object destroyed

The output will be displayed on the screen as follows:

OPERATOR OVERLOADING

Operator overloading is another significant feature provided by C++. In operator overloading, you can overload an operator in the same way as in function overloading. Operator overloading is a technique with which you can provide a new meaning to an operator. This technique helps you to create new definitions for most of the C++ operators. Whenever an operator is overloaded, its original meaning is not lost. For example, the - (unary minus) operator is overloaded and still you can use it to subtract two numbers. While overloading, you need to provide a new definition to an operator but the syntax of the operator remains the same. For example, the * (multiplication) operator is overloaded, but its precedence remains the same (higher than addition(+) and subtraction(-) operator). You can overload almost all the operators except the following:

1. Size operator (**sizeof( )**)
2. Conditional operator (**? :**)
3. Scope resolution operator (**::**)
4. Dot operator (**.**)

Defining Operator Function

You can provide a new definition to an operator with the help of a function, which is known as an operator function. This function defines the operations that the overloaded operator will perform relative to the class to which the operator is applied. The syntax for defining an operator function is as follows:

```
return_type classname :: operator opr(argument list)
{
    body of the function;
}
```

In the above syntax, the **return_type** specifies the type of value returned by the function. The **classname** represents the class to which the operator is applied. Here, **operator** is a keyword and **opr** represents the operator that is to be overloaded.

The operator function may be a member or a non-member function of a class. If it is a non-member function, it is treated as a **friend** function of a class. The main difference between a member and a non-member function is measured by the number of arguments these functions can contain in an argument list. A non-member or a **friend** function will contain one argument for unary operators and two arguments for binary operators. Whereas, a member function will not contain any argument for unary operators and only one argument for binary operators. You should declare an operator function, member or non-member, in the **public** part of a class.

You can invoke an overloaded operator function in the following two ways:

1. For unary operators, the syntax is as follows:

   opr arg1 or arg1 opr;//For member functions
   operator opr(arg1);//For friend functions

Here, **opr** represents a unary operator and **arg1** specifies a value or an object of a class, which is passed as an argument.

2.   For binary operators, the syntax is as follows:

arg1.operator opr (arg2);//For member functions
operator opr (arg1, arg2);//For friend functions

The following example illustrates the use of operator overloading (Unary operators).

Example 5

Write a program to overload a unary increment operator (++).

The following program will overload an ++ operator, decrement all the values passed as arguments by one, and display the resultant values on the screen.

```cpp
//Write a program to overload a unary increment operator        1
#include<iostream>                                              2
using namespace std;                                           3
class overload_demo                                           4
{                                                             5
        int a, b, c;                                         6
        public:                                             7
                void input(int val1, int val2, int val3);  8
                void show( );                              9
                void operator ++( );                      10
};                                                        11
void overload_demo :: input(int val1, int val2, int val3) 12
{                                                         13
        a= val1;                                         14
        b= val2;                                         15
        c= val3;                                         16
}                                                         17
void overload_demo :: show( )                             18
{                                                         19
        cout<<a<<endl;                                   20
        cout<<b<<endl;                                   21
        cout<<c<<endl;                                   22
}                                                         23
void overload_demo :: operator++( )                      24
{                                                         25
        a= --a;                                          26
        b= --b;                                          27
        c= --c;                                          28
}                                                         29
int main( )                                               30
```

```
{                                                                                    31
        overload_demo op;                                                            32
        op.input(10, 20, 30);                                                        33
        cout<<"Values entered are: "<<endl;                                          34
        op.show( );                                                                  35
        ++op;                                                                        36
        cout<<"After invoking the operator function, the values are: "<<endl         37
        op.show( );                                                                  38
        return 0;                                                                    39
}                                                                                    40
```

Explanation
Line 10
void operator ++( );
In this line, an operator function **void operator ++( )** is declared. Here, **void** represents that no value is returned by the operator function. **++** specifies the unary increment operator, which is to be overloaded. In this case, operator function **void operator ++( )** is a member function of the class **overload_demo**. So, no argument is passed while overloading a unary operator.

Line 24 to Line 29
void overload_demo :: operator++( )
{
      a= --a;
      b= --b;
      c= --c;
}
These lines contain the definition of the operator function **operator ++( )**. Here, a new definition is supplied to the unary increment operator (**++**). In the body of the function, the values stored in variables **a**, **b**, and **c** are decremented by one.

Line 32
overload_demo op;
In this line, the variable **op** is declared as an object of the class **overload_demo**.

Line 33
op.input(10, 20, 30);
In this line, the member function **input( )** is invoked with the object **op**. Here, values 10, 20, and 30 are passed as arguments that are assigned to the copy of data members **a**, **b**, and **c** of an object **op**, respectively.

Line 36
++op;
In this line, the overloaded operator function **operator ++( )** is invoked with the object **op**. So, this function will decrement the values of data members of the object **op** by one.

The output of the program is as follows:
Values entered are:
10
20
30
After invoking the operator function, the values are:
9
19
29

The output will be displayed on the screen as follows:

In this program, a unary increment operator (++) is overloaded by using a member function. You can also overload a unary increment operator by using a non-member or a **friend** function. The only difference is that a **friend** function takes only one argument for a unary operator overloading, while a member function takes no argument. The declaration and definition of a friend function is as follows:

```
friend void operator ++(overload_demo &opr);//Declaration
void operator ++(overload_demo &opr)//Definition
{
    opr.a= --opr.a;
    opr.b= --opr.b;
    opr.c= --opr.c;
}
```

In the above definition, a reference to an object of the class **overload_demo** is passed as an argument.

In the above program, you have learned about overloading a unary operator. In the same way, you can also overload a binary operator.

The following example illustrates the use of operator overloading (Binary operator).

Example 6

Write a program to overload a binary minus operator (-).

The following program will overload a - operator and display the resultant values on the screen.

//Write a program to overload a binary minus operator   1

```
#include<iostream>                                          2
using namespace std;                                        3
class bin_demo                                              4
{                                                           5
      int a, b;                                             6
      public:                                               7
            bin_demo( ){}                                   8
            bin_demo(int x, int y)                          9
            {                                              10
                  a=x;                                     11
                  b=y;                                     12
            }                                              13
            bin_demo operator-(bin_demo);                 14
            void show();                                  15
};                                                         16
bin_demo bin_demo :: operator-(bin_demo b1)               17
{                                                          18
      bin_demo temp;                                       19
      temp.a = a - b1.a;                                   20
      temp.b = b - b1.b;                                   21
      return temp;                                         22
}                                                          23
void bin_demo :: show( )                                   24
{                                                          25
      cout<<"Value of a = "<<a<<endl;                      26
      cout<<"Value of b = "<<b<<endl;                      27
}                                                          28
int main( )                                                29
{                                                          30
      bin_demo obj1, obj2, obj3;                           31
      obj1=bin_demo(20, 10);                               32
      obj2=bin_demo(10, 5);                                33
      obj3=obj1- obj2;                                     34
      obj3.show( );                                        35
      return 0;                                            36
}                                                          37
```

Explanation
Line 8
bin_demo( ){}
In this line, a constructor **bin_demo( )** is declared. The empty curly braces {} specify that the body of the constructor does not contain any statement. A call is made to this constructor when no value is passed at the time of object creation.

Lines 9 to 13
bin_demo(int x, int y)
{

```
        a=x;
        b=y;
}
```

These lines contain the definition of the constructor **bin_demo( )**. Here, the argument list contains two integer type arguments. A call is made to this constructor when two integer values are passed at the time of object creation.

Line 14
bin_demo operator-(bin_demo);
In this line, an operator function **operator-(bin_demo)** is declared. Here, **bin_demo** specifies that this function returns an object of the class **bin_demo**. Here, **operator** is the keyword and **-** symbol represents an operator that is to be overloaded. In the argument list, **bin_demo** specifies that an object of the class **bin_demo** is passed as an argument in the function call.

Lines 17 to 23
bin_demo bin_demo :: operator-(bin_demo b1)
```
{
        bin_demo temp;
        temp.a = a - b1.a;
        temp.b = b - b1.b;
        return temp;
}
```

These lines contain the definition of the overloaded operator function **operator-(bin_demo b1)**. In line 16, the first **bin_demo** represents the return type, which specifies that an object of the class **bin_demo** will be returned by this function. The second **bin_demo** represents the class name. In the body of the function, variable **temp** is declared as an object of the class **bin_demo**. Here, a new definition is provided to the **binary minus** operator.

Line 31
bin_demo obj1, obj2, obj3;
In this line, variables **obj1**, **obj2**, and **obj3** are declared as objects of the class **bin_demo**.

Line 34
obj3=obj1- obj2;
In this line, a call is made to the overloaded operator function **operator -( )** and **obj2** is passed as an argument. The values 10 and 5 of data members **a** and **b** of **obj2** are subtracted from the values 20 and 10 of data members **a** and **b** of **obj1**. The resultant values 10 and 5 are assigned to the data members **a** and **b** of **obj3**, respectively.

The output of the program is as follows:
Value of a = 10
Value of b = 5

In this program, a binary minus operator is overloaded by using a member function. You can also overload a binary operator by using a **friend** function. The only difference is that a **friend** function takes two arguments for a binary operator, while a member function takes only one argument.

The following example illustrates the use of operator overloading (Binary operator) by using a **friend** function.

Example 7

Write a program to overload a binary minus operator (-) by using a **friend** function.

The following program will overload a - operator and display the resultant values on the screen.

```
//Write a program to overload a binary minus operator          1
#include<iostream>                                             2
using namespace std;                                          3
class bin_demo                                               4
{                                                           5
      int a, b;                                            6
      public:                                              7
              bin_demo(){}                                8
              bin_demo(int x, int y)                     9
              {                                          10
                     a=x;                               11
                     b=y;                               12
              }                                          13
      friend bin_demo operator-(bin_demo, bin_demo);   14
      void show( );                                     15
};                                                       16
bin_demo operator-(bin_demo b1, bin_demo b2)            17
{                                                       18
      return bin_demo((b1.a - b2.a), (b1.b-b2.b));     19
}                                                       20
void bin_demo :: show( )                                21
{                                                       22
      cout<<"Value of a = "<<a<<endl;                 23
      cout<<"Value of b = "<<b<<endl;                 24
}                                                       25
int main( )                                             26
{                                                       27
      bin_demo obj1, obj2, obj3;                       28
      obj1= bin_demo(20, 10);                          29
      obj2= bin_demo(10, 5);                           30
      obj3=operator-(obj1, obj2);                      31
      obj3.show( );                                     32
      return 0;                                         33
}                                                       34
```

Explanation
Line 14
friend bin_demo operator-(bin_demo, bin_demo);

In this line, a friend operator function **operator-(bin_demo, bin_demo)** is declared. The argument list contains two objects of the class **bin_demo**. These objects specify that the two objects of the same class will be passed when a call is made to this function.

Line 31
obj3=operator-(obj1, obj2);
In this line, a call is made to the overloaded operator function **operator-(obj1, obj2)**. Here, two objects **obj1** and **obj2** are passed as arguments.

The output of the program is as follows:
Value of a = 10
Value of b = 5

Self-Evaluation Test

Answer the following questions and then compare them to the answers given at the end of this chapter:

1. A _____ is used to initialize the objects of a class.

2. A _____ is used to free the memory space.

3. A destructor name is preceded by a _____ symbol.

4. A _____ constructor is used to copy one object into another object of the same class.

5. The mechanism of providing a new definition to an operator is known as _____.

Review Questions

Answer the following questions:

1. Define a constructor and also describe its syntax.

2. Define a copy constructor. How is it different from a default constructor? Explain with a suitable example.

3. Define a destructor and also describe its syntax.

4. What is operator overloading?

5. What is the main difference between overloading a unary operator by using a member function and a **friend** function?

Exercise

Exercise 1

Write a program to create a class **employee** that contains the following constructors and member functions:

1. employee (int emp_id)
2. employee (int emp_id, char name[20])
3. void show( )

The program should use an array of objects to read the information of ten employees and display them on the screen.

Answers to Self-Evaluation Test

1. constructor, **2.** destructor, **3. tlide**, **4.** copy, **5.** operator overloading

Chapter 10

Inheritance

Learning Objectives

After completing this chapter, you will be able to:

- *Understand inheritance.*
- *Understand single inheritance.*
- *Understand multilevel inheritance.*
- *Understand multiple inheritance.*
- *Understand hierarchical inheritance.*
- *Understand hybrid inheritance.*
- *Understand virtual base classes.*

INTRODUCTION

In this chapter, you will learn about another feature of OOP that is known as reusability. Reusability provides a mechanism with which you can reuse something that already exists. This mechanism saves time because you do not need to create the same thing again and again. In C++, reusability is used in the case of classes. Once a class has been written and debugged, it can be used in several ways. In C++, reusability is used by creating a new class from an existing class by reusing its properties. The technique of creating a new class from an old one is known as inheritance or derivation. The new class is known as derived class or subclass and the old class (which is inherited) is known as base class. A derived class can inherit some or all the properties of a base class. A derived class can also add some properties on its own. The syntax for defining a derived class is as follows:

```
class derived_class_name : access_specifier base_class_name
{
    data members;
    access_specifier:
            member functions;
};
```

In the above syntax, the name of the derived class is represented by **derived_class_name**. Here, the colon (**:**) specifies that the derived class represented by **derived_class_name** is derived from the base class represented by **base_class_name**. The **access_specifier** specifies the visibility, which indicates how the data members and member functions of a base class can be accessed by the objects of the derived class. An access specifier can be **public** or **private**. If no access specifier is defined, it is **private** by default.

For example:

```
class derived_demo : public base_demo
{
    data members of derived_demo;
    public:
            member functions of derived_demo;
}
```

In the above example, the base class **base_demo** is publicly inherited by the derived class **derived_demo**. The public members of the base class can be accessed by the objects of the derived class because they become public to the derived class.

A base class can be privately inherited, as shown in the following example:

```
class derived_demo : private base_demo
{
    data members of derived_demo;
    public:
    member functions of derived_demo;
};
```

OR

```
class derived_demo : base_demo//Private by default
{
    data members of derived_demo;
    public:
            member functions of derived_demo;
};
```

You can use any of the above examples for inheriting a base class. The base class **base_demo** is privately inherited by the derived class **derived_demo**. The public members of the class **base_demo** become private to the class **derived_demo**. They can only be accessed by member functions of the derived class but they cannot be directly accessed by its objects.

In C++, inheritance is of the following five types:

1. Single inheritance
2. Multilevel inheritance
3. Multiple inheritance
4. Hierarchical inheritance
5. Hybrid inheritance

Single Inheritance

When a class is inherited from a single base class, it is called single inheritance.

For example:

```
class base_demo
{
    int a;//Private member
    public:
            int b;
            void get(int x, int y)
            {
                    a=x;
                    b=y;
            }
            void show( );
};
class derived_demo : public base_demo
{
    ----------;
    ----------;
    ----------;
};
```

In the above example, the class **derived_demo** publicly inherits the properties from a single base class **base_demo**. The **private** data member **a** of the base class **base_demo** cannot be directly accessed by the objects of the class **derived_demo**. Figure 10-1 represents **single inheritance**. The following example illustrates the use of single inheritance (public).

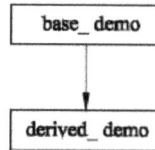

Figure 10-1 *Single inheritance*

Write a program that will calculate the area of a rectangle.

Example 1

The following program will calculate the area of a rectangle and display the resultant value on the screen. The line numbers on the right are not a part of the program and are for reference only.

```
//Write a program to find the area of a rectangle          1
#include<iostream>                                          2
using namespace std;                                        3
class rectangle                                             4
{                                                           5
        int length;                                         6
        public:                                             7
                int width;                                  8
                void getdata( )                             9
                {                                          10
                        length=10;                         11
                        width=10;                          12
                }                                          13
                int getlength( )                           14
                {                                          15
                        return length;                     16
                }                                          17
                void show( )                               18
                {                                          19
                        cout<<"Length = "<<length<<endl;   20
                        cout<<"Width = "<<width<<endl;      21
                }                                          22
};                                                         23
class rect_area : public rectangle                         24
{                                                           25
        int result;                                        26
        public:                                            27
```

```
                    void area( )                                          28
                    {                                                     29
                            result= width * getlength( );                 30
                    }                                                     31
                    void display( )                                       32
                    {                                                     33
                            cout<<"Length = "<<getlength( )<<endl;        34
                            cout<<"Width  = "<<width<<endl;               35
                            cout<<"Area   = "<<result<<endl;              36
                    }                                                     37
};                                                                        38
int main( )                                                               39
{                                                                         40
        rect_area r1;                                                     41
        r1.getdata( );                                                    42
        r1.area( );                                                       43
        r1.getlength( );                                                  44
        r1.display( );                                                    45
        r1.width=20;                                                      46
        r1.area( );                                                       47
        r1.display( );                                                    48
        return 0;                                                         49
}                                                                         50
```

Explanation

Line 6

int length;

In this line, **length** is declared as an integer type variable. The variable **length** is the **private** data member of the class **rectangle**. It can be accessed only with the help of the **public** member functions of the same class.

Lines 14 to 17

int getlength( )
{
      return length;
}

These lines contain the definition of the member function **getlength( )**. Whenever a call is made to this function, it will return a value of the variable **length**.

Line 24

class rect_area : public rectangle

In this line, the class **rect_area** publicly inherits the properties (data member, member functions) of the base class **rectangle**. Only the **public** data members and member functions of the class **rectangle** (base class) are inherited by the objects of the class **rect_area** (derived class). The **private** data members can also be accessed but only with the **public** member functions of the class **rectangle**.

Line 26
int result;
The **result** is declared as an integer type variable. This data member is declared in the **private** section of the class **rect_area**. It can be accessed directly by the objects of the same class.

Lines 28 to 31
void area( )
{
        result= width * getlength( );
}
These lines contain the definition of the member function **area( )**. In the body of the function, the **public** data member **width** of the base class **rectangle** is accessed directly but the **private** data member **length** of the base class is accessed with the help of a **public** member function **getlength( )**. After multiplication, the resultant value is assigned to the variable **result**.

Line 41
rect_area r1;
Here, variable **r1** is declared as an object of the derived class **rect_area**.

Line 46
r1.width=20;
In this line, value 20 is assigned to the **public** data member **width** of the class **rectangle**, which is directly accessed by an object **r1** of the derived class **rect_area**.

The output of the program is as follows:
Length = 10
Width = 10
Area   = 100
Length = 10
Width = 20
Area   = 200

Figure 10-2 represents single inheritance (public), as discussed in Example 1.

In the previous program, the base class **rectangle** was publicly inherited by the derived class **rect_area**. In this section, you will learn about **single inheritance** with **private** derivation. When a class is privately inherited, the **public** data members and member functions of the base class become **private** in the derived class. So, these members are not directly accessed by the objects of the derived class.

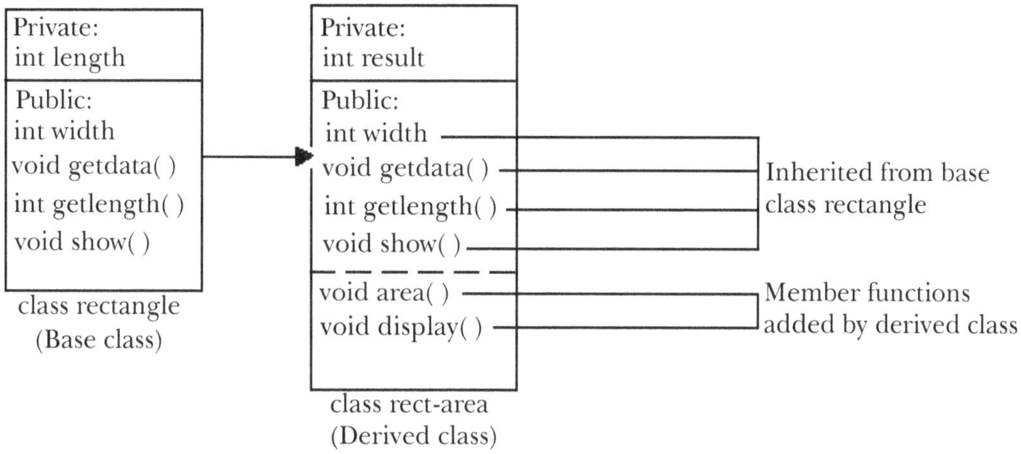

Figure 10-2 *Representation of Example 1*

The following example illustrates the use of single inheritance (private).

Example 2

Write a program to calculate the area of a rectangle.

The following program will calculate the area of a rectangle and display the resultant value on the screen.

```
//Write a program to calculate the area of a rectangle            1
#include<iostream>                                                 2
using namespace std;                                              3
class rectangle                                                   4
{                                                                 5
        int length;                                              6
        public:                                                  7
                int width;                                       8
                void getdata()                                   9
                {                                                10
                        cout<<"Enter the length of a rectangle: ";  11
                        cin>>length;                             12
                        cout<<"Enter the width of a rectangle: ";   13
                        cin>>width;                              14
                }                                                15
        int getlength( )                                         16
        {                                                        17
                return length;                                   18
        }                                                        19
        void show( )                                             20
        {                                                        21
```

```
        cout<<"Length = "<<length<<endl;                    22
        cout<<"Width  = "<<width<<endl;                      23
    }                                                        24
};                                                           25
class rect_area : private rectangle//Private derivation      26
{                                                            27
    int result;                                              28
    public:                                                  29
        void area( )                                         30
        {                                                    31
            getdata( );                                      32
            result= width * getlength( );                    33
        }                                                    34
        void display( )                                      35
        {                                                    36
            show( );                                         37
            cout<<"Result = "<<result<<endl;                 38
        }                                                    39
};                                                           40
int main( )                                                  41
{                                                            42
    rect_area r1;                                            43
    r1.area( );                                              44
    r1.display( );                                           45
    return 0;                                                46
}                                                            47
```

Explanation

Line 26

class rect_area : private rectangle

In this line, the base class **rectangle** is privately inherited by the derived class **rect_area**. Now, the **public** members such as **width**, **getlength( )**, and so on of the class **rectangle** become **private** members of the derived class **rect_area**. So, the objects of the class **rect_area** do not access these members directly.

The output of the program is as follows:
Enter the length of a rectangle: 10
Enter the width of a rectangle: 20
Length =10
Width = 20
Area = 200

The output will be displayed on the screen as follows:

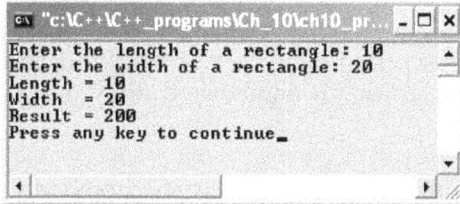

```
cv  "c:\C++\C++_programs\Ch_10\ch10_pr...  _ □ ×
Enter the length of a rectangle: 10
Enter the width of a rectangle: 20
Length = 10
Width  = 20
Result = 200
Press any key to continue_
```

Figure 10-3 represents single inheritance (private), as discussed in Example 2.

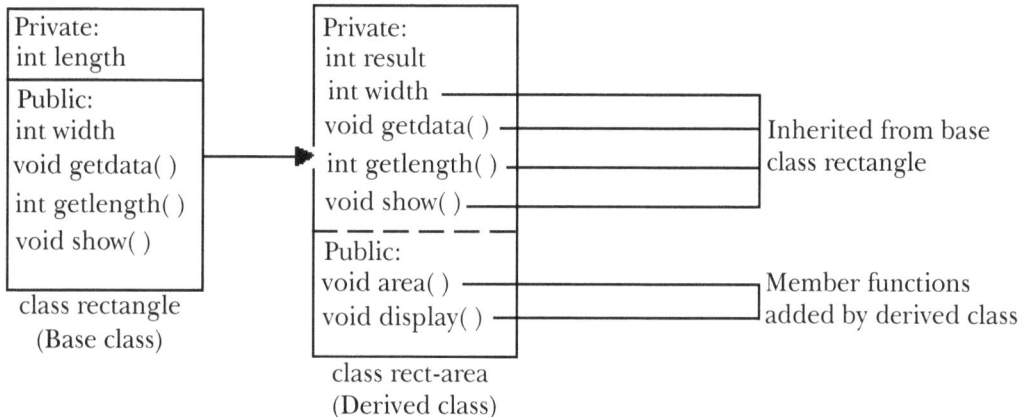

Figure 10-3 *Representation of Example 2*

Making the Private Members of a Base Class Inheritable

In the earlier sections, you have seen that the **private** members of a base class cannot be inherited and are not directly available to the derived class. In case the **private** data needs to be inherited by a derived class, you can simply do it by modifying the visibility limit of a **private** member by making it **public** or **protected**.

When the visibility limit of **private** members of a base class is changed to **public**, the members are accessible by all the functions within the same class and also, by the functions of the other classes. This method makes the members **public**, and this eliminates the feature of data hiding.

Another way is to change the visibility limit of the **private** members of a base class by declaring them as **protected** members. This results in only a limited access to the members of a class. The **protected** members of a class are only accessed by the members of the same class and any class that is immediately derived from it. The syntax for defining **protected** members in the definition of a class is given next.

```
class class_name
{
    protected:
            data members;
```

```
                    member functions( );
    };
```

In the above syntax, the **protected** members can be accessed by the members of the class specified by **class_name** and by the members of the class that is immediately derived from the class **class_name**.

When the **protected** members are inherited in the **public** mode, they become protected in the derived class. So, they are directly accessed by the member functions of the derived class and can be further inherited.

For example:

```
    class rectangle
    {
        protected:
                int length;
        public:
                int width;
                void getdata( );
                void show( );

    };
    class rect_area : public rectangle
    {
        int result;
        public:
        void area( )
        {
                getdata( );
                result=width * length;
        }
        void display( );
    };
```

In the above example, the class **rectangle** is publicly inherited by the class **rect_area**. The **protected** member **length** in the base class **rectangle** becomes **protected** in the derived class **rect_area**, as shown in Figure 10-4. So it can be directly accessed by the member functions of the derived class, as shown in the following statement:

```
    result=width * length;
```

In this statement, the **protected** data member **length** is directly accessed by the member function **area( )** in the derived class.

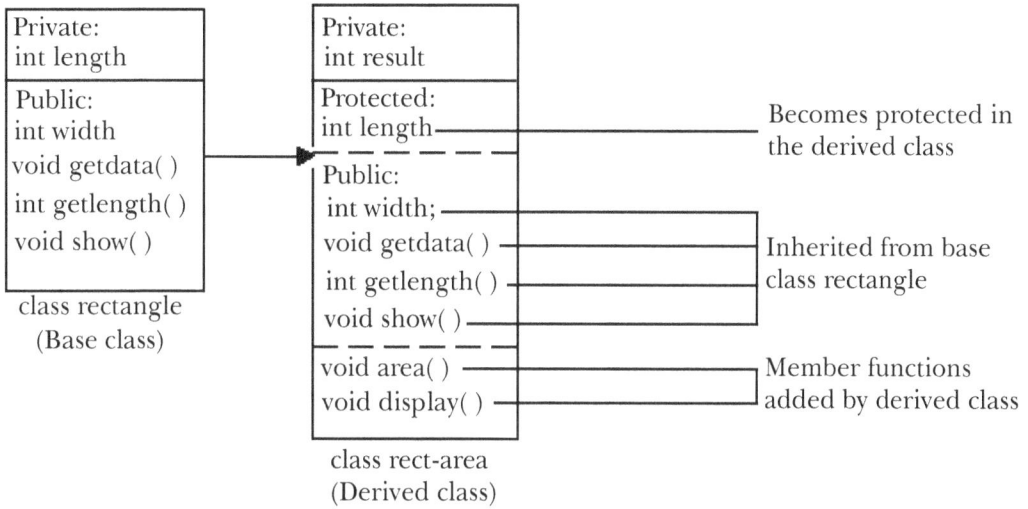

Figure 10-4 *Protected members inherited in the* **public** *mode*

When the **protected** members are inherited in the **private** mode, they become **private** in the derived class. They are accessed by the member functions of the derived class but they cannot be further inherited. Figure 10-5 shows a representation of a protected member inherited in the **private** mode.

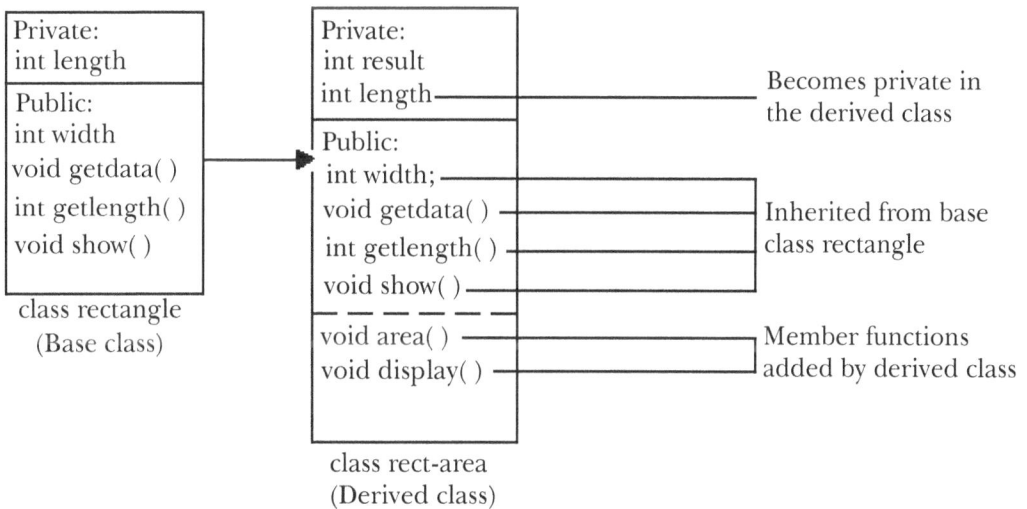

Figure 10-5 *Protected members inherited in the* **private** *mode*

As shown in Figure 10-5, the **protected** data member **length** of the base class became **private** in the derived class.

A base class can also be inherited in the **protected** mode. The **public** and **protected** members of the base class become **protected** in the derived class. So, they are directly accessed by the member functions of the derived class and are also available for further inheritance.

For example:

```
class base_demo
{
    int a;    //By default private
    protected:
            int b;
    public:
            void getdata( );
            void show( );
};
class derived_demo : protected base_demo
{
    int c;
    public:
            int sum( );
            void display( );
};
```

In the above example, the base class **base_demo** is inherited by the class **derived_demo** in the **protected** mode. The **protected** data member **b** and the **public** member functions, **getdata( )** and **show( )** become **protected** members of the class **derived_demo**, as shown in Figure 10-6.

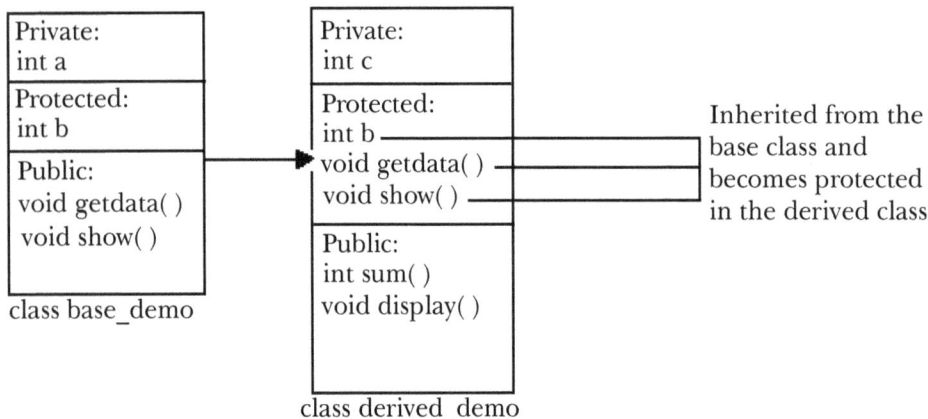

Figure 10-6 *A base class inherited in the* **protected** *mode*

Multilevel Inheritance

When a class is derived from another derived class, it is known as multilevel inheritance, as shown in Figure 10-7.

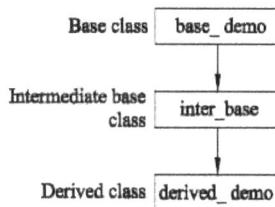

Figure 10-7 *Multilevel inheritance*

In the above figure, the class **base_demo** represents the base class, which is inherited by another class **inter_base**. Now, the derived class **inter_base** is inherited by another class **derived_demo**. Here, the **inter_base** class works as a base class for the class **derived_demo**. The class **inter_base** is also known as the **intermediate base class**.

The syntax for declaring classes that contain multilevel inheritance is as follows:

```
class base_demo
{
    data members;
    public:
            member functions;
};
class inter_demo : public base_demo
{
    data members;
    public:
            member functions;
};
class derived_demo : public inter_demo
{
    data members;
    public:
            member functions;
};
```

In the above syntax, the class **base_demo** represents the base class, which is publicly inherited by another class **inter_demo**. Now, the class **inter_demo** is publicly inherited by another class **derived_demo**. Here, the class **inter_demo** serve as a base class for the class **derived_demo**.

The following example illustrates the use of multilevel inheritance.

Example 3

Write a program to calculate the average of points by using multilevel inheritance.
The following program will prompt the users to enter their information and also the points scored in three subjects. The program will then calculate the average and display the information as well as the average on the screen.

```
//Write a program to calculate the average of the points entered by the user    1
#include<iostream>                                                              2
using namespace std;                                                            3
class student//Base class                                                       4
{                                                                               5
        char name[30];                                                          6
        int stu_id;                                                             7
        char course[10];                                                        8
        public:                                                                 9
                void getdata( );                                                10
                void showdata( );                                               11
};                                                                              12
void student ::  getdata( )                                                     13
{                                                                               14
        cout<<"Enter name: ";                                                   15
        cin>>name;                                                              16
        cout<<"Enter the student ID: ";                                         17
        cin>>stu_id;                                                            18
        cout<<"Enter course: ";                                                 19
        cin>>course;                                                            20
}                                                                               21
void student :: showdata( )                                                     22
{                                                                               23
        cout<<"Name: "<<name<<endl;                                             24
        cout<<"Student ID: "<<stu_id<<endl;                                     25
        cout<<"Course: "<<course<<endl;                                         26
}                                                                               27
class points : public student//First level of inheritance                       28
{                                                                               29
        protected:                                                              30
                float sub[3];                                                   31
        public:                                                                 32
                void get_points( );                                             33
                void show_points( );                                            34
};                                                                              35
void points :: get_points( )                                                    36
{                                                                               37
        for(int i=0; i<3; i++)                                                  38
        {                                                                       39
```

```
                cout<<"Enter the points scored in subject"<<i+1<<": ";        40
                cin>>sub[i];                                                  41
        }                                                                     42
}                                                                             43
void points :: show_points( )                                                 44
{                                                                             45
        for(int j=0; j<3; j++)                                                46
        {                                                                     47
                cout<<"Points scored in subject"<<j+1<<" are: ";              48
                cout<<sub[j]<<endl;                                           49
        }                                                                     50
}                                                                             51
class average : public points//Second level of inheritance                   52
{                                                                             53
        float avrg;                                                          54
        public:                                                              55
                void result( );                                              56
};                                                                           57
void average :: result( )                                                    58
{                                                                             59
        avrg= (sub[0]+sub[1]+sub[2])/3;                                      60
        showdata( );                                                         61
        show_points( );                                                     62
        cout<<"Average: "<<avrg<<endl;                                      63
}                                                                            64
int main( )                                                                  65
{                                                                            66
        average a1;                                                         67
        a1.getdata( );                                                      68
        a1.get_points( );                                                   69
        cout<<"----------------------------------"<<endl;                   70
        a1.result( );                                                       71
        return 0;                                                           72
}                                                                            73
```

Explanation

Lines 4 to 12

class student

{

       char name[30];

       int stu_id;

       char course[10];

       public:

              void getdata( );

              void showdata( );

};

These lines contain the definition of the class **student**, which contains three data members **name**, **stu_id**, **course** and two member functions, **getdata( )** and **showdata( )**. Here, the class **student** is treated as a base class.

Lines 28 to 35
class points : public student
{
        protected:
                float sub[3];
        public:
                void get_points( );
                void show_points( );
};

The class **points** publicly inherits the properties of the base class **student**. So, the private data members of the base class **student** are not directly accessed by the objects of the derived class **points**. The definition of the class **points** contains a **protected** data member **sub**, which is an array of a **float** type with the maximum size 3. It also contains two member functions, **get_points( )** and **show_points( )**. After inheritance, the class **points** contains data members and member functions, as shown in Figure 10-8.

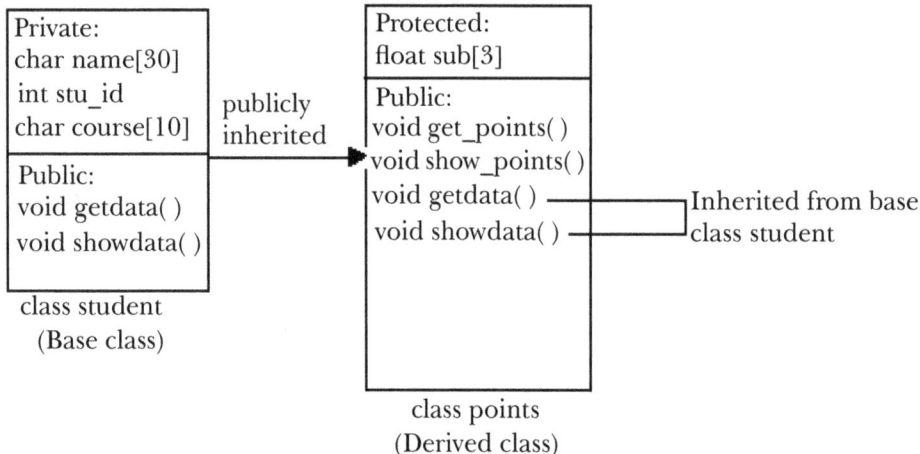

Figure 10-8 *First level of inheritance*

The above figure represents the first level of inheritance in which the base class **student** is inherited by the class **points**. After **public** inheritance, the **public** members of the base class become the **public** members of the derived class.

Lines 52 to 57
class average : public points
{
        float avrg;
        public:
                void result( );
};

The derived class **points** is treated as a base class for the class **average**. The class **average** publicly inherits the properties of the class **points**. So, the **protected** members of the class **points** can be directly accessed by the objects of the derived class **average**. After inheritance, the class **average** contains data members and member functions, as shown in Figure 10-9.

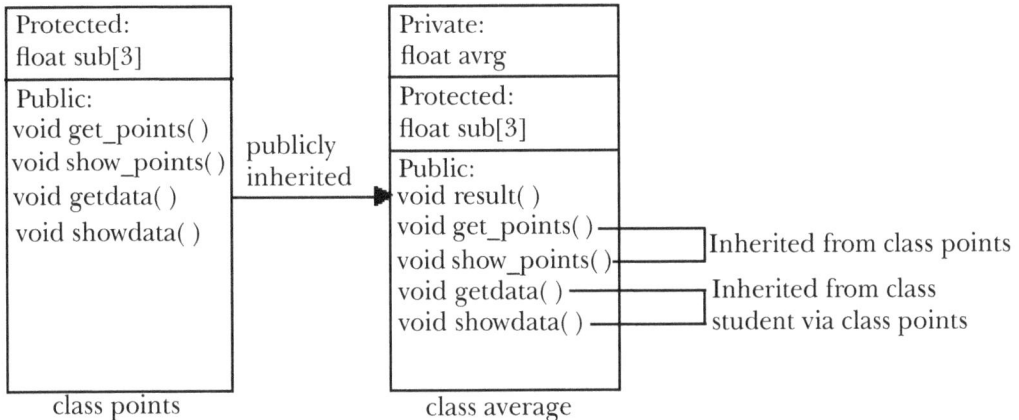

Figure 10-9 *Second level of inheritance*

The above figure represents the second level of inheritance in which the derived class **points** is inherited by another class **average**. Here, the class **points**, which is a derived class, is treated as a base class for the class **average**.

Line 67
average a1;
In this line, the variable **a1** is declared as an object of the class **average**.

Line 68
a1.getdata( );
In the first level of inheritance, all the **public** members of the base class **student** become **public** members of the derived class **points**. In the second level, all the **public** members of the class **points** become **public** members of the class **average**. So now, the **getdata( )** member function is directly accessed by an object **a1** of the class **average**.

The output of the program is as follows:
Enter name: John
Enter the student ID: 201
Enter course: MBA
Enter the points scored in subject1: 78
Enter the points scored in subject2: 80
Enter the points scored in subject3: 82

Name: John
Student ID: 201
Course: MBA

Points scored in subject1 are: 78
Points scored in subject2 are: 80
Points scored in subject3 are: 82
Average: 80

The output will be displayed on the screen as follows:

Multiple Inheritance

When a class inherits the properties from two or more base classes, it is known as multiple inheritance. In multiple inheritance, a class is derived by inheriting the properties of two or more than two base classes, as shown in Figure 10-10.

This figure represents multiple inheritance. In this figure, the derived class, which is specified by **Derived_class**, inherits the properties from the base classes specified by **Base_class1** to **Base_classN**.

The syntax is as follows:

```
class Derived_class : access_specifier Base_class1, ....., access_specifier Base_classN
{
     data_members;
     public:
             member functions;
};
```

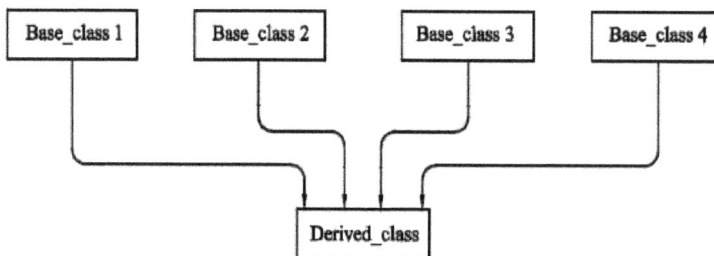

Figure 10-10 Representation of multiple inheritance

In this syntax, the base classes that are specified by **Base_class1** to **Base_classN** are separated by commas.

For example:

```
class average : public student, public points
{
    float avrg;
    public:
            void result( );
};
```

In the above example, the class **average** publicly inherits the properties of two classes **student** and **points**.

The following example illustrates the use of multiple inheritance.
Write a program to calculate the average of points by using multiple inheritance.

The following program will prompt the users to enter their information and also the points scored in three subjects. The program will then calculate the average and display the information as well as the average on the screen.

```
//Write a program to calculate the average of the points entered by the user    1
#include<iostream>                                                              2
using namespace std;                                                           3
class student                                                                   4
{                                                                               5
    char name[30];                                                             6
    int stu_id;                                                                7
```

Example 4

```
    char course[10];                                                           8
    public:                                                                    9
            void getdata( );                                                   10
            void showdata( );                                                  11
};                                                                             12
void student :: getdata( )                                                     13
{                                                                              14
    cout<<"Enter name: ";                                                      15
    cin>>name;                                                                 16
    cout<<"Enter the student ID: ";                                            17
    cin>>stu_id;                                                               18
    cout<<"Enter course: ";                                                    19
    cin>>course;                                                               20
}                                                                              21
void student :: showdata( )                                                    22
{                                                                              23
```

```
        cout<<"Name: "<<name<<endl;                              24
        cout<<"Student ID: "<<stu_id<<endl;                      25
        cout<<"Course: "<<course<<endl;                          26
}                                                                27
class points                                                     28
{                                                                29
        protected:                                               30
                float sub[3];                                    31
        public:                                                  32
                void get_points( );                              33
                void show_points( );                             34
};                                                               35
void marks :: get_points( )                                      36
{                                                                37
        for(int i=0; i<3;i++)                                    38
        {                                                        39
                cout<<"Enter the points scored in subject"<<i+1<<": ";   40
                cin>>sub[i];                                     41
        }                                                        42
}                                                                43
void marks :: show_points( )                                     44
{                                                                45
    for(int j=0; j<3; j++)                                       46
    {                                                            47
        cout<<"Points scored in subject"<<j+1<<" are: ";         48
        cout<<sub[j]<<endl;                                      49
    }                                                            50
}                                                                51
class average : public student, public points                   52
{                                                                53
        float avrg;                                              54
        public:                                                  55
                void result( );                                  56
};                                                               57
void average :: result( )                                        58
{                                                                59
        avrg = (sub[0]+sub[1]+sub[2])/3;                         60
        showdata( );                                             61
        show_points( );                                          62
        cout<<"Average: "<<avrg<<endl;                           63
}                                                                64
int main( )                                                      65
{                                                                66
        average a1;                                              67
        a1.getdata( );                                           68
        a1.get_points( );                                        69
        cout<<"--------------------------------"<<endl;          70
```

```
        a1.result( );                                          71
        return 0;                                              72
}                                                              73
```

Explanation

Line 52

class average : public student, public points

Here, the class **average** publicly inherits the properties of the class **student** and the class **points**. After inheritance, the class **average** contains data members and member functions, as shown in Figure 10-11.

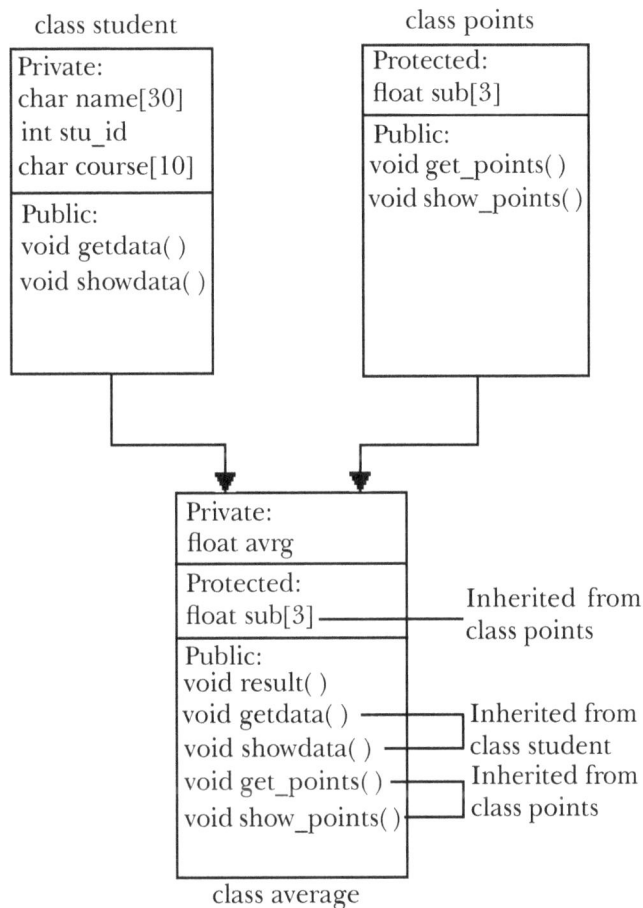

Figure 10-11 *Members of the class average after inheritance*

The output of the program is as follows:

Enter name: John

Enter student ID: 201

Enter course: MBA

Enter the points scored in subject1: 78
Enter the points scored in subject2: 80
Enter the points scored in subject3: 82

Name: John
Student ID: 201
Course: MBA
Points scored in subject1 are: 78
Points scored in subject2 are: 80
Points scored in subject3 are: 82
Average: 80

In multiple inheritance, when a class inherits the properties from more than one base class, the problem of ambiguity may occur. When a function with the same syntax (same name, same return type) exists in more than one base class, it is known as ambiguity.

For example:

```
class A
{
    public:
            void display( )
            {
                    cout<<"You are in class A"<<endl;
            }
};
class B
{
    public:
            void display( )
            {
                    cout<<"You are in class B"<<endl;
            }
};
```

In the above code, both the classes **A** and **B** contain a member function **void display( )** whose syntax is the same in both the classes.

```
class C : public A, public B
{
    public:
            void show( )
            {
                    display( );
            }
};
```

The class **C** publicly inherits the properties from the base classes **A** and **B**. When a call is made to the function **display( )** in the **public** member function **show( )** in class **C**, it will give an error. This error is because of an ambiguity in the program. This ambiguity can be removed by using the name of a class and a scope resolution operator **(::)** with a name of the function, as follows:

```
class C : public A, public B
{
    public:
            void show( )
            {
                    A :: display( );
            }
};
```

In the above code, the class name **A** and the scope resolution operator **(::)** is used with the function **display( )**. This means that the member function **display( )** of the class **A** will be called whenever a call is made to the function **show( )** of the class **C**.

In the above case, you have seen that the problem of ambiguity arises when a single class inherits the properties from more than one base class. This problem can also arise in the case of single inheritance in which a single class inherits the properties from a single base class.

For example:

```
class X
{
    public:
            void show( )
            {
                    cout<<"You are in class A"<<endl;
            }
};
class Y : public X
{
    public:
            void show( )
            {
                    cout<<"You are in class B"<<endl;
            }
};
```

In this example, the member function **show( )** of the derived class **Y** overrides the member function **show( )** of the base class **X**. So, whenever a call is made to the **show( )** function with an object of class **Y**, the compiler will invoke the **show( )** function defined in the derived class.

You can also invoke the function defined in the base class by specifying the class name and a scope resolution operator with the function name as follows:

```
int main( )
{
    Y y1;
    y1.show( );//make a call to show( ) in derived class Y
    y1.X::show( );//make a call to show( ) in base class X
    y1.Y::show( );//make a call to show( ) in derived class Y
    return 0;
}
```

Hierarchical Inheritance

In hierarchical inheritance, the classes are arranged in a hierarchy based on the properties they contain. The base class is at the top of the hierarchy and contains all the properties that are common to the subclasses. A subclass can be derived by inheriting the properties of the base class. In hierarchical inheritance, a subclass can function as a base class for the lower level of classes. Figure 10-12 represents a hierarchical classification of students in a college. In this figure, the **Students** class contains the properties that are common to the subclasses (Management, Computers, and Engineering). The **Management** class serves as a base class for the lower level of classes (Marketing, Finance, and Human Resource).

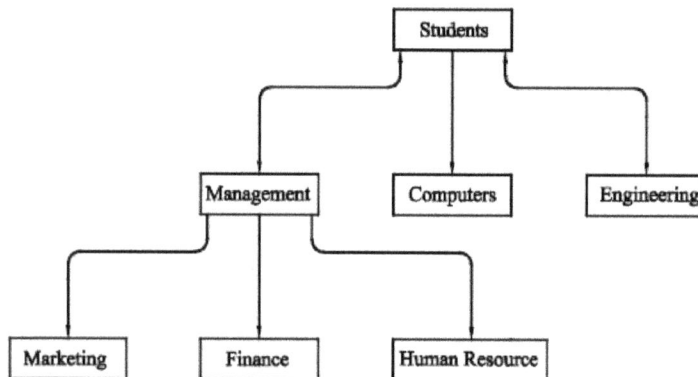

Figure 10-12 Representation of hierarchical inheritance

Hybrid Inheritance

In general terms, a variety, which is a composite of mixed origins is called a hybrid form. In the same way, in C++, when two or more than two types of inheritances are used to design a program, it is known as hybrid inheritance. For example, if in a program two types of inheritance, multilevel and multiple are used, this mixed type of inheritance is known as hybrid inheritance, see Figure 10-13.

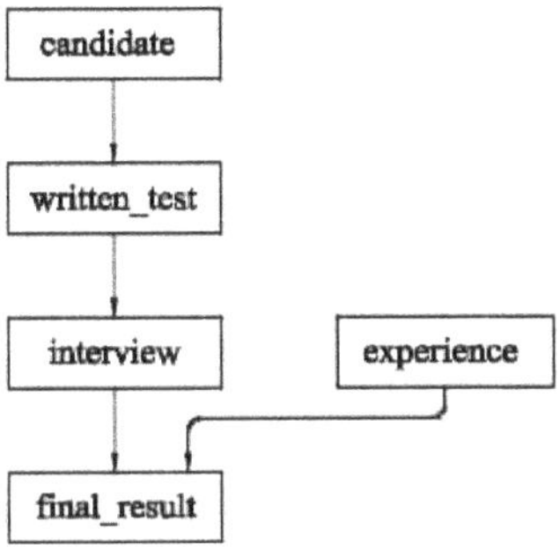

Figure 10-13 Example of hybrid inheritance

The following example illustrates the use of hybrid inheritance.

Example 5

Write a program to calculate the final result of candidates in an interview by using hybrid inheritance.

The following program will prompt the user to enter his information and the points scored in the tests, calculate the final result, and display it on the screen.

```
//Write a program to illustrate the working of hybrid inheritance          1
#include<iostream>                                                          2
using namespace std;                                                       3
class candidate                                                            4
{                                                                          5
        protected:                                                        6
        char name[20];                                                    7
        int ref_num;                                                      8
        public:                                                           9
                void getdata( )                                           10
                {                                                         11
                        cout<<"Enter the name of the candidate: ";        12
                        cin>>name;                                        13
                        cout<<"Enter the reference number: ";             14
                        cin>>ref_num;                                     15
                }                                                         16
                void showdata( )                                          17
                {                                                         18
                        cout<<"Name: "<<name<<endl;                       19
                        cout<<"Reference number: "<<ref_num<<endl;        20
                }                                                         21
};                                                                        22
class written_test : public candidate//Level 1 of multilevel inheritance  23
{                                                                         24
```

```
        protected:                                                          25
        float apt_points;                                                   26
        float tech_points;                                                  27
        public:                                                             28
                void getpoints( )                                           29
                {                                                           30
                        cout<<"Enter the points scored in the Aptitude test: ";   31
                        cin>>apt_points;                                    32
                        cout<<"Enter the points scored in the Technical test: ";  33
                        cin>>tech_points;                                   34
                }                                                           35
                void showpoints( )                                         36
                {                                                           37
                        cout<<"Points scored in the Aptitude test are: "
                           <<apt_points<<endl;                              38
                        cout<<"Points scored in the Technical test are: "
                           <<tech_points;                                   39
                        cout<<endl;                                         40
                }                                                           41
};                                                                          42
class interview: public written_test//Level 2                               43
{                                                                           44
        protected:                                                          45
        float tech_score;                                                   46
        float hr_score;                                                     47
        public:                                                             48
                void getscore( )                                            49
                {                                                           50
                        cout<<"Enter the points scored "
                             "in the Technical interview: ";                51
                        cin>>tech_score;                                    52
                        cout<<"Enter the points scored in the HR interview: ";  53
                        cin>>hr_score;                                      54
                }                                                           55
                void showscore( )                                          56
                {                                                           57
                        cout<<"Points scored in the Technical interview are: "
                           <<tech_score<<endl;                              58
                        cout<<"Points scored  in the HR interview are: "
                           <<hr_score<<endl;                                59
                }                                                           60
};                                                                          61
class experience                                                            62
{                                                                           63
        protected:                                                          64
        float years;                                                        65
        public:                                                             66
```

```
                    void get_exp( )                                  67
                    {                                                68
                            cout<<"Enter experience: ";              69
                            cin>>years;                              70
                    }                                                71
                    void show_exp( )                                 72
                    {                                                73
                            cout<<"Experience in years: "<<years<<endl;  74
                    }                                                75
};                                                                   76
class final_result: public interview, public experience//Multiple inheritance  77
{                                                                    78
        float result;                                                79
        public:                                                      80
        void show_result( );                                         81
};                                                                   82
void final_result:: show_result( )                                   83
{                                                                    84
        result= apt_points + tech_points + tech_score + hr_score + years;  85
        showdata( );                                                 86
        showpoints( );                                               87
        showscore( );                                                88
        show_exp( );                                                 89
        cout<<"Total score: "<<result<<endl;                         90
}                                                                    91
int main( )                                                          92
{                                                                    93
        final_result candidate_1;                                    94
        candidate_1.getdata( );                                      95
        candidate_1.getpoints( );                                    96
        candidate_1.getscore( );                                     97
        candidate_1.get_exp( );                                      98
        candidate_1.show_result( );                                  99
        return 0;                                                    100
}                                                                    101
```

The output of the program is as follows:
Enter the name of the candidate: John
Enter the reference number: 101
Enter the points scored in the Aptitude test: 5
Enter the points scored in the Technical test: 6
Enter the points scored in the Technical interview: 6
Enter the points scored in the HR interview: 7
Enter experience: 1
Name: John
Reference number: 101
Points scored in the Aptitude test are: 5

Points scored in the Technical test are: 6
Points scored in the Technical interview are: 6
Points scored in the HR interview are: 7
Experience in years: 1
Total score: 25

The output will be displayed on the screen as follows:

VIRTUAL BASE CLASSES

In the previous section, you learned about hybrid inheritance, in which two or more than two types of inheritances were used to design a program. But sometimes, when all the three types of inheritances multiple, multilevel, and hierarchical are used in hybrid inheritance to design a program, a problem of ambiguity may occur, see Figure 10-14.

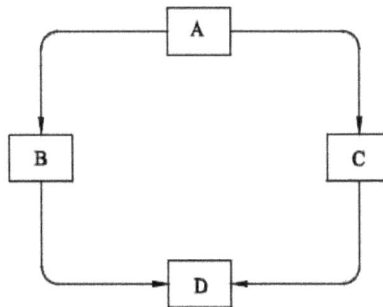

Figure 10-14 *Multipath inheritance*

In the above figure, classes **B** and **C** both inherit the base class **A**, whereas the class **D** inherits the classes **B** and **C**. Here, the class **D** indirectly inherits the properties of the base class **A** twice through classes **B** and **C**. So, all the **public** and the **protected** members of the base class **A** are inherited twice by the class **D**. Therefore, the class **D** contains duplicate copies of the members of the base class **A**. This problem of duplicacy or ambiguity can be solved by declaring the base class **A** as a **virtual** class.

When a common base class is declared as a **virtual** base class, only one copy of that class is inherited by the derived class through all the multiple paths. The syntax for declaring a **virtual** base class is as follows:

```
class A
{
    class definition;
};
class B : public virtual A
{
    class definition;
};
class C : virtual public A
{
    class definition;
};
class D : public B, public C
{
    class definition;
};
```

In the above syntax, the base class **A** is declared as a **virtual** base class, which is publicly inherited by the classes **B** and **C**. Here, class **B** and **C** are publicly inherited by the derived class **D**. The class **D** indirectly inherits the base class **A** through the two paths, but class **D** contains only one copy of the members of the base class **A**. This is because the base class **A** has been declared as a **virtual** base class.

In the previous syntax, the following statements

```
public virtual A
     or
virtual public A
```

are the same. You can use the keyword **virtual** before or after the access specifier.

The following example illustrates the use of the **virtual** base class.

Example 6

Write a program to illustrate the working of the **virtual** base class.

The following program will multiply three numbers and display the resultant value on the screen.

```
//Write a program to multiply three numbers                     1
#include<iostream>                                               2
using namespace std;                                            3
class A                                                          4
{                                                               5
    public:                                                     6
            int a;                                              7
};                                                              8
```

```
class B : public virtual A                                          9
{                                                                   10
        public:                                                     11
                int b;                                              12
};                                                                  13
class C : virtual public A                                          14
{                                                                   15
        public:                                                     16
                int c;                                              17
};                                                                  18
class D : public B, public C                                        19
{                                                                   20
        public:                                                     21
                int mul;                                            22
};                                                                  23
int main( )                                                         24
{                                                                   25
        D d1;                                                       26
        d1.a=10;                                                    27
        d1.b=10;                                                    28
        d1.c=10;                                                    29
        d1.mul= d1.a * d1.b * d1.c;                                 30
        cout<<"The result of multiplication is: "<<d1.mul<<endl;    31
        return 0;                                                   32
}                                                                   33
```

The output of the program is as follows:
The result of multiplication is: 1000

Self-Evaluation Test

Answer the following questions and then compare them to the answers given at the end of this chapter:

1. The technique of creating a new class from an existing class is known as _____.

2. A _____ class can inherit some or all the properties of a _____ class.

3. When a class is privately inherited, the **public** members of the base class become _____ in the derived class.

4. When a class is derived from another derived class, it is known as _____ inheritance.

5. The problem that occurs during multiple inheritance is known as _____.

Review Questions

Answer the following questions:

1. Define inheritance. What is the main advantage of inheritance?

2. Explain the different types of inheritance.

3. Differentiate between **public** and **private** members of a class. Explain the difference with a suitable example.

4. Explain multiple inheritance with a suitable example. What is the main problem that occurs during multiple inheritance?

5. What do you mean by a **virtual** base class?

Exercise

Exercise 1

Write a program to calculate the final result of some students. This program should contain the four classes, which are discussed next.

1. Class **student**, which contains two **protected** data members, **student_id**, and **name**. It should also contain **public** member functions to accept the values of the data members from the user and display them on the screen. The class **student** should be declared as the **virtual** base class.

2. Class **test**, which publicly inherits the properties of the base class **student**. This class should contain a data member, **test_points** and also two member functions to read the points scored from the user and display them on the screen.

3. Class **exam**, which publicly inherits the properties of the base class **student**. This class should contain a data member, **final_points** and also two member functions to read the points scored from the user and display them on the screen.

4. Class **result**, which publicly inherits both the classes, **test** and **exam**. This class should contain a data member, **total_result** and also two member functions to calculate the final result of the student and display it on the screen.

Answers to Self-Evaluation Test

1. inheritance, **2.** derived, base, **3. private**, **4.** multilevel, **5.** ambiguity

Chapter 11

Virtual
Functions
and
Polymorphism

Learning Objectives

After completing this chapter, you will be able to:

- *Understand polymorphism.*
- *Understand virtual functions.*
- *Understand pure virtual functions.*
- *Understand abstract classes.*

INTRODUCTION

In this chapter, you will learn about virtual functions and also about polymorphism, which is another feature of Object-Oriented Programming (OOP). Polymorphism means 'one name many forms'. The virtual function is a member function, which is declared or defined in the base class and again redefined in the derived class.

POLYMORPHISM

Polymorphism is a Greek term that consists of two words, poly and morph. Poly means many and morph means forms. So, polymorphism means 'one name many forms'. The best example of polymorphism is overloading, which is already implemented during function and operator overloading. In overloading, you must have observed that more than one function with the same name is presented in a single program. In C++, polymorphism is of two types, compile time polymorphism and run time polymorphism, see Figure 11-1.

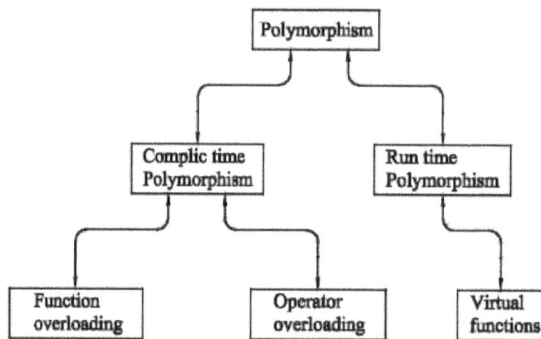

Figure 11-1 *Types of polymorphism*

Compile Time Polymorphism, Early Binding, or Static Binding

When the required information to call a function is known to the compiler at the compile time, it is known as compile time polymorphism, early binding, or static binding. Early binding means that an object is bound to its function call at the compile time. Examples of early binding are overloaded function calls, overloaded operator calls, and so on. The main advantage of early binding is that it is efficient and fast because all the information required to make a call to a function is known by the compiler at the compile time.

Run Time Polymorphism, Late Binding, or Dynamic Binding

When the required information to call a function is known to the compiler at the execution time or runtime, it is known as run time polymorphism, late binding, or dynamic binding. This binding is in complete contrast to early binding. In this type of polymorphism, an appropriate member function is selected dynamically during the execution time. This type of polymorphism is accomplished by using **virtual** functions.

Virtual Functions

A **virtual** function is a member function of the base class, which is overridden by the derived class. In the derived class, the entire body of the function declared in the base class is replaced with a new set of instructions and it performs different operations. A virtual function is declared in the base class with the help of the keyword **virtual**. The syntax for defining a **virtual** function is as follows:

```
virtual return_type fun_name ( list of arguments)
{
    body of the function;
}
```

The main difference between a virtual and a nonvirtual member function is that a nonvirtual member function is selected by the compiler at the compile time, whereas the **virtual** function is selected dynamically at the runtime or execution time.

The following example illustrates the use of the **virtual** functions.

Example 1

Write a program to illustrate the working of the **virtual** functions.

The following program will display the strings, based on a function call, on the screen. The line numbers on the right are not a part of the program and are for reference only.

```
//Write a program to illustrate the use of virtual functions    1
#include<iostream>                                              2
using namespace std;                                           3
class base_demo                                                4
{                                                              5
        public:                                                6
        virtual void vdemo( )                                  7
        {                                                      8
                cout<<"Base class"<<endl;                      9
        }                                                      10
        void show( )                                           11
        {                                                      12
                cout<<"Base class function"<<endl;             13
        }                                                      14
};                                                             15
class derived_demo : public base_demo                          16
{                                                              17
        public:                                                18
        void vdemo( )                                          19
        {                                                      20
                cout<<"Derived class"<<endl;                   21
        }                                                      22
```

```
        void show( )                                              23
        {                                                         24
                cout<<"Derived class function"<<endl;             25
        }                                                         26
};                                                                27
int main( )                                                       28
{                                                                 29
        base_demo b, *base_ptr;                                   30
        derived_demo d;                                           31
        base_ptr = &b;                                            32
        base_ptr->vdemo( );                                       33
        base_ptr->show( );                                        34
        base_ptr = &d;                                            35
        base_ptr->vdemo( );                                       36
        base_ptr->show( );                                        37
        return 0;                                                 38
}                                                                 39
```

Explanation

Lines 7 to 10
virtual void vdemo( )
{
        cout<<"Base class"<<endl;
}
Lines 7 to 10 contain the definition of the **virtual** function **vdemo( )** of the base class **base_demo**.

Lines 11 to 14
void show( )
{
        cout<<"Base class function"<<endl;
}
Lines 11 to 14 contain the definition of the member function **show( )** of the base class
base_demo.

Line 16
class derived_demo : public base_demo
Here, the class **derived_demo** publicly inherits the properties of the base class **base_demo**.

Lines 19 to 22
void vdemo( )
{
        cout<<"Derived class"<<endl;
}
In these lines, the **virtual** function **vdemo( )** of the base class **base_demo** is overridden by
the derived class **derived_demo** and a new definition is provided to the function **vdemo( )**.

Lines 23 to 26

```
void show( )
{
        cout<<"Derived class function"<<endl;
}
```

Here, the **public** member function **show( )** of the base class **base_demo** is overridden by the derived class **derived _demo**.

Line 30
base_demo b, *base_ptr;
In this line, the variable **b** is declared as an object of the base class **base_demo** and the pointer variable ***base_ptr** is declared as a pointer to the base class.

Line 31
derived_demo d;
Here, the variable **d** is declared as an object of the derived class **derived_demo**.

Line 32
base_ptr = &b;
In this line, the starting address of an object **b** of the base class is assigned to the pointer variable **base_ptr**.

Line 33
base_ptr->vdemo( );
In this line, a call is made to the virtual member function **vdemo( )** of the base class with the help of the pointer **base_ptr**. This pointer contains the starting address of an object **b** of the base class. This function will display the following statement on the screen:
Base class

Line 34
base_ptr->show( );
In this line, a call is made to the public member function **show( )** of the base class with the help of the pointer **base_ptr**. This pointer contains the starting address of an object **b** of the base class. This function will display the following statement on the screen:
Base class function

Line 35
base_ptr = &d;
In this line, the starting address of an object **d** of the derived class is assigned to the pointer variable **base_ptr**. Now, the pointer variable points to an object **d** of the derived class.

Line 36
base_ptr->vdemo( );
In this line, a call is made to the overridden virtual member function **vdemo( )** of the derived class with the help of the pointer **base_ptr**, which contains the starting address of an object **d** of the derived class. This function will display the following statement on the screen:
Derived class

Line 37
base_ptr->show( );
The pointer variable **base_ptr** points to an object **d** of the derived class but here it makes a call to the public member function **show( )** of the base class. This is because the member function **show( )** is not declared as a **virtual** function in the base class. This function will display the following statement on the screen:
Base class function

The output of the program is as follows:
Base class
Base class function
Derived class
Base class function

The output will be displayed on the screen as follows:

```
◼ "c:\C++\C++_programs\Ch_11\ch11_...  _ □ ✕
Base class                                    ▲
Base class function
Derived class
Base class function
Press any key to continue
                                              ▼
◄                                          ►  ⁄⁄
```

In the above program, you have observed that the **virtual** member function of the base class is overridden by the derived class. Sometimes, there is a situation when the derived class is not able to override the **virtual** member function of the base class. In that case, whenever an object of the derived class accesses the **virtual** member function, the function defined in the base class is executed.

The following example illustrates the use of the **virtual** functions.

Example 2

Write a program to illustrate the working of the **virtual** functions.

The following program will display the strings, based on a function call, on the screen.

```
//Write a program to illustrate the use of virtual functions    1
#include<iostream>                                               2
using namespace std;                                            3
class base_demo                                                 4
{                                                               5
        public:                                                 6
        virtual void vdemo( )                                   7
        {                                                       8
                cout<<"Base class"<<endl;                       9
```

```
        }                                                          10
        void show( )                                               11
        {                                                          12
                cout<<"Base class function"<<endl;                 13
        }                                                          14
};                                                                 15
class derived_demo1 : public base_demo                             16
{                                                                  17
        public:                                                    18
        void vdemo( )                                              19
        {                                                          20
                cout<<"Derived class"<<endl;                       21
        }                                                          22
        void show( )                                               23
        {                                                          24
                cout<<"First derived class function"<<endl;        25
        }                                                          26
};                                                                 27
class derived_demo2 : public base_demo                             28
{                                                                  29
        public:                                                    30
                void show( )                                       31
                {                                                  32
                        cout<<"Second derived class function"<<endl; 33
                }                                                  34
};                                                                 35
int main( )                                                        36
{                                                                  37
        base_demo b, *base_ptr;                                    38
        derived_demo1 d;                                           39
        derived_demo2 d1;                                          40
        base_ptr = &b;                                             41
        base_ptr->vdemo( );                                        42
        base_ptr->show( );                                         43
        base_ptr = &d;                                             44
        base_ptr->vdemo( );                                        45
        base_ptr->show( );                                         46
        base_ptr = &d1;                                            47
        base_ptr->vdemo( );                                        48
        return 0;                                                  49
}                                                                  50
```

Explanation

Lines 28 to 35

class derived_demo2 : public base_demo
{
        public:
                void show( )
                {

cout<<"Second derived class function"<<endl;
        }
};

These lines contain the definition of the derived class **derived_demo2**, which publicly inherits the properties of the base class **base_demo**. Here, the virtual member function **vdemo( )** of the base class **base_demo** is not overridden by the class **derived_demo2**.

Line 40
derived_demo2 d1;
Here, the variable **d1** is declared as an object of the derived class **derived_demo2**.

Line 47
base_ptr = &d1;
In this line, the starting address of an object **d1** of the derived class **derived_demo2** is assigned to the pointer variable **base_ptr**.

Line 48
base_ptr->vdemo( );
In this line, the pointer variable **base_ptr** points to an object **d1** of the derived class **derived_demo2**. The pointer also makes a call to the **virtual** member function **vdemo( )** of the base class. This is because the **virtual** member function **vdemo( )** is not overridden in the derived class **derived_demo2**. This function will display the following statement on the screen:
Base class

The output of the program is as follows:
Base class
Base class function
Derived class
Base class function
Base class

The output will be displayed on the screen as follows:

```
"c:\C++\C++_programs\Ch_11...
Base class
Base class function
Derived class
Base class function
Base class
Press any key to continue_
```

Pure Virtual Functions

In the previous example, you have observed that the **virtual** member function of the base class is not overridden by the derived class. In such a case, the function defined in the base class is accessed. However, there may be a situation when the **virtual** function is not defined in the base class. In such a case, C++ supports the pure **virtual** function.

A pure **virtual** function is a virtual function, which does not contain any definition within the base class. The syntax for declaring a pure **virtual** function is as follows:

virtual return_type fun_name(list of arguments) =0;

In the case of pure **virtual** function, when a derived class is not able to override the **virtual** member function of the base class, a compile-time error occurs.

The following example illustrates the use of the pure **virtual** functions.

Example 3

Write a program to add and multiply two integer values.

The following program will add and multiply two numbers and display the resultant values on the screen.

```
//Write a program to add and multiply two integer values    1
#include<iostream>                                           2
using namespace std;                                         3
class values                                                 4
{                                                            5
        protected:                                           6
        int a;                                               7
        int b;                                               8
        public:                                              9
                void getvalues(int arg1, int arg2)          10
                {                                           11
                        a=arg1;                             12
                        b=arg2;                             13
                }                                           14
                virtual void result( )=0;//Pure virtual function  15
};                                                          16
class sum : public values                                   17
{                                                           18
        public:                                             19
                void result( )                              20
                {                                           21
                        int c;                              22
                        c = a + b;                          23
                        cout<<"After addition,"
                                "the resultant value is: "<<c<<endl;  24
                }                                           25
};                                                          26
class multiply : public values                              27
```

```
{                                                              28
        public:                                                29
                void result( )                                 30
                {                                              31
                        int c;                                 32
                        c = a * b;                             33
                        cout<<"After multiplication,"
                                "the resultant value is: "<<c<<endl;  34
                }                                              35
};                                                             36
int main( )                                                    37
{                                                              38
        sum s1;                                                39
        multiply m1;                                           40
        s1.getvalues(10,20);                                   41
        s1.result( );                                          42
        m1.getvalues(10,10);                                   43
        m1.result( );                                          44
        return 0;                                              45
}                                                              46
```

Explanation

Line 15
virtual void result( )=0;
In this line, a pure **virtual** function **result( )** of the base class **values** is declared.

Lines 20 to 25
void result( )
{
        int c;
        c = a + b;
        cout<<"After addition,"
                "the resultant value is: "<<c<<endl;
}
In these lines, the pure **virtual** function **result( )** is overridden by the derived class **sum**, which publicly inherits the properties of the base class **values**.

Lines 30 to 35
void result( )
{
        int c;
        c = a * b;
        cout<<"After multiplication,"
                "the resultant value is: "<<c<<endl;
}
In these lines, the pure **virtual** function **result( )** is overridden by the derived class **multiply**, which publicly inherits the properties of the base class **values**.

The output of the program is as follows:
After addition, the resultant value is: 30
After multiplication, the resultant value is: 100

Abstract Classes

An abstract class is a class that contains atleast one pure **virtual** function. These types of classes cannot be used to create objects. You can only create pointers and references to an abstract class. An abstract class acts as a base class on which the other classes can be built. Refer to Example 3, where the class **values** is an abstract class and acts as a base class for the two derived classes, class **sum** and class **multiply**.

Self-Evaluation Test

Answer the following questions and then compare them to the answers given at the end of this chapter:

1. When one name is used in different forms, it is known as _____.

2. In static binding, all the needed information to call a function is known to the compiler at the _____.

3. Operator overloading is an example of _____ binding.

4. A member function of the base class, which is overridden by the derived class, is known as a _____ function.

5. When a base class contains at least one _____ function, it is known as an abstract class.

Review Questions

Answer the following questions:

1. Define polymorphism with a suitable example.

2. Differentiate between compile time and runtime polymorphism.

3. Define **virtual** functions with suitable examples.

4. Define pure **virtual** functions.

5. Define an abstract class with a suitable example.

Exercise

Exercise 1

Write a program to find the area of a rectangle and a triangle by using pure **virtual** functions.

Answers to Self-Evaluation Test
1. polymorphism, 2. compile time, 3. early, 4. virtual, 5. pure virtual

Chapter 12

The C++ Console I/O Operations

Learning Objectives

After completing this chapter, you will be able to:

- *Understand streams.*
- *Understand predefined streams.*
- *Understand the concept of overloaded << and >> operators.*
- *Understand formatted I/O operations.*

INTRODUCTION

In all programming languages, there are certain statements that are used to read the input from the user, process it, and provide the output in the desired form. In C++, the **cin** statement with the **>>** operator is used to read the input from the user and the **cout** statement with the **<<** operator is used to provide the output in the desired form. So, you need to be aware of certain concepts such as how a program extracts the data from an input device or inserts the processed data to an output device. For this purpose, C++ uses the concepts of streams and stream classes. These concepts help in managing the I/O operations with the console (user screen) and disk files. In this chapter, you will learn about the console oriented I/O operations.

A stream is a flow or a sequence of bytes through a system.

The classes, which are used to define the various streams that are used to manage the I/O operations with the console and disk files, are known as the stream classes.

STREAMS IN C++

As you already know that a stream is a flow or a sequence of bytes through a system. It acts as an interface between an input or output device and a program. The following are the two types of streams:

1. Input stream
2. Output stream

Input Stream

A stream from which a program gets the input data is known as an input stream. An input stream can get the data from a keyboard or any other input or storage device. It acts as a source to the program because a program extracts the data from it, as shown in Figure 12-1.

Figure 12-1 *Representation of an input stream*

In the above figure, the data in the input stream comes from the input device and it is extracted by the program.

Output Stream

A stream, which gets the data from a program is known as an output stream. Here, an output stream act as a destination to the program, as shown in Figure 12-2.

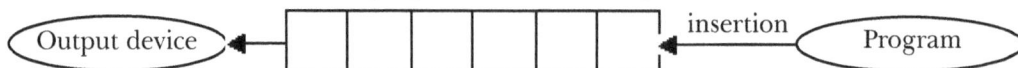

Figure 12-2 *Representation of an output stream*

In Figure 12-2, the processed data in the output stream is inserted by the program and it is provided to the output device.

STREAM CLASSES IN C++

The classes defining various streams that are used to manage the I/O operations with the console and disk files are known as the stream classes. Figure 12-3 represents a hierarchy of the stream classes that are used to manage the console oriented I/O operations.

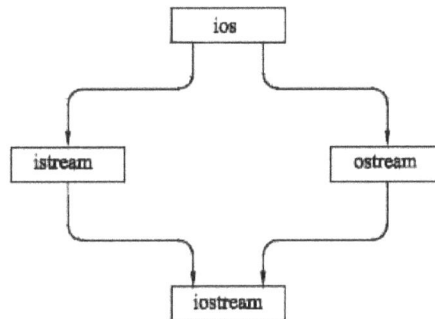

Figure 12-3 *The stream classes that manage the console I/O operations*

In the above figure, there are four main classes **ios**, **istream**, **ostream**, and **iostream**, which are used for managing console oriented I/O operations. The **ios** (Input output stream) class, which acts as a base class for the **istream** (input stream) and the **ostream** (output stream), is declared as a **virtual** base class. So, only a single copy of its members exists. This copy is inherited by the derived classes. The **ios** class contains the member functions that are used for formatted and unformatted console I/O operations. Both the derived classes **istream** and **ostream** act as the base classes for the class **iostream** (Input/Output stream). The **istream** class contains member functions that are used for formatted and unformatted inputs. The **ostream** class contains member functions that are used for formatted and unformatted outputs. The **iostream** class contains the member functions that are used for both the input and output streams.

THE PREDEFINED STREAMS

In C++, whenever a program starts its execution, there are some streams that are automatically included in the program. These streams are known as predefined streams. The following are the predefined streams in C++:

1. cin
2. cout
3. cerr
4. clog

The **cin** is an input stream that is connected to an input device, which can be a keyboard, any other input device, or any storage device.

The **cout** is an output stream that is connected to an output device, which can be a screen or any other output device.

The **cerr** is an error output stream, which is used to write an unbuffered (not saved) output to the standard error device, which is usually a screen.

The **clog** is a buffered version of **cerr**, which is used to write the buffered (saved) output to the standard error device, which is usually a screen.

OVERLOAD >> AND << OPERATORS

You have already learned that the **>>**(extraction) and **<<**(insertion) operators are used with **cin** and **cout** statements, respectively. In C++, these operators are already overloaded when the I/O operations are performed on C++'s built-in types. You can also overload these operators, so that they perform I/O operations on user-defined types. The **>>** operator is overloaded in the **istream** class and the **<<** operator is overloaded in the **ostream** class.

Overload An Insertion (<<) Operator

An insertion operator (**<<**) is overloaded in the **ostream** class. The syntax for overloading an insertion operator (**<<**) is as follows:

```
ostream &operator<<( ostream &stream, class_type obj)
{
    statements;
    return stream;
}
```

In the above syntax, the overloaded **<<** function returns a reference to an object of the **ostream** class. The argument list contains two arguments: the first argument is a reference to the output stream and the second argument is an object of the class, which is specified by the **class_type**. In the second argument, you can also pass the reference to an object of the class. The body of the function contains the statements, which specify the operation that you want to perform. This function should contain a return statement, which returns a stream.

The following example illustrates the concept of overloading an insertion operator (**<<**).

Example 1

Write a program to obtain information about some students from the user and then display it by using the overloaded insertion operator (**<<**).

The following is the program that will display the information of students on the screen. The line numbers on the right are not a part of the program and are for reference only.

```
//Write a program to obtain information about some students
//and display it on the screen                                    1
#include<iostream>                                                 2
```

```
using namespace std;                                              3
class student                                                     4
{                                                                 5
        public:                                                   6
        char name[40];                                            7
        int stu_id;                                               8
        char course[10];                                          9
        student( char *n,  int r,  char *c)                      10
        {                                                        11
                strcpy(name, n);                                 12
                stu_id = r;                                      13
                strcpy(course, c);                               14
        }                                                        15
};                                                               16
ostream &operator <<(ostream &stream, student s1)                17
{                                                                18
        stream <<"Name: "<<s1.name <<endl;                      19
        stream <<"Student ID: "<<s1.stu_id <<endl;              20
        stream <<"Course: "<<s1.course <<endl;                  21
        return stream;                                          22
}                                                                23
int main( )                                                      24
{                                                                25
        student stu1("John", 101, "BBA");                       26
        student stu2("William", 310, "MBA");                    27
        student stu3("Smith", 510, "MS");                       28
        cout<<stu1 <<stu2 << stu3;                              29
        return 0;                                               30
}                                                                31
```

Explanation

Line 10

student(char *n, int r, char *c)

In this line, a constructor **student(char *n, int r, char *c)** of the class **student** is defined and the argument list contains three arguments: a character type pointer **n**, an integer type variable **r**, and a character type pointer **c**.

Line 12

strcpy(name, n);

In this line, the **strcpy** (String copy) function is used to copy the string pointed by the pointer variable **n** into the **public** data member **name**.

Line 13

stu_id = r;

In this line, the value of the variable **r** is assigned to the public data member **stu_id**.

Line 14
strcpy(course, c);
In this line, the **strcpy** (String copy) function is used to copy the string pointed by the pointer variable **c** into the public data member **course**.

Lines 17 to 23
ostream &operator <<(ostream &stream, student s1)
{
        cout <<"Name: "<<s1.name <<endl;
        cout <<"Student ID: "<<s1.stu_id <<endl;
        cout <<"Course: "<<s1.course <<endl;
        return stream;
}
These lines contain the definition of the overloaded operator (**<<**) function. The argument list contains two arguments: the first argument **&stream** is a reference to the output stream **ostream** and the second argument is an object **s1** of the class **student**. This function will return a stream of the type output stream.

Line 26
student stu1("John", 101, "BBA");
In this line, an object **stu1** of the class **student** is declared and three values are passed as arguments. These values are assigned to the copy of the data members **name, stu_id**, and **course** of the object **stu1**.

Line 29
cout<<stu1 <<stu2 << stu3;
In this line, the insertion operator (**<<**) is used three times and so the overloaded operator function will also be called three times. The three objects **stu1, stu2**, and **stu3** are passed to the overloaded operator function one by one.

The output of the program is as follows:
Name: John
Student ID: 101
Course: BBA
Name: William
Student ID: 310
Course: MBA
Name: Smith
Student ID: 510
Course: MS

The output will be displayed on the screen as follows:

In this example, the overloaded **<<** operator function is not a member of the class **student**. So, it can access only the public data members **name**, **stu_id**, and **course** of the class **student**. There are two methods by which this function can access the private data members of the class: the first is to make the private data members **public**, and the second is to declare the overloaded operator function **<<** as a **friend** of the class **student**. The second method is better as compared to the first method for solving a problem as in the first method the data is made **public** and so it can be accessed by anyone.

The following example illustrates the concept of overloading an insertion operator (**<<**).

Example 2

Write a program to obtain information about some students and then display it by using an overloaded insertion operator (**<<**) function (friend of the class).

The following program will display the information of some students on the screen.

```
//Write a program to display the information of some students
//and display it on the screen                                    1
#include<iostream>                                                 2
using namespace std;                                              3
class student                                                     4
{                                                                 5
        char name[40];                                            6
        int stu_id;                                               7
        char course[10];                                          8
        public:                                                   9
        student( char *n,  int r,  char *c)                      10
        {                                                        11
                strcpy(name, n);                                 12
                stu_id = r;                                      13
                strcpy(course, c);                               14
        }                                                        15
        friend ostream &operator <<(ostream &stream, student s1); 16
};                                                               17
```

```
ostream &operator <<(ostream &stream, student s1)              18
{                                                               19
        stream <<"Name: "<<s1.name <<endl;                     20
        stream <<"Student ID: "<<s1.roll_num <<endl;           21
        stream <<"Course: "<<s1.course <<endl;                 22
        return stream;                                         23
}                                                              24
int main( )                                                    25
{                                                              26
        student stu1("John", 101, "BBA");                      27
        student stu2("William", 310, "MBA");                   28
        student stu3("Smith", 510, "MS");                      29
        cout<<stu1 <<stu2 << stu3;                             30
        return 0;                                              31
}                                                              32
```

Explanation
Line 16
friend ostream &operator <<(ostream &stream, student s1);
In this line, the overloaded operator function **<<** is declared as the **friend** of the class **student**.
Now, it can access the private data members **name, stu_id, and course** of the class **student**.

The output of the program is as follows:
Name: John
Student ID: 101
Course: BBA
Name: William
Student ID: 310
Course: MBA
Name: Smith
Student ID: 510
Course: MS

Overload An Extraction >> Operator
You can also overload an extraction operator (**>>**) in the same way as the insertion operator (**<<**). The extraction operator (**>>**) is overloaded in the **istream** class. The syntax for overloading an insertion operator (**<<**) is as follows:

```
istream &operator >>(istream &stream, class_type &obj)
{
    statements;
    return stream;
}
```

In the above syntax, the overloaded operator **>>** function returns a reference to an object of the **istream** class. The argument list contains two arguments: the first argument is a reference to a stream of the type **istream** and the second argument is a reference to an object of the class, which is specified by the **class_type**. The body of the function contains the statements, which specify the operation that you want to perform. This function should contain a return statement, which returns a stream.

The following example illustrates the concept of overloading an extraction operator (**>>**).

Example 3

Write a program to obtain information about the account holders of a bank and then display it by using an overloaded extraction operator (**>>**).

The following program will display the information of the account holders of a bank on the screen.

```
//Write a program to obtain information about the account holders of a bank   1
#include<iostream>                                                            2
using namespace std;                                                          3
class acc_details                                                             4
{                                                                             5
      char name[40];                                                          6
      int acc_num;                                                            7
      public:                                                                 8
            acc_details( ) { };                                               9
            acc_details(char *n, int a)                                       10
            {                                                                 11
                  strcpy(name, n);                                            12
                  acc_num=a;                                                  13
            }                                                                 14
            friend ostream &operator <<(ostream &stream, acc_details a1);     15
            friend istream &operator >>(istream &stream, acc_details &a1);    16
};                                                                            17
ostream &operator <<(ostream &stream, acc_details a1)                         18
{                                                                             19
      stream <<"Name: " <<a1.name<<endl;                                      20
      stream <<"Account Number: " <<a1.acc_num<<endl;                         21
      return stream;                                                          22
}                                                                             23
istream &operator >>(istream &stream, acc_details &a1)                        24
{                                                                             25
      cout<<"Enter name: ";                                                   26
      stream>>a1.name;                                                        27
      cout<<"Enter account number: ";                                        28
      stream>>a1.acc_num;                                                     29
      return stream;                                                          30
}                                                                             31
```

```
int main( )                                                          32
{                                                                    33
        acc_details acc1;                                            34
        cin >> acc1;                                                 35
        cout << acc1;                                                36
        return 0;                                                    37
}                                                                    38
```

Explanation

Line 15

friend ostream &operator <<(ostream &stream, acc_details a1);

In this line, the overloaded operator **<<** function is declared as the **friend** of the class **acc_details**. Now, it can access the private data members **name** and **acc_num** of the class **acc_details**. The argument list contains two arguments, a reference to a stream of type **ostream**, and an object **a1** of the class **acc_details**.

Line 16

friend istream &operator >>(istream &stream, acc_details &a1);

In this line, the overloaded operator **>>** **function** is declared as the **friend** of the class **acc_details**. Now, it can access the private data members **name** and **acc_num** of the class **acc_details**. The argument list contains two arguments, a reference to a stream of type **istream**, and a reference to an object **a1** of the class **acc_details**.

Line 34

acc_details acc1;

In this line, the variable **acc1** is declared as an object of the class **acc_details**.

Line 35

cin >> acc1;

In this line, when the extraction operator (**>>**) is encountered, a call is made to the overloaded operator **>>** function and the control is transferred to line 24.

Line 36

cout << acc1;

In this line, when the insertion operator (**<<**) is encountered, a call is made to the overloaded operator **<<** function and the control is transferred to line 18.

The output of the program is as follows:
Enter name: Smith
Enter account number: 1002
Name: Smith
Account Number: 1002

The output will be displayed on the screen as follows:

```
 ▄ "c:\C++\C++_programs\Ch_12\ch..   _ □ ✕
Enter name: Smith                          ▲
Enter account number: 1002                 ▨
Name: Smith
Account Number: 1002
Press any key to continue_


                                           ▼
◄                              ►
```

FORMATTED I/O OPERATIONS

The input/output (I/O) system in C++ also provides you facilities with which you can format the I/O operations. You can format these operations in the following two ways:

1. By using the member functions and the flags of the **ios** class.
2. By using manipulators.

Formatting the Output by Using the ios Members

The **ios** class contains a number of member functions, which are used to format the input/output operations. The following list contains some important functions that are widely used.

1. width( )
2. precision( )
3. fill( )
4. setf( )
5. unsetf( )

The width( ) Function

Whenever an output is produced, the space occupied by the output value is equal to the number of characters it contains to display it (default specification). You can also specify a minimum field size to display an output by using the **width( )** function. The syntax for defining the **width( )** function is as follows:

    cout.width(size);

In the above syntax, the argument **size** represents the field width (number of columns). The **width( )** function is used to specify the field width for the value that immediately follows it. This function can only specify the field width for a single value at a time.

For example:

    cout.width(10);
    cout<< "Hello";

This example will produce the output, as shown in Figure 12-4.

					H	e	l	l	o

Figure 12-4 *Representation of the output*

In the above example, an integer value 10 (Number of columns in which the output will be printed) is passed to the **width( )** function, which specifies the field width size. The string **Hello** is printed at the right end of the field, as shown in Figure 12-4.

Also, the **width(10)** function is used for a single value **Hello**. After printing **Hello**, the next output will be printed by using the default specifications.

For example:

```
cout.width(10);
cout<<"Hello";
cout<<"Hi";
```

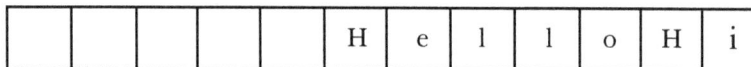

					H	e	l	l	o	H	i

Figure 12-5 *Representation of the output*

The above example will produce the output, as shown in Figure 12-5.

In the above figure, you have observed that after printing **Hello**, the next value **Hi** is printed by using the default specifications because the field width size is not specified for it. You can also pass an integer value as the field width size for the value **Hi**, as shown in the following example:

```
cout.width(10);
cout<<"Hello";
cout.width(5);
cout<<"Hi";
```

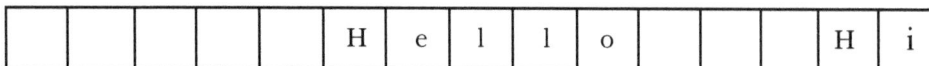

					H	e	l	l	o				H	i

Figure 12-6 *Representation of the output*

The above example will produce the output, as shown in Figure 12-6.

In the above example, the field width size 10 is specified for the value **Hello** and the field width size 5 is specified for the value **Hi**.

If the field width size specified by you is smaller than the size of the value to be printed, the field size will be expanded automatically by C++ to fit the value.

For example:

```
cout.width(5);
cout<<"You";
cout.width(2);
cout<<"and";
cout.width(2);
cout<<"Me";
```

In the above example, the value 2 is specified as the field width size for **and**, but it requires a wider field size 3 to print the value **and**. In this case, C++ automatically expands the field width size by one to print the value **and**. The above example will produce the output, as shown in Figure 12-7.

		Y	o	u	a	n	d	m	e

Figure 12-7 *Representation of the output*

The following example illustrates the use of the **width( )** function.

Example 4

Write a program to display the points scored by the students by using the **width( )** function.

The following program will display the points scored by the students on the screen.

```
//Write a program to display the points scored by the students        1
#include<iostream>                                                     2
using namespace std;                                                   3
int main( )                                                            4
{                                                                      5
      int stu_id[5]= {101, 102, 103, 104, 105};                        6
      int points_1[5] = {45, 40, 55, 50, 46};                          7
      int points_2[5] = {55, 50, 48, 56, 52};                          8
      int i;                                                           9
      cout.width(11);                                                  10
      cout<<"Student ID";                                              11
      cout.width(27);                                                  12
      cout<<"Points scored in Data Structure";                         13
      cout.width(17);                                                  14
      cout<<"Points scored in DBMS"<<endl;                             15
      for( i=0; i<=4; i++)                                             16
      {                                                                17
```

cout.width(11);	18
cout<<stu_id[i];	19
cout.width(35);	20
cout<<points_1[i];	21
cout.width(25);	22
cout<<points_2[i]<<endl;	23
}	24
return 0;	25
}	26

Explanation

Line 10
cout.width(11);
In this line, an integer value 11 is passed as an argument to the **width( )** function. This value will be set as the field width size for the value that immediately follows this line.

Line 11
cout<<"Student ID";
In line 10, the field width size for the value **Student ID** is set to **11**. Now, the value **Student ID** is printed at the right end of the field.

Line 18
cout.width(11);
In this line, an integer value 11 is passed as an argument to the **width( )** function. This value will be set as the field width size for the value that immediately follows this line.

Line 19
cout<<stu_id[i];
In line 10, the field width size for the first value of an array **stu_id[5]** is set to 11. Now, the first value 101 is printed at the right end of the field.

The output of the program is as follows:

Student ID	Points scored in Data Structure	Points scored in DBMS
101	45	55
102	40	50
103	55	48
104	50	56
105	46	52

The output will be displayed on the screen as follows:

The precision( ) Function

In C++, when a floating-point value is printed, by default six digits are printed after the decimal point. You can also specify the number of digits that are printed after the decimal point by using the **precision( )** function. The syntax for defining the **precision( )** function is as follows:

    cout.precision(number of digits);

In the above syntax, the argument **number of digits** is an integer value, which specifies the number of digits that are printed after the decimal point.

For example:

    cout.precision(3);
    cout<<3.745;
    cout<<4.758;

The above statements will produce the following output:

    3.74
    4.76

In the above example, you have observed that a single **precision( )** function sets the same precision 3 for two floating-point values 3.745 and 4.758. If you want to set different precisions for different floating-point values, you can do so, as shown in the following example:

    cout.precision(3);
    cout<<3.745<<endl;
    cout.precision(2);
    cout<<4.758;

In the above example, the integer value 3 and value 2 are set as the precision for the floating-point values 3.745 and 4.758, respectively.

This example will produce the following output:

    3.75
    4.8

The following example illustrates the use of the **precision( )** function.

Example 5

Write a program to multiply two **float** type arrays.

The following program will multiply two **float** type arrays, store the resultant values in the third array, and display it on the screen.

```
//Write a program to multiply two float type arrays            1
#include<iostream>                                             2
using namespace std;                                          3
int main( )                                                   4
{                                                             5
        float a[5]={7.4, 8.5, 6.3, 2.1, 7.9};               6
        float b[5]={5.6, 3.4, 5.9, 1.4, 4.1};               7
        float c[5];                                          8
        int i;                                               9
        cout.precision(3);                                   10
        cout.width(6);                                       11
        cout<<"A";                                           12
        cout.width(7);                                       13
        cout<<"B";                                           14
        cout.width(10);                                      15
        cout<<"C"<<endl;                                     16
        for(i=0; i<=4; i++)                                  17
        {                                                    18
                cout.width(6);                               19
                cout<<a[i];                                  20
                cout.width(7);                               21
                cout<<b[i];                                  22
                c[i] = a[i] * b[i];                          23
                cout.width(10);                              24
                cout<<c[i]<<endl;                            25
        }                                                    26
        return 0;                                            27
}                                                            28
```

Explanation
Line 10
cout.precision(3);
In this line, the **precision(3)** function sets the precision to 3 digits for all the floating-point arrays (a[5], b[5], and c[5]).

Line 11
cout.width(6);
In this line, the **width(6)** function sets the field width size to 6 for the value that immediately follows it (line 12).

The output of the program is as follows:

A	B	C
7.4	5.6	41.4
8.5	3.4	28.9
6.3	5.9	37.2
2.1	1.4	2.94
7.9	4.1	32.4

The output will be displayed on the screen as follows:

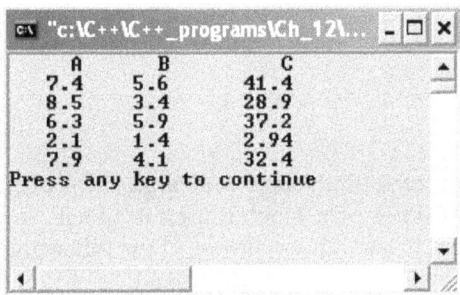

The fill( ) Function

You have already learned that the **width( )** function is used to specify the field width size for a value. If the field width size is larger than the width required by the value, the unused space is filled by blank spaces, as shown in Figure 12-8.

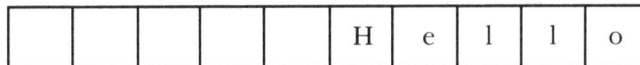

					H	e	l	l	o

*Figure 12-8 Representation of the **width( )** function*

In the above figure, the field width size **10** is larger than the required width for **Hello**, which is five. The unused space is filled by blank spaces.

If you want to fill the unused space with any character, you can do it by using the **fill( )** function. The syntax for defining the **fill( )** function is as follows:

    cout.fill(char);

In the above syntax, the argument **char** represents a character, which is used to fill the unused space in the field width.

For example:

```
cout.fill( '#');
cout.width(10);
cout<<"Hello";
```

The output of this example is as shown in Figure 12-9.

#	#	#	#	#	H	e	l	l	o

Figure 12-9 Representation of the output

The setf( ) Function

The **setf( )** function is used to format the output in a specific manner such that the text or the numeric values are displayed as justified or left-aligned and so on. By using this function, you can also display or print the floating-point numbers in scientific notations. The syntax for defining the **setf( )** function is as follows:

    cout.setf (arg1, arg2);

In the above syntax, the argument list contains two arguments **arg1** and **arg2**. The **arg1** represents a flag (used to indicate that if something is on or off), which is used to specify the format action that is applied to the output. The **arg1** is a flag and it can be one of the following:

ios::left

If the **ios::left** flag is set, the fill characters (blank space by default) are appended after the value.

For example:

    cout.fill('#');
    cout.setf(ios::left, ios::adjustfield);
    cout.width(18);
    cout<<"Left Aligned"<<endl;

The above example will produce the output as shown in Figure 12-10.

L	e	f	t		A	l	i	g	n	e	d	#	#	#	#	#	#

Figure 12-10 Representation of the output

In the above example, the **setf( )** function contains two arguments: **ios::left** and **ios::adjustfield**. The **ios::left** flag is set, which will produce the left-aligned output in the total field width size of 18 columns. The value **Left Aligned** uses only 12 columns and the remaining columns are filled with the **#** character. The second argument **ios::adjustfield** specifies the group of flags that are used to control padding such as left, right, and so on.

ios::right

If the **ios::right** flag is set, the fill characters (blank space by default) are appended before the value.

For example:

```
cout.fill('#');
cout.setf(ios::right, ios::adjustfield);
cout.width(18);
cout<<"Right Aligned"<<endl;
```

This example will produce the output as shown in Figure 12-11.

#	#	#	#	#	R	i	g	h	t		A	l	i	g	n	e	d

Figure 12-11 *Representation of the output*

In this example, the **setf( )** function contains two arguments: **ios::right** and **ios::adjustfield**. The **ios::right** flag is set, which will produce the right-aligned output in the total field width size of 18 columns. The value **Right Aligned** uses only 13 columns and the remaining columns are filled with the **#** character.

ios::internal

If the **ios::internal** flag is set, the fill characters (blank space by default) are appended after any leading sign or base indicator but before the specified value.

For example:

```
cout.fill('$');
cout.setf(ios::internal, ios::adjustfield);
cout.width(12);
cout<<-25.123<<endl;
```

-	$	$	$	$	$	2	5	.	1	2	3

Figure 12-12 *Representation of the output*

The above example will produce the output as shown in Figure 12-12.

In the above example, the **setf( )** function contains two arguments: **ios::internal** and **ios::adjustfield**. The **ios::internal** flag is set, which will append the character **$** after the minus **(-)** sign but before the value 25.123, as shown in Figure 12-12.

ios::scientific

If the **ios::left** flag is set, it converts the floating-point value into the scientific notation. In scientific notation, there is only one digit before the decimal point and the digits after the decimal point depend upon the **precision( )** function.

```
cout<<-25.12345<<endl;
```

This example will produce the output as shown in Figure 12-13.

-	$	$	$	$	$	$	2	.	5	1	e	+	0	1

Figure 12-13 *Representation of the output*

In this example, the second **setf( )** function contains two arguments: **ios::scientific** and **ios::floatfield**. The **ios::scientific** flag is set, which will convert the floating-point value -25.12345 into -2.51e+01. The second argument **ios::floatfield** specifies the group of flags that are used for floating-point conversions.

ios::fixed
If the **ios::fixed** flag is set, it converts the floating-point value into decimal notations but not in the scientific notations.

For example:

```
cout.fill('$');
cout.precision(2);
cout.setf(ios::internal, ios::adjustfield);
cout.setf(ios::fixed, ios::floatfield);
cout.width(15);
cout<<-25.12345<<endl;
```

-	$	$	$	$	$	$	$	$	$	2	5	.	1	2

Figure 12-14 *Representation of the output*

The above example will produce the output as shown in Figure 12-14.

In the above example, the **ios::fixed** flag is set, which will convert the floating-point value 25.12345 into the decimal notation 25.12.

Displaying Trailing Zeros and Decimal Points
Whenever a floating-point value is shown in the output, the trailing zeros (zeros after the decimal point) are not displayed with the value.

For example:

```
cout.precision(2);
cout.width(8);
cout<<25.00<<endl;
```

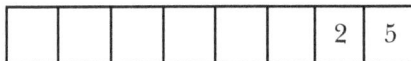

Figure 12-15 *Representation of the output*

The above example will produce the output as shown in Figure 12-15.

In this example, the trailing zeros and the decimal point are truncated from the value 25.00 and only the value 25 is printed.

In certain cases, such as in the case of the list of prices of items, it is required to display the trailing zeros. For this purpose, the base class **ios** provides some flags that are used to display the trailing zeros, a **+** sign before a positive value, and so on. These flags are as follows:

ios::showpoint
If the **ios::showpoint** flag is set, it will display the decimal point and also the trailing zeros while printing a floating-point value. As discussed in the earlier examples, this flag is also used as an argument in the **setf( )** function.

For example:

```
cout.setf(ios::showpoint);
cout<<1.22<<endl;
```

The above example will produce the output as shown in Figure 12-16.

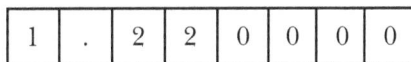

Figure 12-16 *Representation of the output*

In the above example, the **ios::showpoint** is set, which will cause the floating-point value 1.220000 to be printed instead of the value 1.22.

ios::showpos
If the **ios::showpos** is set, a **+** sign will be printed before the positive numbers.

For example:

```
cout.width(8);
cout.setf(ios::showpos);
cout<<12<<endl;
```

This example will produce the output as shown in Figure 12-17.

In the above example, the **ios::showpos** is set, and so a **+** sign will be printed before the integer value 12.

Figure 12-17 *Representation of the output*

The unsetf( ) Function

The **unsetf( )** function is contrary to the **setf( )** function. The **unsetf( )** function is used to clear the flags, which were earlier set by using the **setf( )** function.

For example:

```
cout.width(8);
cout.setf(ios::showpos);
cout<<12<<endl;
cout.width(8);
cout.unsetf(ios::showpos);
cout<<14<<endl;
```

Figure 12-18 *Representation of the output*

The above example will produce the output as shown in Figure 12-18.

In the above example, the **ios::showpos** is set, and so a **+** sign will be printed with the integer value 12. After that, the **unsetf( )** function is used to clear the **ios::showpos** flag, which was earlier set by using the **setf( )** function. Now, the **+** sign is not printed while printing the next integer value 14.

Formatting the Output by Using Manipulators

In the previous section, you have learned to format the output by using the members of the **ios** base class. In this section, you will learn to format the output by using the manipulators. The manipulators are the functions, which are defined in the **iomanip** header file. So, you must include the **iomanip** header file whenever you want to access these manipulators to format the output. The following list contains the manipulators that are widely used.

1. setw(int width)
2. setprecision(int precision)
3. setfill(char c)
4. setiosflags(int flag)
5. resetiosflags(int flag)

All these manipulators provide the same features as that of the base class **ios** member functions. Also, flags such as the **setw(int width)** are used to set the field width size as the same as of **width( )**, which is the member function of the **ios** base class. Table 12-1 contains all the manipulators and their equivalents in the **ios** base class.

S. No.	Manipulators	Equivalent(in the ios base class)
1.	setw(int width)	width( )
2.	setprecision(int p)	precision( )
3.	setfill(char c)	fill( )
4.	setiosflags(int f)	setf( )
5.	resetiosflags(int f)	unsetf( )

Table 12-1

The syntax for using the manipulators is as follows:

cout<<manipulator_name<<value;

In the above syntax, the **manipulator_name** represents a manipulator, which is used to format the output as per the user requirement. The **value** represents the data, which is to be formatted by using the manipulator.

For example:

cout<<setw(10)<<12.23;

The above example will produce the output as shown in Figure 12-19.

Figure 12-19 *Representation of the output*

In the above example, the **setw( )** manipulator sets the field width size 10 for the value 12.23.

You can also use more than one manipulator in a single output statement, as shown follows:

cout<<manp_1<<value<<manp_2<<value;

For example:

cout<<setw(10)<<12.23<<setw(8)<<1.23;

In the above example, in a single **cout** statement, two **setw( )** manipulators are used for two different values 12.23 and 1.23, respectively. The first **setw(10)** sets the field width size 10 for the value 12.23 and the second **setw(8)** sets the field width size **8** for the value 1.23. The above example will produce the output as shown in Figure 12-20.

					1	2	.	2	3					1	.	2	3

Figure 12-20 *Representation of the output*

Self-Evaluation Test

Answer the following questions and then compare them to the answers given at the end of this chapter:

1. The flow or sequence of bytes through a system is known as _____.

2. When a program starts its execution, some streams are automatically opened. These types of streams are known as _____ streams.

3. The _____ is an error output stream.

4. You can set the field width size of a value by using the _____ or _____ function.

5. If the _____ flag is set, it will display the decimal point and also the trailing zeros, while printing a floating-point value.

Review Questions

Answer the following questions:

1. Define streams and its types.

2. Define predefined streams.

3. Explain the **width( )** member function with a suitable example.

4. Explain the **fill( )** member function with a suitable example.

5. Explain the working of the **ios::showpoint** with a suitable example.

Exercise

Exercise 1

Write a program to find the square root of the numbers from 1 to 10 using the **width( )** and **precision( )** functions. The program should produce the output as shown below:

VALUE	SQUARE ROOT
1	1
2	1.41
3	1.73
4	2
5	2.24
6	2.45
7	2.65
8	2.83
9	3
10	3.16

Answers to Self-Evaluation Test
1. stream, **2.** predefined, **3. cerr, 4. width( ), setw( ), 5. ios::showpoint**

Chapter 13

Exception Handling

Learning Objectives

After completing this chapter, you will be able to:
- *Understand exceptions and their types.*
- *Understand the concept of exception handling.*

INTRODUCTION

During execution of a program, generally two types of errors are encountered. These are as follows:

1. Logical errors
2. Syntactical errors

The logical errors are those errors that are encountered because of the improper understanding of the problems and their solutions. The syntactical errors are those errors that are encountered because of the improper understanding of the language syntax. These errors are detected and handled during the compilation time. But sometimes, during the program execution, some problems are encountered that are other than the logical and syntactical errors. These errors are known as exceptions. An exception is a runtime error or an abnormal condition that terminates the program abnormally. C++ provides the mechanism of exception handling to manage these exceptions. In this chapter, you will learn about the concept of exception handling.

EXCEPTION HANDLING

The exceptions are divided into the following two categories:

1. Synchronous
2. Asynchronous

The exceptions such as divided by zero, out of range, and so on are known as synchronous exceptions. These exceptions occur repeatedly at the same place in a program and with the same data each time the program is executed. The exceptions that occur because of the external hardware devices such as keyboard are known as asynchronous exceptions. These exceptions are beyond the control of the program. In C++, the exception handling mechanism is used to manage only the synchronous exceptions.

You already know that the exception handling mechanism is used to manage the exceptions, so that a program can work normally. The exception handling mechanism is carried out in the following steps:

1. In the first step, an exception is detected, or in other words, the statements due to which the program was terminated abnormally are searched. This process is also known as hit the exception.

2. After detection, the exception is thrown. This means information is sent to the system that an error has occurred. This process is also known as **throw** the exception.

3. The thrown exception is caught by the block of code, which handles the exception. This process is also known as **catch** the exception.

4. Finally, the corrective action is taken.

Fundamentals of Exception Handling Mechanism

In C++, the exception handling mechanism is built upon the following three keywords:

1. try
2. throw
3. catch

The **try** block contains the statement or statements, which are monitored for the exception. The syntax for defining the **try** block is as follows:

```
try
{
    statement or statements;
}
```

When an exception is detected in the **try** block, it can be thrown by using the **throw** statement. The syntax for declaring the **throw** statement is as follows:

```
throw exception_type;
```

In the above syntax, the **throw** is a keyword and **exception_type** represents an exception. Whenever an exception occurs in the **try** block, as represented by the **exception_type**, it is thrown with the help of **throw** keyword. The **throw** statement is used in the **try** block as follows:

```
try
{
    statement;
    throw exception;
    statement;
}
```

The **catch** block contains the statement or statements, which should be executed whenever an exception occurs in the **try** block. This block is used to catch the exception, which is thrown by the **throw** statement in the **try** block. Each **try** block should be followed by at least one **catch** block. The syntax for defining the **catch** block is as follows:

```
try
{
    statement or statements;
}
catch(type arg1)
{
    statement or statements;
}
```

In this syntax, the **type** represents the type of exception and **arg1** represents an object of the given type. Here, only a particular type of exception can be caught by the **catch** statement.

More than one **catch** block can also be associated with a single **try** block, as follows:

```
try
{
    statement;
    throw exception;
    statement;
}
catch(type arg1)
{
    statement;
    ----------;
}
catch(type arg2)
{
    statement;
    ----------;
}



catch(type argN)
{
    statement;
    ----------;
}
```

In the above syntax, more than one **catch** block is associated with a **try** block. The execution of the **catch** block depends on the type of exception thrown in the **try** block. If the data type specified by a **catch** matches the data type of the exception, that particular **catch** block will be executed and the remaining **catch** blocks will be skipped. If no match is found, a call is made to the **abort( )** function, which will terminate the program abnormally. If no exception is detected and thrown, the control transfers to the statement, which is immediate to the **catch** blocks.

The following program illustrates the use of exception handling mechanism.

Example 1

Write a program to handle an exception (divide by zero) by using the exception handling mechanism.

The program given next will prompt the user to enter two numbers, divide them, handle the exception, and display the value of the variable **result** on the screen. The line numbers on the right are not a part of the program and are for reference only.

```
//Write a program to handle an exception (divide by zero)
//by using the exception handling mechanism                          1
#include<iostream>                                                    2
using namespace std;                                                 3
int main( )                                                          4
{                                                                    5
        int var1, var2, result;                                     6
        cout<<"Enter two numbers:";                                 7
        cin>>var1>>var2;                                            8
        cout<<"Value of var1 is: "<<var1<<endl;                    9
        cout<<"Value of var2 is:  "<<var2<<endl;                   10
        try                                                         11
        {                                                           12
                if(var2==0)                                         13
                {                                                   14
                        cout<<"Attempted to divide by zero"<<endl;  15
                        throw var2;                                 16
                }                                                   17
                else                                                18
                {                                                   19
                        result=var1/var2;                          20
                        cout<<"After division,"
                            " the resultant value is: "<<result<<endl;  21
                }                                                   22
        }                                                           23
        catch(int x)                                                24
        {                                                           25
                cout<<"Exception caught"<<endl;                    26
        }                                                           27
        cout<<"End of the program"<<endl;                          28
        return 0;                                                   29
}                                                                   30
```

Explanation

Line 11

try

This line contains the keyword **try**, which represents the start of the **try** block. This block contains the statements that are monitored for an exception.

Lines 13 to 17

if(var2==0)
{
        cout<<"Attempted to divide by zero"<<endl;
        throw var2;
}

These lines contain the **if** block and the value of the variable **var2** is verified whether it is equal to zero. If the value is equal to zero, it is thrown as an exception by using the **throw** statement. Otherwise, the control will be transferred to the **else** block.

Lines 18 to 22
else
{

      result=var1/var2;
      cout<<"After division,"
           " the resultant value is: "<<result<<endl;

}

If the condition in the **if** statement is evaluated to false, the control transfers to the **else** block. The value of the variable **var1** is divided by the value of the variable **var2**. Next, the quotient value is assigned to the variable **result** and displayed on the screen.

Lines 23 to 26
catch(int x)
{

      cout<<"Exception caught"<<endl;

}

The exception thrown by using the **throw** statement in the **try** block is caught by the **catch** statement. In the parentheses, the **int** specifies the type of exception and the variable **x** represents an object of the specified type. When an exception occurs in the **try** block, the **throw** statement throws the variable **result** as an exception, which is caught by the **catch** statement. After that, the next statement (Line 25) will be executed. If no exception occurs, the **catch** block will be skipped and the control will be directly transferred to the next statement that immediately follows it.

The output of the program is as follows:
Enter two numbers: 10 0
Value of var1 is: 10
Value of var2 is: 0
Attempted to divide by zero
Exception caught
End of the program

The output will be displayed on the screen as follows:

In this program, an integer value 10 is assigned to the variable **var1** and the value 0 is assigned to the variable **var2**. When the value of the variable **var2** is equal to 0, it is thrown as an exception by using the **throw** statement. After that, the thrown exception is caught by the **catch** statement and the next statement will be executed and it is displayed on the screen as follows:

Exception caught

In the previous program, the exception is thrown from inside the **try** block. You can also throw an exception from outside the **try** block. In such case, the function that generates the exception will be invoked from inside the **try** block.

The following example illustrates the concept of throwing an exception from outside the **try** block.
Write a program to handle an exception (divide by zero) by using the concept of throwing an exception from outside the **try** block.

The following program will prompt the user to enter two numbers, divide them, handle the exception, and display the value of the variable **result** on the screen.

Example 2

```
//Write a program to handle an exception (divide by zero)
//by using the concept of throwing an exception                    1
#include<iostream>                                                  2
using namespace std;                                                3
void division(int i, int j)                                         4
{                                                                   5
        if(j== 0)                                                   6
        {                                                           7
                cout<<"Attempted to divide by zero"<<endl;          8
                throw j;                                            9
        }                                                          10
        else                                                       11
        {                                                          12
                int result=i/j;                                    13
                cout<<"After division,"
                        " the resultant value is: "<<result<<endl; 14
        }                                                          15
}                                                                  16
int main( )                                                        17
{                                                                  18
        try                                                        19
        {                                                          20
                division(10,0);                                    21
        }                                                          22
        catch(int x)                                               23
        {                                                          24
                cout<<"Exception caught"<<endl;                    25
        }                                                          26
        cout<<"End of the program"<<endl;                          27
        return 0;                                                  28
}                                                                  29
```

The working of this program is the same as the previous program except that in this program, the **throw** statement is used in the function **division( )**, which is defined outside the **try** block. The **division( )** function is invoked within the **try** block and the values 10 and 0 are assigned to the variables **i** and **j**, respectively. In the **division( )** function, when an exception occurs, it is thrown by using the **throw** statement. The thrown exception is caught and handled by the **catch** statement in the **main( )** function.

The output of the program is as follows:
Attempted to divide by zero
Exception caught
End of the program

Multiple catch Statements

You have already learned that more than one **catch** can be associated with a single **try** block. When multiple **catch** statements are used in a program, each **catch** statement is used to catch different types of exceptions.

The following example illustrates the use of multiple **catch** statements.

Example 3

Write a program to illustrate the working of multiple **catch** statements.

The following program will handle the exceptions using multiple **catch** statements. It will also display the value of the variable **var** on the screen, which is based on the value entered by the user.

```
//Write a program to illustrate the working of multiple catch statements    1
#include<iostream>                                                          2
using namespace std;                                                        3
void handler(int i)                                                         4
{                                                                           5
        try                                                                 6
        {                                                                   7
                if(i==0)                                                    8
                        throw "Value is zero";                              9
                else if(i==1)                                               10
                        throw 'A';                                          11
                else if(i==2)                                               12
                        throw i;                                            13
                else                                                        14
                        throw i=10;                                         15
        }                                                                   16
        catch(float var)                                                    17
        {                                                                   18
                cout<<"Caught: "<<var<<endl;                                19
        }                                                                   20
```

```
        catch(char var)                                          21
        {                                                        22
                cout<<"Caught: "<<var<<endl;                     23
        }                                                        24
        catch(char * var)                                        25
        {                                                        26
                cout<<"Caught: "<<var<<endl;                     27
        }                                                        28
        catch(int var)                                           29
        {                                                        30
                cout<<"Caught: "<<var<<endl;                     31
        }                                                        32
}                                                                33
int main( )                                                      34
{                                                                35
        cout<<"Multiple catch statements"<<endl;                 36
        handler(1);                                              37
        handler(0);                                              38
        handler(2);                                              39
        handler(5);                                              40
        return 0;                                                41
}                                                                42
```

Explanation

Lines 6 to 16

try
{
        if(i==0)
                throw "Value is zero";
        else if(i==1)
                throw 'A';
        else if(i==2)
                throw i;
        else
                throw i;
}

These lines contain the definition of the **try** block. In this block, the value of the variable **i** is compared with the specified values 0, 1, and 2. If the value of the variable **i** is equal to zero, an exception **Value is zero** is thrown by using the **throw** statement. If the value of the variable **i** is equal to one, an exception **A** is thrown by using the **throw** statement, and so on. If any value except 0, 1, and 2 is passed during a function call, the value of the variable **i** will be thrown.

Lines 17 to 20
catch(float var)
{
        cout<<"Caught: "<<var<<endl;
}

These lines contain the definition of the **catch** statement. Only the floating-point exception is caught by this **catch** statement because in the parentheses it contains a float type argument. So, whenever a floating type exception is thrown by the **try** block, it is caught by the **catch** statement and the statements associated with the **catch** block are executed.

Note
*In this program, multiple **catch** statements are used. So, whenever an exception is thrown by the **try** block, the type of thrown exception is matched with the type of catch statements one by one. When a suitable match is found, the particular **catch** block is executed and the remaining **catch** blocks are skipped.*

Line 37
handler(1);
In this line, a call is made to the function **handler(1)** and an integer value 1 is passed as an argument, which is assigned to the variable **i** in the function definition (line 4). Now, the value of the variable **i** is compared to the **if** and **else-if** statements. The comparison is evaluated to true in line 10 and an exception '**A**' is thrown.

Line 40
handler(5);
In this line, a call is made to the function **handler(5)** and an integer value 5 is passed as an argument, which is assigned to the variable **i** in the function definition (line 4). Now, the value of the variable **i** is compared to the **if** and **else-if** statements. After comparison, the **else** block is executed because value 5 does not match to the **if** and **else-if** statements. In the **else** block, the value of the variable **i** is thrown as an exception.

The output of the program is as follows:
Multiple catch statements
Caught: A
Caught: Value is zero
Caught: 2
Caught: 10

The output will be displayed on the screen as follows:

Using catch(...) to Catch All Types of Exceptions

In the above program, you observed that multiple **catch** statements were used to catch different types of exceptions. In certain cases, you are not able to define independent **catch** statements for different types of exceptions. In such cases, you can define the **catch(...)** statement, which is able to catch all types of exceptions. The syntax for defining the **catch(...)** statement is as follows:

```
catch(...)
{
    statements;
}
```

The following program illustrates the use of the **catch(...)** statement.

Example 4

Write a program to illustrate the working of the **catch(...)** statement.

The following program will handle the exceptions by using one **catch(...)** statement and display a message on the screen.

```
//Write a program to illustrate the working of the catch(...) statement    1
#include<iostream>                                                         2
using namespace std;                                                       3
void handler(int i)                                                        4
{                                                                          5
        try                                                                6
        {                                                                  7
                if(i==0)                                                   8
                        throw "Value is zero";                             9
                else if(i==1)                                             10
                        throw 'A';                                        11
                else if(i==2)                                             12
                        throw 1.23;                                       13
                else                                                      14
                        throw i;                                          15
        }                                                                 16
        catch(...)                                                        17
        {                                                                 18
                cout<<"Caught an exception"<<endl;                        19
        }                                                                 20
}                                                                         21
int main( )                                                               22
{                                                                         23
        cout<<"Multiple catch statements"<<endl;                         24
        handler(1);                                                      25
        handler(0);                                                      26
```

```
        handler(2);                                              27
        handler(5);                                              28
        return 0;                                                29
}                                                                30
```

The working of the above program is the same as the previous program except that whenever an exception is thrown, it will be caught by the **catch(...)** statement. But in the previous program different types of exceptions were caught by different types of **catch** statements.

The output of the program is as follows:
Multiple catch statements
Caught an exception
Caught an exception
Caught an exception
Caught an exception

Rethrowing an Exception

In all the previous programs, the **catch** statements handled all the exceptions thrown by the **try** block. But if you want that the **catch** statement should rethrow an exception without handling it, you can use the keyword **throw** without any argument inside the **catch** block. The syntax for rethrowing an exception is as follows:

```
    catch(type arg_name)
    {
        statements;
        throw;
    }
```

In the above syntax, the **throw** keyword rethrows the exception, which was earlier caught by the **catch** statement. This causes the current exception to be passed to the next enclosing **try-catch** sequence.

The following program illustrates the use of rethrowing an exception.

Example 5

Write a program to illustrate the working of rethrowing an exception.

The following program will handle an exception by rethrowing it. It will also display the resultant value on the screen.

```
//Write a program to illustrate the working of rethrowing an exception   1
#include<iostream>                                                        2
using namespace std;                                                      3
void handler(int i)                                                       4
{                                                                         5
        try                                                              6
        {                                                                7
```

```
            if(i==0)                                                8
                    throw 'x';                                      9
            else                                                    10
                    throw i;                                        11
        }                                                           12
    catch(char a)                                                   13
    {                                                               14
            cout<<"Character "<<a<<" caught inside handler"<<endl;  15
            throw;//rethrow the exception                           16
    }                                                               17
    catch(int j)                                                    18
    {                                                               19
            cout<<"Caught: "<<j<<endl;                              20
    }                                                               21
}                                                                   22
int main( )                                                         23
{                                                                   24
    cout<<"Inside main"<<endl;                                      25
    try                                                             26
    {                                                               27
            handler(0);                                             28
            handler(1);                                             29
    }                                                               30
    catch(char a)                                                   31
    {                                                               32
            cout<<"Character "<<a<<" caught inside main"<<endl;     33
    }                                                               34
    cout<<"End"<<endl;                                              35
    return 0;                                                       36
}                                                                   37
```

Explanation

In this program, when a call is made to the function **handler( )** and the value 0 is passed as an argument, an exception **'x'** is detected and thrown by the **try** block. Now, the thrown exception is caught by the **catch** statement (line 13). In the **catch** block, the caught exception is not handled and it is rethrown by using the **throw** statement (line 16). After rethrowing, the exception **'x'** is handled by the next **catch** block (line 31) in the **main** function.

The output of the program is as follows:
Inside main
Caught: 1
Character x caught inside handler
Character x caught inside main
End

The output will be displayed on the screen as follows:

```
"c:\C++\C++_programs\Ch_13\ch13_...  _ □ ×
Inside main
Caught: 1
Character x caught inside handler
Character x caught inside main
End
Press any key to continue_
```

Specifying the Exceptions

In the previous programs, you have observed that a function can throw any type of exception. In some cases, it may be required that a function throws only some particular types of exceptions. You can accomplish these restrictions by adding the throw clause to a function definition. The syntax for specifying some particular types of exceptions for a function is given next.

```
return_type fun_name(argument list) throw(type_list)
{
    statement;
    ----------;
    ----------;
}
```

In the above syntax, the function specified by the **fun_name** can throw only those exceptions whose types are specified in the **type_list** and are separated by commas.

For example:

```
void demo(int i, int j) throw(int, char, double)
{
    body of the function;
}
```

In the above example, the type list contains three types of exceptions **int, char**, and **double**. The function **demo( )** can only throw these three types of exceptions. If any other type of exception is thrown by the function **demo( )**, it will cause an abnormal termination of the program.

To ensure that a function does not throw any exception, use an empty type list as follows:

```
void demo(int i, int j) throw( )
{
    body of the function;
}
```

In the above example, the function **demo( )** cannot throw any exception because the type list is empty.

The following program restricts a function to throw only certain types of exceptions.

Example 6

Write a program to restrict a function **demo( )** to throw only **int, char,** and **double** types of exceptions.

The following program will define a function that can throw only certain types of exceptions. It will also display a statement based on the value caught by a catch statement on the screen.

```
//Write a program to restrict a function to throw only certain types of exceptions   1
#include<iostream>                                                                   2
using namespace std;                                                                 3
void demo(int i) throw(int, char, double)                                            4
{                                                                                    5
        try                                                                          6
        {                                                                            7
                if(i==0)                                                             8
                        throw i;                                                     9
                else if(i==1)                                                       10
                        throw 'x';                                                  11
                else if(i==2)                                                       12
                        throw 10.234;                                               13
        }                                                                           14
        catch(char a)                                                               15
        {                                                                           16
                cout<<"Caught: "<<a<<endl;                                          17
        }                                                                           18
        catch(int a)                                                                19
        {                                                                           20
                cout<<"Caught: "<<a<<endl;                                          21
        }                                                                           22
        catch(double a)                                                             23
        {                                                                           24
                cout<<"Caught: "<<a<<endl;                                          25
        }                                                                           26
}                                                                                   27
int main( )                                                                         28
{                                                                                   29
        demo(0);                                                                    30
        demo(1);                                                                    31
        demo(2);                                                                    32
        return 0;                                                                   33
}                                                                                   34
```

Explanation

Line 4

void demo(int i) throw(int, char, double)

In this line, the function **demo( )** is defined. The type list contains three types of exceptions, **int**, **char** and **double**. The function **demo( )** can throw only these three types of exceptions.

The output of the above program is as follows:

Caught: 0

Caught: x

Caught: 10.234

Self-Evaluation Test

Answer the following questions and then compare them to the answers given at the end of this chapter:

1. Errors that are encountered because of the improper understanding of the problem and its solution are known as _____ errors.

2. An _____ is a runtime error or an abnormal condition that will terminate the program abnormally.

3. The exception handling is based upon the _____, _____, and _____ keywords.

4. The _____ statement is used to catch all types of exceptions.

5. The _____ function is used to terminate the program abnormally.

Review Questions

Answer the following questions:

1. What is an exception?

2. Explain different types of exceptions.

3. Explain the term exception handling with a suitable example.

4. Explain the concept of multiple **catch** statements with a suitable example.

5. Explain the working of the **catch(...)** statement.

Exercises

Exercise 1

Write a program that illustrates the concept of multiple **catch** statements.

Exercise 2

Write a program that illustrates the use of the **catch(...)** statement.

Answers to Self-Evaluation Test

1. logical, **2.** exception, **3. try, throw, catch**, **4. catch(...)**, **5. abort( )**

Chapter 14

The File I/O System

Learning Objectives

After completing this chapter, you will be able to:

- *Understand the file I/O system.*
- *Understand the classes used for file I/O operations.*
- *Understand the concept of opening and closing a file.*
- *Understand the concept of reading and writing text files.*
- *Understand the file pointers.*
- *Understand the file I/O operations.*
- *Understand the concept of checking I/O status.*
- *Understand the command-line arguments.*
- *Learn about some important functions.*

INTRODUCTION

In the chapter **The C++ Console I/O Operations**, you studied that the data communication takes place between the console unit and the program by using the input and the output streams. This type of data communication is used when the data is not voluminous. If the data is voluminous, it is stored in the hard disk or the floppy disk by using the concept of files. A file is a collection of related data stored in a particular area of the disk. In this chapter, you will learn how the data communication takes place between the files and the programs by using the file streams.

THE FILE I/O SYSTEM

In the file I/O system, the input and output operations are performed in the same way as in the console I/O system, except that in the file I/O system, the file streams are used rather than the streams used in the console I/O system. The file streams are used as an interface between the programs and the files. The stream that reads the files from the disk and supplies it to the program is known as the input stream. The stream that receives data from the program and provides it to the disk is known as the output stream, see Figure 14-1.

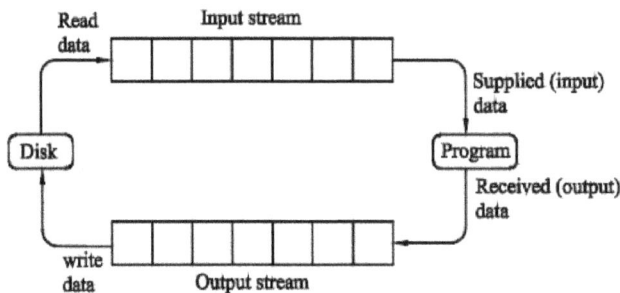

Figure 14-1 *Representation of File I/O streams*

THE CLASSES USED FOR FILE I/O OPERATIONS

You can perform the file I/O operations in the program by using certain predefined methods or functions. These methods are defined in certain classes. These classes are **ifstream**, **ofstream**, and **fstream**. They are derived from the classes **istream**, **ostream**, and **iostream**, respectively and also from the **fstreambase** class, see Figure 14-2. Whenever you want to perform the file I/O operations, these classes should be included by including the header file **fstream** in the program. These classes perform certain functions that are as follows:

The fstreambase class

This class serves as a base class for the **ifstream**, **ofstream**, and **fstream** classes. The **fstreambase** class contains the **open( )** and the **close( )** functions and it also provides the functions that are common to both the input and the output file streams.

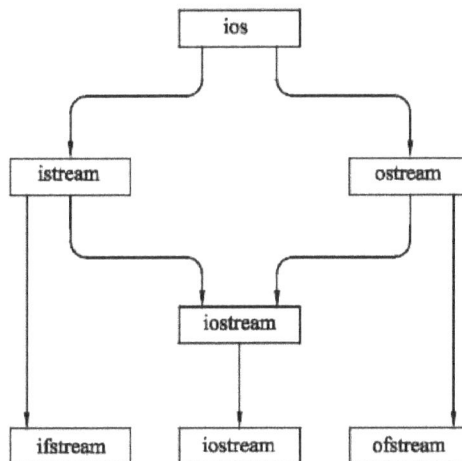

Figure 14-2 *Classes used for file I/O operations*

The ifstream class

The **ifstream** class provides a stream interface, which is used to read the data from the file. It also inherits the functions **get( )**, **getline( )**, **read( )**, and so on from the **istream** class, and is used for the input operations.

The ofstream class

The **ofstream** class provides a stream interface, which is used to write the data into the file. It also inherits the functions **put( )**, **write( )**, and so on from the **ostream** class, and is used for the output operations.

The fstream class

The **fstream** class provides a stream interface, which is used to perform both read and write operations. It also inherits the properties of the **istream** and **ostream** classes through the **iostream** class.

OPENING AND CLOSING A FILE

To perform any file I/O operation in a program, the specified file should be opened. To open a file, it should be linked with a stream. The stream can be any one of the following:

1. ifstream (Input stream)
2. ofstream (Output stream)
3. fstream (Input and output stream)

To perform only the input operations on a file, you should create an input stream. You can create an input stream object, as shown in the following statement:

    ifstream in;

In this statement, the **in** is declared as a stream of the class **ifstream**.

To perform only the output operations on a file, you should create an output stream. You can create an output stream object, as shown in the following statement:

    ofstream out;

In the above statement, the **out** is declared as a stream of the class **ofstream**.

To perform both the input and the output operations, you should create a stream that can perform both the operations. You can create an Input/Output stream, as shown in the following statement:

    fstream io;

In the above statement, the **io** is declared as a stream of the class **fstream**.

After the creation of the stream, you can open a file by using the **open( )** function, which is the member of all the three stream classes. The syntax for using the **open( )** function is as follows:

    stream_class object("filename", ios::openmode);

        OR

    stream_class object;
    object.open("filename", ios::openmode);

In the above syntax, the **stream_class** represents the stream class, which can be any one of the following three: **ifstream**, **ofstream**, and **fstream**. The **object** represents a stream of the class specified by the **stream_class**. Here, the **open( )** function is called with the stream **object** and two arguments are passed: **filename** and **ios::openmode**. The **filename** specifies the name of the file on which the operations are performed. The second argument **ios::openmode** is optional, which specifies the type of the operations that you can perform on a file. The **ios::openmode** can be any one of the following:

1. ios::app   //Appends the output of the program at the end of the file
2. ios::in   //Only the input operations can be performed
3. ios::out   //Only the output operations can be performed
4. ios::trunc   //Discards the contents of the file, if they exist
5. ios::binary   //Opens a file in the binary mode
6. ios::ate   //Enables data to be written anywhere in the file
7. ios::nocreate   //If the file does not exist, the open operation fails
8. ios::noreplace //If the file already exists, the open operation fails

If the second argument **ios::openmode** is not specified in the **open( )** function, the default values are provided for each type of streams such as **ios::in** for **ifstream**, **ios::out** or **ios::trunc** for **ofstream**, and **ios::in|ios::out** for **fstream**.

For example:

```
ifstream in;
in.open("Test");
```

In the above example, the open mode for the file **Test** is not specified. So, the default mode **ios::in** is provided, which specifies that only the input operations are performed on the file **Test**.

As you already know that the **open( )** function is used to open a file. But sometimes the **open( )** function fails to open a file and generates an error. This error should be handled properly. To handle this error, type the following:

```
ifstream in;
in.open("Test");
if(!Test)
{
    cout<<"Cannot open the test file"<<endl;
}
```

In the above example, the **open( )** function is used to open the **Test** file. If the **open( )** function fails, the stream **in** will evaluate to false and the statement associated with the **if** statement will be executed.

To verify that the specified file is successfully opened, use the **is_open( )** function. This function is the member function of the classes **fstream**, **ifstream**, and **ofstream**. The syntax for using the **is_open( )** is as follows:

```
if(file_name.is_open( ))
{
    statements;
}
```

In the above syntax, if the file specified by the **file_name** is successfully opened, it will return true and the statements associated with the **if** statement will be executed. Otherwise, it will return false and the statements associated with the **if** statement will be skipped.

When all the operations have been performed within a file, it should be closed. You can close a file by using the **close( )** function. The **close( )** function neither takes any arguments nor returns any value. The syntax for using the **close( )** function is as follows:

```
stream_object.close( );
```

For example:

```
in.close( );
```

In this example, the **close( )** function closes the file linked to a stream **in**, which is of the **ifstream** type.

READING AND WRITING TEXT FILES

To perform the read and write operations on a text file, the **<<** and **>>** operators are used in the same way as in the console I/O system. In this case, instead of using the **cin** and **cout** statements, a stream that is linked to a file is used.

For example (Write operation):

```
ofstream out;
out.open("Test");
----------;
----------;
out<< "This is written in the file"<<endl;
----------;
out.close( );
```

The above example illustrates that the write operation is performed on a text file. In this example, the **out** is declared as a stream of the type **ofstream**. Next, the stream **out** is linked with the text file **Test**, which is opened in the write mode. Now, the write operation is performed by using the stream **out** with the **<<** operator and the statement **This is written in the file** is written on the file **Test**.

For example (Read operation):

```
ifstream in;
in.open("Test");
----------;
----------;
in>> var1>> var2;
----------;
```

The above example illustrates that the read operation is performed on a text file. In this example, the **in** is declared as a stream of the type **ifstream**. Next, the stream **in** is linked with the text file **Test**, which is opened in the read mode. Now, the read operation is performed and the values of the variables **var1** and **var2** will be read by using the stream **in** with the **>>** operator.

The following example illustrates the read and write operations on a text file.

Example 1

Write a program to illustrate the read and write operations on a text file.

The program given next will write some details of the employees in a text file, read the contents of the file, and display them on the screen. The line numbers on the right are not a part of the program and are for reference only.

```
//Write a program that will perform the read and write operations on a text file    1
#include<iostream>                                                                   2
#include<fstream>                                                                    3
using namespace std;                                                                 4
int main( )                                                                          5
{                                                                                    6
        int emp_id;                                                                  7
        char emp_name[50];                                                           8
        ifstream in;                                                                 9
        ofstream out;                                                               10
        out.open("Test");                                                           11
        if(!out)                                                                    12
        {                                                                           13
                cout<<"File not opened"<<endl;                                      14
                return 1;                                                           15
        }                                                                           16
        out<< "John" << 45262 << endl;                                             17
        out<< "Smith" << 45165 << endl;                                            18
        out<< "William" << 44500 << endl;                                          19
        out.close( );                                                              20
        in.open("Test");                                                           21
        if(!in)                                                                    22
        {                                                                           23
                cout<<"File not opened"<<endl;                                      24
                return 1;                                                           25
        }                                                                           26
        in>> emp_name >> emp_id;                                                    27
        cout<< emp_name << emp_id << endl;                                          28
        in>> emp_name >> emp_id;                                                    29
        cout<< emp_name << emp_id << endl;                                          30
        in>> emp_name >> emp_id;                                                    31
        cout<< emp_name << emp_id << endl;                                          32
        in.close( );                                                               33
        return 0;                                                                  34
}                                                                                   35
```

Explanation

Line 3

#include<fstream>

This line contains the header file **fstream**, which contains the functions and streams that are used to perform I/O operations on the files.

Line 9

ifstream in;

In this line, the **in** is declared as a stream of the class **ifstream**. This stream is treated as an input stream.

Line 10
ofstream out;
In this line, the **out** is declared as a stream of the class **ofstream**. This stream is treated as an output stream.

Line 11
out.open("Test");
In this line, the **open( )** function is used to open the file **Test** in the write mode (default for **ofstream** class) so that the write operation can be performed on it.

Lines 12 to 16
if(!out)
{
         cout<<"File not opened"<<endl;
         return 1;
}
The statements associated with the **if** block will be executed when the text file **Test** is not successfully opened. Otherwise, these lines will be skipped.

Line 17
out<< "John" << 45262 << endl;
In this line, the data (John and 45262) is written into the text file **Test** by using the output stream **out** and the extraction (**>>**) operator.

Line 20
out.close( );
In this line, the **close( )** function is used to close the text file **Test**. Now, the link that was created earlier between the **out** stream and the text file **Test** will be terminated.

Line 21
in.open("Test");
In this line, the text file **Test** is again opened but in the read mode (default for **ifstream** class) with an input stream **in**.

Line 27
in>> emp_name >> emp_id;
In this line, the values of the variables **emp_name** and **emp_id** are read from the text file **Test**.

Line 33
in.close( );
In this line, the **close( )** function is used to close the text file **Test**, which was earlier opened in the read mode.

The output of the program is as follows:
John 45262
Smith 45165
William 44500

THE FILE POINTERS

The pointers that are associated with each file in the C++ file system are known as the file pointers. These pointers are used to move the cursor in between the contents of a file. The following are the two pointers that are associated with each file:

1. Input pointer
2. Output pointer

The input pointer is used to perform the read operation. It can read the contents of a file from a specified location. Whenever a file is opened in the read mode, by default the input pointer is set at the start of the file, so that the read operation can begin from the start of the file. The input pointer is also known as the get pointer. The output pointer is used to perform the write operation. Whenever a file is opened in the write mode, the existing contents are deleted and the output pointer is set at the start of the file. This ensures that the write operation begins from the start of the file. To edit a file, you need to open it in the append mode. In this mode, the output pointer moves to the end of the file and the new data is added there. The output pointer is also known as the put pointer.

You can also manipulate these pointers (control the movement of the pointers) by using the functions that are given next.

1. seekg( )
2. seekp( )
3. tellg( )
4. tellp( )

The seekg( ) Function

The **seekg( )** function is used to move the input or get pointer to a specified location. The syntax for using the **seekg( )** function is as follows:

    stream.seekg(offset);

In the above syntax, the **stream** specifies an object of the stream class **ifstream**, **ofstream**, and **fstream**. The **offset** specifies the number of bytes that the file pointer will move from the beginning (default) of the file.

For example:

    ifstream in;
    in.open("Test");
    in.seekg(20);

In this example, the text file **Test** is opened in the read mode (default for the **ifstream** class). In the **seekg( )** function, the value 20 is passed as an argument, which specifies the **offset value**. Now, the input pointer moves to the byte number 20 in the file **Test** and the read operation starts from the 21st byte of the file.

You can also use the **seekg( )** function in the following way:

    stream.seekg(offset, seek_direction);

In the above syntax, the **offset** specifies the number of bytes that the file pointer has to move from the position, which is specified by the **seek_direction**. The **seek_direction** takes any one value from the following:

1. ios::beg   //offset from the start of the file
2. ios::cur   //offset from the current position of the pointer
3. ios::end   //offset from the end of the file

The above three constants are defined in the **ios** class.

For example:

    ifstream in;
    in.open("Test");
    in.seekg(0, ios::beg);

In the above example, the **ios::beg** will set the output or the put pointer at the start of the file from where the reading operation begins.

If you pass a negative value for the first argument (offset), the read or write operations will be performed in the backward direction from the position specified by the **seek_direction**.

For example:

    ifstream in;
    in.open("Test");
    in.seekg(-2, ios::cur);

In the above example, the **ios::cur** sets the input pointer at the current position in the file. Now, it will move 2 bytes backward from the current position because the offset value is -2.

The seekp( ) Function

As you already know that the **seekg( )** function is used to move the input pointer to a specified location. Similarly, the **seekp( )** function is used to move the output pointer to a specified location. You can use the **seekp( )** function in the same way as the **seekg( )** function.

For example:

    ofstream out;
    out.open("Test");
    out.seekp(0, ios::end);

In the above example, the **ios::end** sets the output pointer at the end of the file.

The tellg( ) Function

The **tellg( )** function is used to get the current position of the input pointer in the file. This function returns an integer value.

For example:

```
ifstream in;
in.open("Test");
in.seekg(10, ios::beg);
int num = in.tellg( );
```

In the above example, the **seekg( )** function moves the input pointer to the 10th byte from the start of the file **Test**. The function **tellg( )** returns the current position of the input pointer and the resultant value is assigned to the variable **num**.

The tellp( ) Function

The **tellp( )** function is used to get the current position of the output pointer in the file. This function also returns an integer value.

For example:

```
ofstream out;
out.open("Test");
in.seekp(10, ios::beg);
int num = in.tellp( );
```

In the above example, the **seekp( )** function moves the output pointer to the 10th byte from the start of the file **Test**. The function **tellp( )** returns the current position of the output pointer and the resultant value is assigned to the variable **num**.

FILE INPUT/OUTPUT OPERATIONS

To perform certain I/O operations on files, a number of functions are used, which are provided by the file stream classes such as **ifstream**, **ofstream**, and so on. The list of these functions is as follows:

1. get( )
2. put( )
3. read( )
4. write( )

The **get( )** and the **put( )** functions operate on a single character, whereas the **read( )** and the **write( )** functions operate on a binary data (data which is represented in the form of 0's and 1's).

The get( ) and put( ) Functions

The **get( )** and **put( )** functions operate on a single character. The **get( )** function is used to read a single character from a file and the **put( )** function is used to write a character on it. The syntax for using the **get( )** and **put( )** functions is as follows:

```
stream_obj.get(char ch);
stream_obj.put(ch);
```

In the above syntax, the **get( )** function reads a character from the calling stream. Here, the calling stream is represented by the **stream_obj**. The resultant character is assigned to the character variable **ch**. The **put( )** function writes the value of the character variable **ch** on the file.

For example:

```
fstream finout;
finout.open("Test", ios::in|ios::out);
finout.put(ch);
----------;
----------;
finout.get(ch);
```

In the above example, **finout** is declared as a stream of the class **fstream**, which can be used to perform both the read and the write operations. This stream is linked with the text file **Test**, which is opened in both the read and the write mode. The **put( )** function writes a character (value of the character variable **ch**) to the calling stream **finout**. After the write operation is completed, the **get( )** function is used to read a character one by one from the calling stream (**finout**) and the resultant character value is assigned to the character variable **ch**.

The following example illustrates the use of the **get( )** and **put( )** functions.

Example 2

Write a program to perform the read and write operations on a text file by using the **get( )** and **put( )** functions.

The following program will prompt the user to enter a string, write it in a text file, read the string from the text file, and display it on the screen.

```
//Write a program that performs the read and write operations on a file      1
#include<iostream>                                                           2
#include<fstream>                                                            3
#include<string>                                                             4
using namespace std;                                                         5
int main( )                                                                  6
{                                                                            7
        fstream file;                                                        8
        char str[80];                                                        9
```

```
        char ch;                                                    10
        cout<<"Enter a string"<<endl;                               11
        cin>>str;                                                   12
        int len = strlen(str);                                      13
        file.open("C:\\demo3.txt", ios::in | ios::out);             14
        for(int i=0; i<len; i++)                                    15
        {                                                           16
                file.put(str[i]);                                   17
        }                                                           18
        file.seekg(0);                                              19
        while(file.get(ch))                                         20
                cout<<ch;                                           21
        file.close( );                                              22
        return 0;                                                   23
}                                                                   24
```

Explanation

Line 8

fstream file;

In this line, the **file** is declared as a stream of the class **fstream**. The **file** stream is used as an input and an output stream.

Line 13

int len = strlen(str);

In this line, the **strlen( ) (string length)** function is used to calculate the length of the string **(str)**, which will be entered by the user.

Line 14

file.open("C:\\demo3.txt", ios::in | ios::out);

In this line, the **open( )** function is used to open the text file **demo3**. The **open( )** function contains two arguments: **C:\\demo3.txt** and **ios::in | ios::out**. The first argument specifies the path of the text file **demo3**. The second argument specifies that the file is opened in both the read and the write mode. This means that you can perform both the read and write operations on the file.

> **Note**
> *You can also specify a new path for the text file, which is created by you.*

Line 17

file.put(str[i]);

This line is associated with the **for** loop (line 15). In this line, the **put( )** function is called with the stream **file**, which can write the characters (character by character) of the string **str** to the calling stream **file**.

Line 19

file.seekg(0);

In this line, the **seekg( )** function is used to set the file input pointer at the start of the file.

Line 20
while(file.get(ch))
Here, the **get( )** function reads the entire contents of the file **demo3**, character by character as long as the end of the file is not encountered and it also displays all the contents by using the **cout** statement given in line 21.

Line 22
file.close( );
In this line, the **close( )** function closes the file **demo3**. As a result, the connection, which was created earlier, between the file **demo3** and the stream **file** will be terminated.

The output of the program is as follows:
Enter a string
Smith
Smith

The read( ) and write( ) Functions

You can read or write the binary data by using the **read( )** and **write( )** functions. The syntax for using the **read( )** and **write( )** functions is as follows:

```
stream_obj.read((char *buf) &var, sizeof(var));
stream_obj.write((char *buf) &var, sizeof(var));
```

In the above syntax, the **read( )** and **write( )** functions contain two arguments: **&var** and **sizeof(var)**. The first argument **&var** provides the address of the variable **var**. The resultant address must be transformed into the character type pointer **char *buf**. The second argument is the length of the variable **var** in terms of bytes. The **read( )** function reads the data from the calling stream, which is represented by the **stream_obj**. The **write( )** function writes the data on the calling stream **stream_obj**.

The following example illustrates the use of the **read( )** and **write( )** functions.

Example 3

Write a program to perform the read and write operations on the binary data by using the **read( )** and **write( )** functions.

The following program will write some data on the text file, read it, and then display it on the screen.

```
//Write a program to perform operation on the binary data          1
#include<iostream>                                                  2
#include<fstream>                                                   3
#include<string>                                                    4
using namespace std;                                               5
struct employee                                                    6
{                                                                  7
```

```
        char name[40];                                          8
        int emp_id;                                             9
};                                                              10
int main( )                                                     11
{                                                               12
        employee emp1;                                          13
        strcpy(emp1.name, "Smith");                             14
        emp1.emp_id = 1022;                                     15
        ofstream out;                                           16
        out.open("C:\\demo3.txt", ios::out|ios::binary);        17
        if(!out)                                                18
        {                                                       19
                cout<<"Cannot open file"<<endl;                 20
                return 1;                                       21
        }                                                       22
        out.write((char *) &emp1, sizeof(employee));            23
        out.close( );                                           24
        ifstream in;                                            25
        in.open("C:\\demo3.txt", ios::in|ios::binary);          26
        if(!in)                                                 27
        {                                                       28
                cout<<"Cannot open file"<<endl;                 29
                return 1;                                       30
        }                                                       31
        in.read((char *) &emp1, sizeof(employee));              32
        cout<<emp1.name<<endl;                                  33
        cout<<emp1.emp_id;                                      34
        in.close();                                             35
        return 0;                                               36
}                                                               37
```

The output of the program is as follows:
Smith
1022

The output will be displayed on the screen as follows:

CHECKING THE I/O STATUS

In C++, the I/O system contains the information about the status of every I/O operation. In the I/O system, the current status is held by an object of the type **iostate**, which is an enumerated type defined in the **ios** class. The object **iostate** can have any one of the following values, as shown in the Table 14.1

S.No.	Name	Meaning
1.	goodbit	When no error occurs
2.	failbit	When an input or output operation fails
3.	eofbit	When the end of file is encountered
4.	badbit	When a fatal I/O error occurs

Table 14.1 *Represents the values of iostate*

You can obtain the I/O status in the following two ways:

1. By using the **rdstate( )** function
2. By using one of the following functions:

    a.   bool bad( )
    b.   bool eof( )
    c.   bool fail( )
    d.   bool good( )

By Using the rdstate( ) Function

You can use the **rdstate( )** function to obtain the information about the I/O status. The syntax for using the **rdstate( )** function is as follows:

    rdstate( );

The **rdstate( )** function returns the current status of the error flags (**ios::eof**, **ios::bad**, and **ios::fail**). If no error occurs, the **rdstate( )** function returns **goodbit**. Otherwise, it returns an error flag according to the type of error. The error can be any one of the following:

1. eofbit
2. failbit
3. badbit

For example:

```
----------;
----------;
ifstream in;
in.open("Test");
----------;
----------;
if(in.rdstate( ) ==ios::badbit)
    cout<<"Fatal I/O error"<<endl;
else if(in.rdstate( ) ==ios::failbit)
    cout<<"I/O operation fails"<<endl;
else if(in.rdstate( ) ==ios::eofbit)
    cout<<"End of file"<<endl;
else
    cout<<"No error occured"<<endl;
----------;
----------;
```

In the above example, the **rdstate( )** function is called with a stream **in** within the **if** statement. The value, which is returned by the function is compared with the value such as **ios::badbit**, **ios::failbit**, and so on. If a match is found, the statements associated with that particular block will be executed. For example, if the **rdstate( )** function returns **eofbit**, the statement **End of file** is displayed on the screen.

By Using the good( ), eof( ), bad( ), and fail( ) Functions

You can also use the **good( )**, **eof( )**, **bad( )**, and **fail( )** functions to obtain information about the I/O status and also for error handling. These functions are the member functions of the **ios** base class. They are of boolean type and return a true or false value. These functions are described as follows:

Function	Description
good( )	It will return true (other than zero), if no error occurs during the file operations. Also, all the operations can be carried out normally. If it returns false, no further operation can be performed.
eof( )	It will return true, if the end of a file is encountered. Otherwise, it will return false.
bad( )	It will return true, if any fatal I/O operation is performed. Otherwise, it will return false.
fail( )	It will return true, if any I/O operation fails. Otherwise, it will return false.

The syntax for using any of the given functions is as follows:

    stream_obj.fun_name( );

In the above syntax, the **stream_obj** specifies a **stream**, which is either an **input** or **output** stream. The **fun_name** specifies the function, which can be any one from **good( )**, **eof( )**, **bad( )**, and **fail( )** functions, depending on the requirement.

For example:

```
----------;
----------;
ifstream in;
in.open("Test");
----------;
----------;
if(in.eof( ))
{
     statements;        //Which terminates the program normally
}
----------;
----------;
```

In the above example, if the end of the file is encountered, the **eof( )** function returns the value true. As a result, the statements associated with the **if** statement are executed and this results in the normal termination of the program.

If an error occurs during the file operation, the error flags should be cleared before the continuation of the program. You can clear all the error flags by using the **clear( )** member function. The syntax for using the **clear( )** function is as follows:

    stream_obj.clear( );

The **clear( )** function resets all the error flags such as **ios::badbit**, **ios::eofbit**, and so on.

COMMAND LINE ARGUMENTS

In all the previous examples, the **main( )** function did not contain any parameter list. Also, no arguments were supplied to it. To supply arguments to a **main( )** function in a program, you can use the command line arguments. The command line arguments are passed at the time of invoking the program. Whenever you want to pass the command line arguments in a program, the **main( )** function is defined as follows:

    int main(int argc, char * argv[ ])

In the definition given above, the argument list of the **main( )** function contains two arguments: **argc** and **argv[ ]**. The first argument **argc** (argument counter) specifies the number of arguments, which are passed in the command line. The second argument **argv[ ]** (argument vector) is an array of character type pointers. The maximum size of the array is equal to the value stored in the first argument **argc**.

The syntax for passing command line arguments is as follows:

C:\> filename arg1 arg2 .....argN

In this syntax, the **filename** is the name of the file, which contains the program. The **arg1** to **argN** specify the arguments, which are passed into the command line. The command line arguments are entered by the user and separated by a blank space. The first argument should always be the name of a file. The command line arguments are basically used to pass the names of the files during the file I/O operations.

For example:

C:\> demo Test

In the above example, **demo** is the file name and it contains the program, which is to be executed. The second argument **Test** is the file name, which is passed as a command-line argument to the program. So, the value of **argc** is two and the size of the array **argv[ ]** is also two. The **argv[0]** points to the first argument **demo** and the **argv[1]** points to the second argument **Test**.

IMPORTANT FUNCTIONS

There are some other functions that are useful during the file I/O operations. These functions are described below:

1. ignore( )
2. peek( )
3. putback( )
4. _unlink( )
5. getline( )
6. flush( )

The ignore( ) Function

The **ignore( )** function is basically used during the read operation. It is used to extract and discard certain number of characters from the input stream. The syntax for using the **ignore( )** function is given next.

stream_obj.ignore(int count, delimiter);

In the above syntax, the **ignore( )** function continues to extract and discard characters from the input stream until the **count** characters are discarded or the character specified by the **delimiter** is encountered.

For example:

```
---------;
---------;
ifstream in;
in.open("Test");
---------;
---------;
in.ignore(5, 'h');
---------;
---------;
```

In the above example, the **ignore( )** function contains two arguments: integer value 5 and a character value h. The **ignore( )** function continues to extract and discard characters until either 5 characters have been discarded or the character h is encountered.

The peek( ) Function

The **peek( )** function is used to read the next character from an input file stream. But unlike the **get( )** function, it does not move the input pointer to the next character. The syntax for using the **peek( )** function is as follows:

```
stream_obj.peek( );
```

In the above syntax, the **peek( )** function will return the next character or **EOF** if the end of the file is encountered.

For example:

```
---------;
---------;
ifstream in;
in.open("C:\\demo4.txt");
in.get(ch);
---------;
---------;
cout<< in.peek( ) <<endl;
---------;
```

In the above example, the **get( )** function reads a single character from the input file stream and moves the input pointer to the next character. Next, the **peek( )** function is called, which will return the next character from the input file stream but the input pointer will not move from the current position.

The putback( ) Function

The **putback( )** function, used with the input streams, returns the previously read character to the input streams. The syntax for using the **putback( )** function is as follows:

```
stream_obj.putback(char ch);
```

In the above syntax, the **putback( )** function returns the character **ch**, which was previously read from the input stream **stream_obj**. Next, the resultant character **ch** is assigned to the input stream **stream_obj** and the input pointer moves one position backward.

For example:

```
----------;
----------;
ifstream in;
in.open("C:\\demo4.txt");
in.get(ch);
in.putback(ch);
----------;
----------;
```

In the above example, the **get( )** function reads a character from the input stream **in**. In the next statement, the **putback( )** function is called and it returns the character **ch**, which was previously read by the **get( )** function. The returned character **ch** will be assigned to the input stream **in** and the input pointer moves one position backward.

The _unlink( ) Function

You can delete a file during the file I/O operations in a program by using the **_unlink( )** member function. The **_unlink( )** function is defined in the **io** base class. So, whenever you want to use this function in a program, you must include the **io** base class in the header files. The syntax for using the **_unlink( )** function is as follows:

```
_unlink("Filename");
```

In the above syntax, the **_unlink( )** function deletes the file, which is specified by the **Filename**.

For example:

```
----------;
----------;
ofstream out;
out.open("C:\\demo4.txt");
----------;
_unlink("C:\\demo4.txt");
----------;
```

In the above example, the **_unlink( )** function deletes the text file **demo4**.

The getline( ) Function

The **getline( )** function is used for the read operation. The **getline( )** function reads the contents of a file line by line from an input stream. The syntax for using the **getline( )** function is as follows:

> stream_obj.getline(char *ar, streamsize n);
> stream_obj.getline(char *ar, streamsize n, char delim);

In this syntax (first type), the **ar** is a pointer to an array of characters. The **streamsize n** specifies the maximum number of characters that can be stored in a successive position in an array, which is pointed by the pointer **ar**. The **getline( )** function continues to read characters from an input stream until **n-1** characters have been extracted or the end of the file has been encountered.

In this syntax (second type), the **getline( )** function continues to read characters from an input stream until **n-1** characters have been extracted, the end of the file has been encountered, or the **delim** character has been read. If the **delim** character is encountered, it is extracted but not stored in the array.

For example:

```
----------;
----------;
ifstream in;
in.open("C:\\demo4.txt");
----------;
----------;
in.getline(arr, 10, 'i');
----------;
```

In the above example, the **getline( )** function continues to read characters until 10 characters are read, the end of the file is encountered, or the character **i** specified by the **delimiter** is encountered.

The flush( ) Function

Whenever you perform write operation on a file, the contents are not written directly but they are saved in a buffer (storage space). When the buffer is full, the contents are written on the specified file of the physical device such as hard disk, floppy disk, and so on. If you want to write the contents directly on the linked device, even if the buffer is not full, you can do so by using the **flush( )** function. The syntax for using the **flush( )** function is as follows:

> stream_obj.flush( );

The **flush( )** function is used during the write operation.

Self-Evaluation Test

Answer the following questions and then compare them to the answers given at the end of this chapter:

1. The _____ class serves as a base class for the classes such as **ifstream**, **ofstream**, and so on.

2. The _____ provides a stream interface, which is used to write the data on a file.

3. The _____ open mode is used to open a file in the binary mode.

4. The _____ pointer is used for the read operation.

5. The _____ function is used to get the current position of the output pointer in a file.

Review Questions

Answer the following questions:

1. Describe the input and output streams.

2. Explain the classes used for the file I/O operations.

3. Explain the **seekg( )** and **seekp( )** functions with a suitable example.

4. Explain the functions that are used during the read and write operations with suitable examples.

5. Explain the working of the **rdstate( )** function.

Exercise

Exercise 1

Write a program to read the contents of a text file and write them onto another text file by using the **get( )** and **put( )** functions.

Answers to Self-Evaluation Test
1. fstreambase, 2. ofstream, 3. ios::binary, 4. input, 5. tellp( )

Index

Other Publications by CADCIM Technologies

The following is the list of some of the publications by CADCIM Technologies. Please visit *www.cadcim.com* for the complete listing.

3ds Max Textbooks
- Autodesk 3ds Max 2016: A Comprehensive Guide, 16th Edition
- Autodesk 3ds Max 2015: A Comprehensive Guide, 15th Edition
- Autodesk 3ds Max 2014: A Comprehensive Guide
- Autodesk 3ds Max 2013: A Comprehensive Guide
- Autodesk 3ds Max 2012: A Comprehensive Guide

Autodesk Maya Textbooks
- Autodesk Maya 2016: A Comprehensive Guide, 8th Edition
- Autodesk Maya 2015: A Comprehensive Guide, 7th Edition
- Character Animation: A Tutorial Approach
- Autodesk Maya 2014: A Comprehensive Guide
- Autodesk Maya 2013: A Comprehensive Guide
- Autodesk Maya 2012: A Comprehensive Guide

ZBrush Textbook
- Pixologic ZBrush 4R6: A Comprehensive Guide

CINEMA 4D Textbooks
- MAXON CINEMA 4D Studio R16: A Tutorial Approach, 3rd Edition
- MAXON CINEMA 4D Studio R15: A Tutorial Approach
- MAXON CINEMA 4D Studio R14: A Tutorial Approach

Fusion Textbooks
- The eyeon Fusion 6.3: A Tutorial Approach
- Black Magic Design Fusion 7 Studio: A Tutorial Approach

Flash Textbooks
- Adobe Flash Professional CC: A Tutorial Approach
- Adobe Flash Professional CS6: A Tutorial Approach

Premiere Textbooks
- Adobe Premiere Pro CC: A Tutorial Approach, 3rd Edition
- Adobe Premiere Pro CS6: A Tutorial Approach
- Adobe Premiere Pro CS5.5: A Tutorial Approach

3ds Max Design Textbooks
• Autodesk 3ds Max Design 2015: A Tutorial Approach, 15th Edition
• Autodesk 3ds Max Design 2014: A Tutorial Approach
• Autodesk 3ds Max Design 2013: A Tutorial Approach
• Autodesk 3ds Max Design 2012: A Tutorial Approach
• Autodesk 3ds Max Design 2011: A Tutorial Approach

Softimage Textbook
• Autodesk Softimage 2014: A Tutorial Approach
• Autodesk Softimage 2013: A Tutorial Approach

AutoCAD Textbooks
• AutoCAD 2016: A Problem-Solving Approach, Basic and Intermediate, 22nd Edition
• AutoCAD 2016: A Problem-Solving Approach, 3D and Advanced, 22nd Edition
• AutoCAD 2015: A Problem-Solving Approach, Basic and Intermediate, 21st Edition
• AutoCAD 2015: A Problem-Solving Approach, 3D and Advanced, 21st Edition
• AutoCAD 2014: A Problem-Solving Approach

Autodesk Inventor Textbooks
• Autodesk Inventor 2016 for Designers, 16th Edition
• Autodesk Inventor 2015 for Designers, 15th Edition
• Autodesk Inventor 2014 for Designers
• Autodesk Inventor 2013 for Designers
• Autodesk Inventor 2012 for Designers
• Autodesk Inventor 2011 for Designers

AutoCAD MEP Textbooks
• AutoCAD MEP 2016 for Designers, 3rd Edition
• AutoCAD MEP 2015 for Designers
• AutoCAD MEP 2014 for Designers

Solid Edge Textbooks
• Solid Edge ST7 for Designers, 12th Edition
• Solid Edge ST6 for Designers
• Solid Edge ST5 for Designers
• Solid Edge ST4 for Designers
• Solid Edge ST3 for Designers
• Solid Edge ST2 for Designers

NX Textbooks
• NX 9.0 for Designers, 8th Edition
• NX 8.5 for Designers
• NX 8 for Designers
• NX 7 for Designers

SolidWorks Textbooks
- SOLIDWORS 2015 for Designers, 13th Edition
- SolidWorks 2014 for Designers
- SolidWorks 2013 for Designers
- SolidWorks 2012 for Designers
- SolidWorks 2014: A Tutorial Approach
- SolidWorks 2012: A Tutorial Approach
- Learning SolidWorks 2011: A Project Based Approach
- SolidWorks 2011 for Designers

CATIA Textbooks
- CATIA V5-6R2014 for Designers, 12th Edition
- CATIA V5-6R2013 for Designers
- CATIA V5-6R2012 for Designers
- CATIA V5R21 for Designers
- CATIA V5R20 for Designers
- CATIA V5R19 for Designers

Creo Parametric and Pro/ENGINEER Textbooks
- PTC Creo Parametric 3.0 for Designers, 3rd Edition
- Creo Parametric 2.0 for Designers
- Creo Parametric 1.0 for Designers
- Pro/Engineer Wildfire 5.0 for Designers
- Pro/ENGINEER Wildfire 4.0 for Designers
- Pro/ENGINEER Wildfire 3.0 for Designers

ANSYS Textbooks
- ANSYS Workbench 14.0: A Tutorial Approach
- ANSYS 11.0 for Designers

Creo Direct Textbook
- Creo Direct 2.0 and Beyond for Designers

Autodesk Alias Textbooks
- Learning Autodesk Alias Design 2016, 5th Edition
- Learning Autodesk Alias Design 2015, 4th Edition
- Learning Autodesk Alias Design 2012
- Learning Autodesk Alias Design 2010
- AliasStudio 2009 for Designers

AutoCAD LT Textbooks
- AutoCAD LT 2015 for Designers, 10th Edition
- AutoCAD LT 2014 for Designers
- AutoCAD LT 2013 for Designers
- AutoCAD LT 2012 for Designers
- AutoCAD LT 2011 for Designers

EdgeCAM Textbooks
• EdgeCAM 11.0 for Manufacturers
• EdgeCAM 10.0 for Manufacturers

AutoCAD Electrical Textbooks
• AutoCAD Electrical 2015 for Electrical Control Designers, 6th Edition
• AutoCAD Electrical 2014 for Electrical Control Designers
• AutoCAD Electrical 2013 for Electrical Control Designers
• AutoCAD Electrical 2012 for Electrical Control Designers
• AutoCAD Electrical 2011 for Electrical Control Designers
• AutoCAD Electrical 2010 for Electrical Control Designers

Autodesk Revit Architecture Textbooks
• Autodesk Revit Architecture 2016 for Architects and Designers, 12th Edition
• Autodesk Revit Architecture 2015 for Architects and Designers, 11th Edition
• Autodesk Revit Architecture 2014 for Architects and Designers
• Autodesk Revit Architecture 2013 for Architects and Designers
• Autodesk Revit Architecture 2012 for Architects and Designers

Autodesk Revit Structure Textbooks
• Exploring Autodesk Revit Structure 2016, 6th Edition
• Exploring Autodesk Revit Structure 2015, 5th Edition
• Exploring Autodesk Revit Structure 2014
• Exploring Autodesk Revit Structure 2013
• Exploring Autodesk Revit Structure 2012

AutoCAD Civil 3D Textbooks
• Exploring AutoCAD Civil 3D 2016, 6th Edition
• Exploring AutoCAD Civil 3D 2015, 5th Edition
• Exploring AutoCAD Civil 3D 2014
• Exploring AutoCAD Civil 3D 2013

AutoCAD Map 3D Textbooks
• Exploring AutoCAD Map 3D 2016, 6th Edition
• Exploring AutoCAD Map 3D 2015, 5th Edition
• Exploring AutoCAD Map 3D 2014
• Exploring AutoCAD Map 3D 2013
• Exploring AutoCAD Map 3D 2012

Revit MEP Textbooks
• Exploring Autodesk Revit MEP 2016, 3rd Edition
• Exploring Autodesk Revit MEP 2015
• Exploring Autodesk Revit MEP 2014

STAAD Pro Textbook
•Exploring Bentley STAAD.Pro V8i

Navisworks Textbooks
- Exploring Autodesk Navisworks 2015, 3rd Edition
- Exploring Autodesk Navisworks 2015
- Exploring Autodesk Navisworks 2014

Computer Programming Textbooks
- Learning Oracle 11g
- Learning ASP.NET AJAX
- Learning Java Programming
- Learning Visual Basic.NET 2008
- Learning C++ Programming Concepts
- Learning VB.NET Programming Concepts

AutoCAD Textbooks Authored by Prof. Sham Tickoo and Published by Autodesk Press
- AutoCAD: A Problem-Solving Approach: 2013 and Beyond
- AutoCAD 2012: A Problem-Solving Approach
- AutoCAD 2011: A Problem-Solving Approach
- AutoCAD 2010: A Problem-Solving Approach
- Customizing AutoCAD 2010
- AutoCAD 2009: A Problem-Solving Approach

Textbooks Authored by CADCIM Technologies and Published by Other Publishers

3D Studio MAX and VIZ Textbooks
- Learning 3DS Max: A Tutorial Approach, Release 4
  Goodheart-Wilcox Publishers (USA)
- Learning 3D Studio VIZ: A Tutorial Approach
  Goodheart-Wilcox Publishers (USA)

CADCIM Technologies Textbooks Translated in Other Languages

SolidWorks Textbooks
- SolidWorks 2008 for Designers (Serbian Edition)
  Mikro Knjiga Publishing Company, Serbia
- SolidWorks 2006 for Designers (Russian Edition)
  Piter Publishing Press, Russia
- SolidWorks 2006 for Designers (Serbian Edition)
  Mikro Knjiga Publishing Company, Serbia

NX Textbooks
- NX 6 for Designers (Korean Edition)
  Onsolutions, South Korea
- NX 5 for Designers (Korean Edition)
  Onsolutions, South Korea

Pro/ENGINEER Textbooks
- Pro/ENGINEER Wildfire 4.0 for Designers (Korean Edition)
  HongReung Science Publishing Company, South Korea
- Pro/ENGINEER Wildfire 3.0 for Designers (Korean Edition)
  HongReung Science Publishing Company, South Korea

Autodesk 3ds Max Textbook
- 3ds Max 2008: A Comprehensive Guide (Serbian Edition)
  Mikro Knjiga Publishing Company, Serbia

AutoCAD Textbooks
- AutoCAD 2006 (Russian Edition)
  Piter Publishing Press, Russia
- AutoCAD 2005 (Russian Edition)
  Piter Publishing Press, Russia
- AutoCAD 2000 Fondamenti (Italian Edition)

Coming Soon from CADCIM Technologies
- Solid Edge ST8 for Designers
- NX 10.0 for Designers
- NX Nastran 9.0 for Designers
- SOLIDWORKS Simulation 2015 for Designers
- Exploring Primavera P6 V8
- Exploring Risa 3D 12.0
- Exploring Autodesk Raster Design 2016 for Image Processing

Online Training Program Offered by CADCIM Technologies
CADCIM Technologies provides effective and affordable virtual online training on animation, architecture, and GIS softwares, computer programming languages, and Computer Aided Design and Manufacturing (CAD/CAM) software packages. The training will be delivered 'live' via Internet at any time, any place, and at any pace to individuals, students of colleges, universities, and CAD/CAM training centers. For more information, please visit the following link: *www.cadcim.com*